ARCO

Everything you need to score high on

POSTAL
EXAMS

Fourth Edition

E.P. Steinberg

Macmillan • USA

Fourth Edition

Macmillan Reference USA
A Simon & Schuster Macmillan Company
1633 Broadway
New York, NY 10019-6785

An ARCO Book

Library of Congress Number 97-071472

ISBN: 0-02-861934-X

Manufactured in the United States of America
10 9 8 7 6 5 4 3 2 1

C o n t e n t s

Applying for Postal Positions   85

Test-Taking Techniques   89

Part II — Five Model Examinations

Model Examination 1

Model Examination 2

Model Examination 3

Model Examination 4

Model Examination 5

Working for the Post Office

The United States Postal Service is an independent agency of the Federal Government. As such, employees of the Postal Service are federal employees who enjoy the very generous benefits offered by the government. These benefits include an automatic raise at least once a year, regular cost-of-living adjustments, liberal paid vacation and sick leave, life insurance, hospitalization, and the opportunity to join a credit union. At the same time, the operation of the Postal Service is businesslike and independent of politics. A postal worker's job is secure even though presidential administrations may change. An examination system is used to fill vacancies. This system provides opportunities for those who are able and motivated to enter the Postal Service and to move within it.

Since postal employment is so popular, entry is very competitive. In some parts of the country certain exams are given as seldom as once every three years. The resulting list is used to fill vacancies as they occur during the next three years. An individual who has been employed by the Postal Service for at least a year may ask to take the exam for any position and, if properly qualified, may fill a vacancy ahead of a person whose name is on the regular list. (The supervisor does not need to grant the request to take a special exam to fill a vacancy, but most supervisors readily grant such permission to employees with good performance records who have served an adequate period in their current positions.) It is even possible to change careers within the Postal Service. A custodian, for instance, might take a city carrier exam; a stenographer might choose to become a letter-sorting machine operator; or a mail handler might take an exam to enter personnel work. If the exam for the precise position that you want will not be administered for some time, it might be worthwhile to take the exam for another position in hopes of entering the Postal Service and then moving from within. There is never a fee for applying for a postal examination, so if you want to work for the Postal Service take every exam for which you are qualified.

Salaries, hours, and other working conditions as well are subject to frequent change. Postal workers have very effective unions that bargain for them and gain increasingly better conditions. At the time of your employment, you should make your own inquiry as to salary, hours, and other conditions as they apply to you. Job descriptions and requirements are less subject to change.

As you can see, the best way to get the job you want with the Postal Service is first to get any job with the Postal Service. This book will help you get started on your career.

The book begins with an overview of the most popular postal positions. It describes the jobs themselves, the qualifications necessary for each position, and the exams applicants must pass. Following the overview are instructions for applying for postal positions and samples of some actual forms that must be filled out. Then, the next chapter offers proven advice on how to be a better test-taker. The second part of the book provides five full-length model exams for 18 different postal positions. Of course, it is most important that you practice with the exam for the job that you really want. If you have time, however, it might be worthwhile to try the other exams in the book. In this way you will be prepared for any examination that may be given.

ONE

About the Jobs and the Qualifying Exams

Occupations in the Postal Service

The U.S. Postal Service handles billions of pieces of mail a year, including letters, magazines, and parcels. Close to a million workers are required to process and deliver this mail. The vast majority of Postal Service jobs are open to workers with four years of high school or less. The work is steady. Some of the jobs, such as mail carrier, offer a good deal of personal freedom. Other jobs, however, are more closely supervised and are more routine.

WHO WORKS FOR THE POSTAL SERVICE?

Most people are familiar with the duties of the city carrier and the post-office window clerk. Yet few are aware of the many different tasks required in processing mail and of the variety of occupations in the Postal Service.

At all hours of the day and night, a steady stream of letters, packages, magazines, and papers moves through the typical large post office. City carriers have collected some of this mail from neighborhood mailboxes; some has been trucked in from surrounding towns or from the airport. When a truck arrives at the post office, mail handlers unload the mail. Postal clerks then sort it according to destination. After being sorted, outgoing mail is loaded into trucks for delivery to the airport or nearby towns. Local mail is left for carriers to deliver the next morning.

To keep buildings and equipment clean and in good working order, the Postal Service employs a variety of service and maintenance workers, including janitors, laborers, truck mechanics, electricians, carpenters, and painters. Some workers specialize in repairing machines that process mail.

Postal inspectors audit the operations of post offices to see that they are run efficiently, that funds are spent properly, and that postal laws and regulations are observed. They also prevent and detect crimes such as theft, forgery, and fraud involving use of the mail.

Postmasters and supervisors are responsible for the day-to-day operation of the post office, for hiring and promoting employees, and for setting up work schedules.

The Postal Service also contracts with private businesses to transport mail. There are more than 12,500 of these "Star" route contracts. Most "Star" route carriers use trucks to haul mail, but in some remote areas horses or boats are used instead.

The Postal Service has historically utilized many technological innovations to improve mail distribution and delivery. The first extensive application of technology started in the late 1960s when Multi-Position Letter Machines or MPLSMs began replacing manual mail-sorting equipment. Mechanized MPLSMs represented a significant change in the way mail was processed. In the early 1980s more advanced automated technology, Optical Character Readers and Bar Code Sorters, were introduced and are now essential components in the mail processing environment. These machines are not the ultimate creation. New technologies continue to evolve at an ever-increasing rate. Mail processing by automation is critical to future postal success.

The latest technical advance is the Remote Bar Coding System (RBCS), and the newest job title in the Postal Service is that of Data Conversion Operator.

Almost 85 percent of all postal workers are in jobs directly related to processing and delivering mail. This group includes postal clerks, city carriers, mail handlers, rural carriers, and truck drivers. Postmasters and supervisors make up nearly 10 percent of total employment, and maintenance workers about 4 percent. The remainder includes such workers as postal inspectors, guards, personnel workers, and secretaries.

WHERE ARE THE JOBS?

The Postal Service operates more than 41,000 installations. Most are post offices, but some serve special purposes such as handling payroll records or supplying equipment.

Although every community receives mail service, employment is concentrated in large metropolitan areas. Post offices in cities such as New York, Chicago, and Los Angeles employ a great number of workers because they not only process huge amounts of mail for their own populations but also serve as mail-processing points for the smaller communities that surround them. These large city post offices have sophisticated machines for sorting the mail. In these post offices, distribution clerks who have qualified as machine operators quickly scan addresses and send letters on their way automatically by pushing the proper button.

The first move toward decentralization of postal operations is the development of the Remote Bar Coding System at Remote Encoding Centers. The Remote Encoding Centers, as their name implies, are being established outside the most congested population centers in smaller cities where land, construction, and operating expenses are far lower. At the time of this writing, hiring is underway in Salt Lake City, Utah; Lehigh Valley, Pennsylvania; Northern New Jersey; Greensboro, North Carolina; Charleston, West Virginia; Birmingham, Alabama; Chattanooga, Tennessee; Wichita, Kansas; Akron, Ohio; Des Moines, Iowa; Beaumont, Texas; Little Rock, Arkansas; and Syracuse and Albany, New York. For information about areas in which you may seek this employment when you are ready to apply, call (800) 276–5627.

TRAINING, OTHER QUALIFICATIONS, AND ADVANCEMENT

An applicant for a Postal Service job must pass an examination and meet minimum age requirements. Generally, the minimum age is 18 years, but a high school graduate may begin work at 16 years if the job is not hazardous and does not require use of a motor vehicle. Many Postal Service jobs do not require formal education or special training. Applicants for these jobs are hired on the basis of their examination scores.

Some postal jobs do have special education or experience requirements, and some are open only to veterans. Any special requirements will be stated on the announcement of examination.

Male applicants born after December 31, 1959, unless for some reason they are exempt, must be registered with the Selective Service System.

The Immigration Reform and Control Act of 1986 applies to postal workers. All postal workers must be citizens of the United States or must be able to prove identity and right to work in the United States (permanent resident alien status—Green Card).

Applicants should apply at the post office where they wish to work and take the entrance examination for the job they want. Examinations for most jobs include a written test. A physical examination, including drug testing, is required as well. Applicants for jobs that require strength and stamina are sometimes given a special test. For example, mail handlers must be able to lift mail sacks weighing up to 70 pounds. The names of applicants who pass the examinations are placed on a list in the order of their scores. Separate eligibility lists are maintained for each post office. Five extra points are added to the score of an honorably discharged veteran and 10 extra points to the score of a veteran wounded in combat or disabled. Disabled veterans who have a compensable, service-connected disability of 10 percent or more are placed at the top of the eligibility list. When a job opens, the appointing officer chooses one of the top three applicants. Others are left on the list so that they can be considered for future openings.

New employees are trained either on the job by supervisors and other experienced employees or in local training centers. Training ranges from a few days to several months, depending on the job. For example, mail handlers and mechanics' helpers can learn their jobs in a relatively short time. Postal inspectors, on the other hand, need months of training.

Advancement opportunities are available for most postal workers because there is a management commitment to provide career development. Also, employees can get preferred assignments, such as the day shift or a more desirable delivery route, as their seniority increases. When an opening occurs, employees may submit written requests, called "bids," for assignment to the vacancy. The bidder who meets the qualifications and has the most seniority gets the job.

In addition, postal workers can advance to better-paying positions by learning new skills. Training programs are available for low-skilled workers who wish to become technicians or mechanics.

Applicants for supervisory jobs must pass an examination. Additional requirements for promotion may include training or education, a satisfactory work record, and appropriate personal characteristics such as leadership ability. If the leading candidates are equally qualified, length of service is also considered.

Although opportunities for promotion to supervisory positions in smaller post offices are limited, workers may apply for vacancies in a larger post office and thus increase their chances of promotion.

EMPLOYMENT OUTLOOK

Employment in the Postal Service is expected to grow more slowly than the average for all industries through the 1990s. Mechanization of mail processing and more efficient delivery should allow the Postal Service to handle increasing amounts of mail without corresponding increases in employment. Nevertheless, thousands of job openings will result as workers retire, die, or transfer to other fields.

EARNINGS AND WORKING CONDITIONS

Postal Service employees are paid under several separate pay schedules depending upon the duties of the job and the knowledge, experience, or skill required. For example, there are separate schedules for production workers such as clerks and mail handlers, for rural carriers, for postal managers, and for postal executives. In all pay schedules, except that of executives, employees receive periodic "step" increases up to a specified maximum if their job performance is satisfactory.

The conditions that follow are subject to collective bargaining and may well be different by the time you are employed by the Postal Service.

Full-time employees work an 8-hour day, 5 days a week. Both full-time and part-time employees who work more than 8 hours a day or 40 hours a week receive overtime pay of one-and-a-half times their hourly rate. In addition, pay is higher for those on the night shift.

Postal employees earn 13 days of annual leave (vacation) during each of their first 3 years of service, including prior federal civilian and military service; 20 days each year for 3 to 15 years of service; and 26 days after 15 years. In addition, they earn 13 days of paid sick leave a year regardless of length of service.

Other benefits include retirement and survivorship annuities, free group life insurance, and optional participation in health insurance programs supported in part by the Postal Service.

Most post office buildings are clean and well-lit, but some of the older ones are not. The Postal Service is in the process of replacing and remodeling its outmoded buildings, and conditions are expected to improve.

Most postal workers are members of unions and are covered by a national agreement between the Postal Service and the unions.

The Jobs and Sample Questions

As you have already learned, there are a great many different occupations within the Postal Service. These include those that come readily to mind, such as window clerk, city carrier, sorting machine operator, rural carrier, truck driver, and special delivery messenger, as well as some you may never have considered, such as machine maintenance and repair worker, vehicle maintenance and repair worker, security guard, cleaner and custodian, secretary, auditor, postal inspector, and, of course, postmaster, classed according to the size of the post office. On the following pages, you will find descriptions of some of these positions and official sample questions for some required examinations. Official sample questions are sent to job applicants along with the examination appointment and admission card.

POSTAL CLERK

Duties of the Job

People are most familiar with the window clerk who sits behind the counter in post office lobbies selling stamps or accepting parcel post. However, the majority of postal clerks are distribution clerks who sort incoming and outgoing mail in workrooms. Only in a small post office does a clerk do both kinds of work.

When mail arrives at the post office it is dumped on long tables where distribution clerks and mail handlers separate it into groups of letters, parcel post, and magazines and newspapers. Clerks feed letters into stamp-canceling machines and cancel the rest by hand. The mail is then taken to other sections of the post office to be sorted by destination. Clerks first separate the mail into primary destination categories: mail for the local area, for each nearby state, for groups of distant states, and for some of the largest cities. This primary distribution is followed by one or more secondary distributions. For example, local mail is combined with mail coming in from other cities and is sorted according to street and number. In post offices with electronic mail-sorting machines, clerks simply push a button, corresponding to the letter's destination, and the letter drops into the proper slot.

The clerks at post office windows provide a variety of services in addition to selling stamps and money orders. They weigh packages to determine postage and check to see if their size, shape, and condition are satisfactory for mailing. Clerks also register and insure mail and answer questions about postage rates, mailing restrictions, and other postal matters. Occasionally they may help a customer file a claim for a damaged package. In large post offices a window clerk may provide only one or two of these services and be called a registry, stamp, or money order clerk.

Working Conditions

Working conditions of clerks differ according to the specific work assignments and the amount and kind of labor-saving machinery in the post office. In small post offices clerks must carry heavy mail sacks from one part of the building to another and sort the mail by hand. In large post offices, chutes and conveyors move the mail, and much of the sorting is done by machine. In either case, clerks are on their feet most of the time, reaching for sacks of mail, placing packages and bundles into sacks while sorting, and walking around the workroom.

Distribution clerks may become bored with the routine of sorting mail unless they enjoy trying to improve their speed and accuracy. They also may have to work at night, because most large post offices process mail around the clock.

A window clerk, on the other hand, has a greater variety of duties, has frequent contact with the public, generally has a less strenuous job, and never has to work a night shift.

New clerks are trained on the job. Most clerks begin with simple tasks to learn regional groupings of states, cities, and ZIP codes. To help clerks learn these groupings, many post offices offer classroom instruction. A good memory, good coordination, and the ability to read rapidly and accurately are important. These traits are measured by performance on Exam 470.

Distribution clerks work closely with other clerks, frequently under the tension and strain of meeting deadlines. Window clerks must be tactful when dealing with the public, especially when answering questions or receiving complaints.

CITY CARRIER

Duties of the Job

Most city carriers travel planned routes delivering and collecting mail. Carriers start work at the post office early in the morning, where they spend a few hours arranging their mail for delivery, readdressing letters to be forwarded, and taking care of other details.

A carrier typically covers the route on foot, toting a heavy load of mail in a satchel or pushing it in a cart. In outlying suburban areas where houses are far apart, a car or small truck is sometimes needed to deliver mail. Residential carriers cover their routes only once a day, but carriers assigned a business district may make two or more trips. Deliveries are made house to house except in large buildings, such as apartment houses, which have all the mailboxes on the first floor.

Besides making deliveries, carriers collect c.o.d. fees and obtain signed receipts for registered and sometimes for insured mail. If a customer is not home, the carrier leaves a notice that tells where special mail is being held. Carriers also pick up letters to be mailed.

After completing their routes, carriers return to the post office with mail gathered from street collection boxes and homes. They may separate letters and parcels so that stamps can be canceled easily, and they turn in the receipts and money collected during the day.

Many carriers have more specialized duties than those just described. Some deliver only parcel post. Others collect mail from street boxes and office mail chutes.

Working Conditions

Most carriers begin work early in the morning, in some cases as early as 6 A.M., if they have routes in the business district. Carriers spend most of their time outdoors in all kinds of weather, walking from house to house with their heavy mailbags. Even those who drive must walk when making deliveries and must lift heavy sacks of parcel post when loading their vehicles.

The job, however, has its advantages. Carriers who begin work early in the morning are through by early afternoon. They are also free to work at their own pace as long as they cover their routes within a certain period of time. Moreover, full-time postal employees have more job security than workers in most other industries.

Applicants must have a driver's license and pass a road test if the job involves driving. They also must pass a physical examination and may be asked to show that they can lift and handle mail sacks weighing up to 70 pounds. Applicants who have had health conditions that might interfere with work must have a special review to determine their eligibility.

City carrier applicants must take Exam 470.

DISTRIBUTION CLERK, MACHINE (LETTER-SORTING MACHINE OPERATOR)

Duties of the Job

Distribution clerks work indoors. Often clerks must handle sacks of mail weighing as much as 70 pounds. They sort mail and distribute it by using a complicated scheme that must be memorized. Machine distribution clerks must learn computer codes for the automatic routing of mail. Clerks may be on their feet all day. They also have to stretch, reach, and throw mail. The work of the distribution clerk is more routine than that of other postal clerks; however, the starting salary is higher. Distribution clerks begin at postal pay level six while other clerks and carriers begin at level five. Increasing automation within the postal service has made the job of the distribution clerk quite secure.

Although the amount of mail post offices handle is expected to grow as both the population and the number of businesses grow, modernization of post offices and installation of new equipment will increase the amount of mail each clerk can handle. For example, machines that semiautomatically mark destination codes on envelopes are now being introduced. These codes can be read by computer-controlled letter-sorting machines, which automatically drop each letter into the proper slot for its destination. With this system, clerks read addresses only once, at the time they are coded, instead of several times, as they do now. Eventually this equipment will be installed in all large post offices.

Applicants must be physically able to perform the duties described. Any physical condition that causes the applicant to be a hazard to him/herself or to others will be a disqualification for appointment.

The distant vision for clerk positions must test at least 20/30 (Snellen) in one eye (glasses are permitted). Some distribution clerk positions may be filled by the deaf.

A physical examination, drug test, and psychological interview are required before appointment.

Letter-sorting machine operator applicants must take Exam 470.

FLAT SORTING MACHINE OPERATOR

Duties of the Job

The work of the Flat Sorting Machine Operator is very similar to that of the Letter-Sorting Machine Operator except that the Flat Sorting Machine Operator works with large, bulky packages. Greater physical strength and stamina are required in this position. The postal pay level at entry is level six, and with ever-increasing automation and mechanization of post offices, job security is virtually assured.

Flat sorting machine operator applicants must take Exam 470.

MAIL HANDLER

Duties of the Job

The mail handler loads, unloads, and moves bulk mail, and he or she performs duties incidental to the movement and processing of mail. Duties may include separation of mail sacks; facing letter mail; canceling stamps on parcel post; operating canceling machines, addressographs, and mimeographs; operating a fork-lift truck; rewrapping parcels; and so forth.

Mail handler applicants must take Exam 470.

Strength and Stamina Test

A physical examination is required before appointment. Persons who have had an arm, leg, or foot amputated should not apply.

When eligibles are within reach of appointment, they are required to pass a test of strength and stamina. In this test they are required to lift, shoulder, and carry two 70-pound sacks 15 feet—one at a time—and load them on a hand truck. They are required to push the truck to an area containing some 40-, 50-, and 60-pound sacks. They are required to load the sacks onto the truck. They next have to unload the truck and return the truck to its original location. Eligibles are notified when and where to report for the test of strength and stamina.

Persons with certain physical conditions are not permitted to take the test of strength and stamina without prior approval of a physician. These physical conditions include hernia or rupture, back trouble, heart trouble, pregnancy, or any other condition that makes it dangerous to the eligible to lift and carry 70-pound weights. Persons with these physical conditions are given special instructions at the time they are notified to report for the strength and stamina test.

An eligible being considered for an appointment who fails to qualify on the strength and stamina test is not tested again in the same group of hires. If the eligible fails the test a second time, his or her eligibility for the position of mail handler is canceled.

MAIL PROCESSOR

Duties of the Job

A mail processor performs such tasks as:

1. Operating mail-processing equipment, including bar code sorters and optical bar code readers;
2. Acting as minor trouble-shooter for the equipment;
3. Collating and bundling processed mail and transferring it from one work area to another;
4. Processing by hand mail that cannot be handled by the machines;
5. Loading mail into bins and onto trucks;
6. Other related tasks.

Mail processor applicants must take Exam 470.

Physical requirements for mail processors are not as stringent as those for mail handlers because the work is not as strenuous. Since the demands of the work are less, mail processors enter at postal pay level three rather than at the level four of mail handlers.

MARK-UP CLERK, AUTOMATED

Duties of the Job

The mark-up clerk, automated, operates an electro-mechanical machine to process mail that is classified as "undeliverable as addressed." In doing this, the mark-up clerk operates the keyboard of a computer terminal to enter and extract data to several databases including change of address, mailer's database, and address-correction file. The mark-up clerk must select the correct program and operating mode for each application, must affix labels to mail either manually or with mechanical devices, and must prepare forms for address-correction services. Other duties may include distribution of processed mark-ups to appropriate separations for further handling, operation of a photocopy machine, and other job-related tasks in support of primary duties.

Qualification Requirements

An applicant for a mark-up clerk position must have had either six months of clerical or office-machine-operating experience or have completed high school or have had a full academic year (36 weeks) of business school. The record of experience and training must show ability to use reference materials and manuals; ability to perform effectively under pressure; ability to operate any office equipment appropriate to the position; ability to work with others; and ability to read, understand, and apply certain regulations and procedures commonly used in processing mail that is undeliverable as addressed.

For appointment, a mark-up clerk must be 18 years old, or 16 years old if a high school graduate. An applicant who will reach his or her eighteenth birthday within two years from the date of the exam may participate. A mark-up clerk must be able to read, without strain, printed material the size of typewritten characters and must have 20/40 (Snellen) vision in one eye. Glasses are permitted. In addition, the applicant must pass a computer-administered alpha-numeric typing test. Candidates with high scores on the competitive exam, Exam 470, and with the requisite experience are called to the alpha-numeric typing test, Exam 715, individually as openings occur and hiring is likely. The exam is administered on a personal computer with its numeric keyboard disabled so that the candidate must use only the main keyboard. The Postal Service does not distribute sample questions for Exam 715, but the instructions at the test site are very clear and ample time is allowed for preparation. The alpha-numeric typing test is not a competitive test. The candidate needs only to pass to qualify.

RURAL CARRIER

Duties of the Job

The work of the rural carrier combines the work of the window clerk and the letter carrier but also has special characteristics of its own. The rural carrier's day begins with sorting and loading the mail for delivery on his or her own route. Then comes a day's drive, which may be over unpaved roads and rough terrain. The rural carrier does most deliveries and pickups of outgoing mail from the car. Occasionally, however, bulky packages must be delivered directly to the homeowner's door. Since rural postal patrons may be far from the nearest post office, the rural carrier sells stamps, weighs and charges for packages to be mailed, and performs most other services performed by window clerks in post offices. At the end of the day, the rural carrier returns to the post office with outgoing mail and money collected in various transactions. The rural carrier must be able to account for the stamps, postcards, and other supplies with which he or she left in the morning and must "balance the books" each day.

A rural carrier enjoys a great deal of independence. No supervisor looks over his or her shoulder. On the other hand, there is no supervisor to turn to for advice on how to handle a new situation that may come up.

Since the rural carrier's job requires driving, the minimum age for a rural carrier is 18. The rural carrier must have a valid driver's license, good eyesight, and the ability to hear ordinary conversation (glasses and hearing aid are permitted). In addition, the rural carrier must demonstrate physical stamina and ability to withstand the rigors of the job.

Rural carrier applicants must take Exam 460, which is identical in every way to Exam 470.

OFFICIAL SAMPLE QUESTIONS FOR EXAMINATIONS 470 AND 460

This section discusses exams 470 and 460, for people who are applying for the following positions:

City Carrier
Clerk
Distribution Clerk, Machine (LSM Operator)
Flat Sorting Machine Operator
Mail Handler
Mail Processor
Mark-Up Clerk
Rural Carrier

Examinations 470 and 460 are identical, and so the official sample questions are the same. Examination 460 is offered whenever a postal district is prepared to establish a new list of eligible candidates to fill positions as rural carriers. Examination 470 is offered when a postal district needs to establish a list of eligibles for any one of the seven titles that are covered by Examination 470. At the time of taking the examination, a test-taker may check off as few as one job title or as many as all seven, thereby taking one examination for as many of these jobs as the test-taker wishes to apply for. The same exam and the same score may then find their way onto a number of hiring lists, and the applicant will have a better chance of actually being hired.

Test Instructions

During the test session, it will be your responsibility to pay close attention to what the examiner has to say and to follow all instructions. One of the purposes of the test is to see how quickly and accurately you can work. Therefore, each part of the test will be carefully timed. You will not START until you are told to do so. Also, when you are told to STOP, you must immediately STOP answering the questions. When you are told to work on a particular part of the examination, regardless of which part, you are to work on that part ONLY. If you finish a part before time is called, you may review your answers for that part, but you will not go on or back to any other part. Failure to follow ANY directions given to you by the examiner may be grounds for disqualification. Instructions read by the examiner are intended to ensure that each applicant has the same fair and objective opportunity to compete in the examination.

Sample Questions

Study carefully before the examination.

The following questions are like the ones that will be on the test. Study these carefully. This will give you practice with the different kinds of questions and show you how to mark your answers.

Part A: Address Checking

In this part of the test, you will have to decide whether two addresses are alike or different. If the two addresses are exactly *Alike* in every way, darken circle A for the question. If the two addresses are *Different* in any way, darken circle D for the question.

Mark your answers to these sample questions on the Sample Answer Grid at the right.

1 ...2134 S 20th St   2134 S 20th St

Since the two addresses are exactly alike, mark A for question 1 on the Sample Answer Grid.

2 ...4608 N Warnock St   4806 N Warnock St

3 ...1202 W Girard Dr   1202 W Girard Rd

4 ...Chappaqua NY   10514   Chappaqua NY   10514

5 ...2207 Markland Ave   2207 Markham Ave

Sample Answer Grid	
1 ● Ⓓ	
2 Ⓐ ●	
3 Ⓐ ●	
4 ● Ⓓ	
5 Ⓐ ●	

The correct answers to questions 2 to 5 are: 2D, 3D, 4A, and 5D.

Your score on Part A of the actual test will be based on the number of wrong answers as well as on the number of right answers. Part A is scored right answers minus wrong answers. Random guessing should not help your score. For the Part A test, you will have six minutes to answer as many of the 95 questions as you can. It will be to your advantage to work as quickly and as accurately as possible. You will not be expected to be able to answer all the questions in the time allowed.

Part B: Memory for Addresses

In this part of the test, you will have to memorize the locations (A, B, C, D, or E) of 25 addresses shown in five boxes, like those below. For example, "Sardis" is in Box C, "6800–6999 Table" is in Box B, and so forth. (The addresses in the actual test will be different.)

A	B	C	D	E
4700–5599 Table	6800–6999 Table	5600–6499 Table	6500–6799 Table	4400–4699 Table
Lismore	Kelford	Joel	Tatum	Ruskin
5600–6499 West	6500–6799 West	6800–6999 West	4400–4699 West	4700–5599 West
Hesper	Musella	Sardis	Porter	Nathan
4400–4699 Blake	5600–6499 Blake	6500–6799 Blake	4700–5599 Blake	6800–6999 Blake

Study the locations of the addresses for five minutes. As you study, silently repeat these to yourself. Then cover the boxes and try to answer the questions below. Mark your answers for each question by darkening the circle as was done for questions 1 and 2

1. Musella

2. 4700–5599 Blake

3. 4700–5599 Table

4. Tatum

5. 4400–4699 Blake

6. Hesper

7. Kelford

8. Nathan

9. 6500–6799 Blake

10. Joel

11. 4400–4699 Blake

12. 6500–6799 West

13. Porter

14. 6800–6999 Blake

Sample Answer Grid			
1 Ⓐ ● Ⓒ Ⓓ Ⓔ	5 Ⓐ Ⓑ Ⓒ Ⓓ Ⓔ	9 Ⓐ Ⓑ Ⓒ Ⓓ Ⓔ	13 Ⓐ Ⓑ Ⓒ Ⓓ Ⓔ
2 Ⓐ Ⓑ Ⓒ ● Ⓔ	6 Ⓐ Ⓑ Ⓒ Ⓓ Ⓔ	10 Ⓐ Ⓑ Ⓒ Ⓓ Ⓔ	14 Ⓐ Ⓑ Ⓒ Ⓓ Ⓔ
3 Ⓐ Ⓑ Ⓒ Ⓓ Ⓔ	7 Ⓐ Ⓑ Ⓒ Ⓓ Ⓔ	11 Ⓐ Ⓑ Ⓒ Ⓓ Ⓔ	
4 Ⓐ Ⓑ Ⓒ Ⓓ Ⓔ	8 Ⓐ Ⓑ Ⓒ Ⓓ Ⓔ	12 Ⓐ Ⓑ Ⓒ Ⓓ Ⓔ	

The correct answers for questions 3 to 14 are: 3A, 4D, 5A, 6A, 7B, 8E, 9C, 10C, 11A, 12B, 13D, and 14E.

During the examination, you will have three practice exercises to help you memorize the location of addresses shown in the five boxes. After the practice exercises, the actual test will be given. Part B is scored right answers minus one-fourth of the wrong answers. Random guessing should not help your score, but if you can eliminate one or more alternatives, it is to your advantage to guess. For the Part B test, you will have five minutes to answer as many of the 88 questions as you can. It will be to your advantage to work as quickly and as accurately as you can. You will not be expected to be able to answer all the questions in the time allowed.

Part C: Number Series

For each *Number Series* question there is at the left a series of numbers that follow some definite order and at the right five sets of two numbers each. You are to look at the numbers in the series at the left and find out what order they follow. Then decide what the next two numbers in that series would be if the same order were continued. Mark your answers on the Sample Answer Grid.

1. 1 2 3 4 5 6 7 .... (A) 1 2   (B) 5 6   (C) 8 9   (D) 4 5   (E) 7 8

The numbers in this series are increasing by 1. If the series were continued for two more numbers, it would read: 1 2 3 4 5 6 7 8 9. Therefore the correct answer is 8 and 9 and you should have darkened C for question 1.

2. 15 14 13 12 11 10 9 .... (A) 2 1   (B) 17 16 (C) 8 9   (D) 8 7   (E) 9 8

The numbers in this series are decreasing by 1. If the series were continued for two more numbers, it would read: 15 14 13 12 11 10 9 8 7. Therefore the correct answer is 8 and 7 and you should have darkened D for question 2.

3. 20 20 21 21 22 22 23 .... (A) 23 23 (B) 23 24 (C) 19 19 (D) 22 23 (E) 21 22

Each number in this series is repeated and then increased by 1. If the series were continued for two more numbers, it would read: 20 20 21 21 22 22 23 23 24. Therefore the correct answer is 23 and 24 and you should have darkened B for question 3.

4. 17 3 17 4 17 5 17 .... (A) 6 17   (B) 6 7   (C) 17 6   (D) 5 6   (E) 17 7

This series is the number 17 separated by numbers increasing by 1, beginning with the number 3. If the series were continued for two more numbers, it would read: 17 3 17 4 17 5 17 6 17. Therefore the correct answer is 6 and 17 and you should have darkened A for question 4.

5. 1 2 4 5 7 8 10 .... (A) 11 12 (B) 12 14 (C) 10 13 (D) 12 13 (E) 11 13

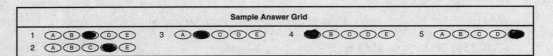

Sample Answer Grid			
1 Ⓐ Ⓑ ● Ⓓ Ⓔ	3 Ⓐ ● Ⓒ Ⓓ Ⓔ	4 ● Ⓑ Ⓒ Ⓓ Ⓔ	5 Ⓐ Ⓑ Ⓒ Ⓓ ●
2 Ⓐ Ⓑ Ⓒ ● Ⓔ			

The numbers in this series are increasing first by 1 (plus 1) and then by 2 (plus 2). If the series were continued for two more numbers, it would read: 1 2 4 5 7 8 10 (plus 1) <u>11</u> and (plus 2) <u>13</u>. Therefore the correct answer is 11 and 13 and you should have darkened E for question 5.

Now read and work sample questions 6 through 10 and mark your answers on the Sample Answer Grid.

6. 21 21 20 20 19 19 18 .... (A) 18 18   (B) 18 17   (C) 17 18   (D) 17 17   (E) 18 19

7. 1 22 1 23 1 24 1 .... (A) 26 1   (B) 25 26   (C) 25 1   (D) 1 26   (E) 1 25

8. 1 20 3 19 5 18 7 .... (A) 8 9   (B) 8 17   (C) 17 10   (D) 17 9   (E) 9 18

9. 4 7 10 13 16 19 22 .... (A) 23 26   (B) 25 27   (C) 25 26   (D) 25 28   (E) 24 27

10. 30 2 28 4 26 6 24 .... (A) 23 9   (B) 26 8   (C) 8 9   (D) 26 22   (E) 8 22

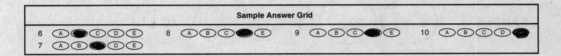

The correct answers to sample questions 6 to 10 are: 6B, 7C, 8D, 9D and 10E. Explanations follow.

6. Each number in the series repeats itself and then decreases by 1 or minus 1; <u>21</u> (repeat) <u>21</u> (minus 1) <u>20</u> (repeat) <u>20</u> (minus 1) <u>19</u> (repeat) <u>19</u> (minus 1) <u>18</u> (repeat) <u>?</u> (minus 1) <u>?</u>

7. The number 1 is separated by numbers that begin with 22 and increase by 1; <u>1 22 1</u> (increase 22 by 1) <u>23 1</u> (increase 23 by 1) <u>24 1</u> (increase 24 by 1) ?

8. This is best explained by two alternating series—one series starts with 1 and increases by 2 or plus 2; the other series starts with 20 and decreases by 1 or minus 1.

1	^	3	^	5	^	7	^	?
20		19		18		?		

9. This series of numbers increases by 3 (plus 3) beginning with the first number—<u>4</u> <u>7</u> <u>10</u> <u>13</u> <u>16</u> <u>19</u> <u>22</u> ? ?

10. Look for two alternating series—one series starts with 30 and decreases by 2 (minus 2): the other series starts with 2 and increases by 2 (plus 2).

Now try questions 11 to 15.

11. 5 6 20 7 8 19 9 .... (A) 10 18   (B) 18 17   (C) 10 17   (D) 18 19   (E) 10 11

12. 4 6 9 11 14 16 19 .... (A) 21 24   (B) 22 25   (C) 20 22   (D) 21 23   (E) 22 24

13. 8 8 1 10 10 3 12 .... (A) 13 13   (B) 12 5   (C) 12 4   (D) 13 5   (E) 4 12

14. 10 12 50 15 17 50 20 .... (A) 50 21   (B) 21 50   (C) 50 22   (D) 22 50   (E) 22 24

15. 20 21 23 24 27 28 32 33 38 39.. (A) 45 46   (B) 45 52   (C) 44 45   (D) 44 49   (E) 40 46

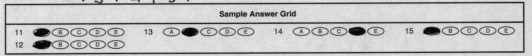

The correct answers to the sample questions above are: 11A, 12A, 13B, 14D and 15A.

It will be to your advantage to answer every question in Part C that you can, since your score on this part of the test will be based on the number of questions that you answer correctly. Answer first those questions that are easiest for you. For the Part C test, you will have 20 minutes to answer as many of the 24 questions as you can.

Part D: Following Oral Directions

In this part of the test, you will be told to follow directions by writing in a test booklet and then on an answer sheet. The test booklet will have lines of material like the following five samples:

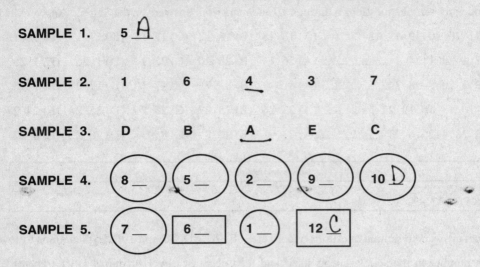

SAMPLE 1.   5 _A_

SAMPLE 2.   1   6   _4_   3   7

SAMPLE 3.   D   B   _A_   E   C

SAMPLE 4.   (8 __)   (5 __)   (2 __)   (9 __)   (10 _D_)

SAMPLE 5.   (7 __)   [6 __]   (1 __)   [12 _C_]

To practice this part of the test, tear out the page of instructions to be read. Then have somebody read the instructions to you, while you follow them. When he or she tells you to darken the space on the Sample Answer Grid, use the one on this page.

Your score for Part D will be based on the number of questions that you answer correctly. Therefore, if you are not sure of an answer, it will be to your advantage to guess. Part D will take about 25 minutes.

	Sample Answer Grid		
1 Ⓐ Ⓑ Ⓒ Ⓓ Ⓔ	5 ● Ⓑ Ⓒ Ⓓ Ⓔ	9 ● Ⓑ Ⓒ Ⓓ Ⓔ	
2 Ⓐ Ⓑ Ⓒ Ⓓ Ⓔ	6 Ⓐ Ⓑ Ⓒ Ⓓ Ⓔ	10 Ⓐ Ⓑ Ⓒ ● Ⓔ	
3 Ⓐ Ⓑ Ⓒ Ⓓ Ⓔ	7 Ⓐ Ⓑ Ⓒ Ⓓ Ⓔ	11 Ⓐ Ⓑ Ⓒ Ⓓ Ⓔ	
4 Ⓐ ● Ⓒ Ⓓ Ⓔ	8 Ⓐ Ⓑ Ⓒ Ⓓ Ⓔ	12 Ⓐ Ⓑ ● Ⓓ Ⓔ	

Instructions to be read for Part D. (The words in parentheses should NOT be read aloud.)

You are to follow the instructions that I shall read to you. I cannot repeat them.

Look at the samples. Sample 1 has a number and a line beside it. On the line write A as in ace. **(Pause 2 seconds.)** Now, on the Sample Answer Grid, find number 5 **(pause 2 seconds)** and darken the letter you just wrote on the line. **(Pause 2 seconds.)**

Look at Sample 2. (Pause slightly.) Draw a line under the third number. **(Pause 2 seconds.)** Now, on the Sample Answer Grid, find the number under which you just drew a line and darken B as in boy. **(Pause 5 seconds.)**

Look at the letters in Sample 3. (Pause slightly.) Draw a line under the third letter in the line. **(Pause 2 seconds.)** Now, on your Sample Answer Grid, find number 9 **(pause 2 seconds)** and darken the letter under which you drew a line. **(Pause 5 seconds.)**

Look at the five circles in Sample 4. (Pause slightly.) Each circle has a number and a line in it. Write D as in dog on the line in the last circle. **(Pause 2 seconds.)** Now, on the Sample Answer Grid, darken the number-letter combination that is in the circle you just wrote in. **(Pause 5 seconds.)**

Look at Sample 5. (Pause slightly.) There are two circles and two boxes of different sizes with numbers in them. **(Pause slightly.)** If 4 is more than 2 and if 5 is less than 3, write A as in ace in the smaller circle. **(Pause slightly.)** Otherwise write C as in car in the larger box. **(Pause 2 seconds.)** Now, on the Sample Answer Grid, darken the number-letter combination in the box or circle in which you just wrote. **(Pause 5 seconds.)**

Now look at the Sample Answer Grid. (Pause slightly.) You should have darkened 4B, 5A, 9A, 10D, and 12C on the Sample Answer Grid. **(If the person preparing to take the examination made any mistakes, try to help him or her see why he or she made wrong marks.)**

TEAR HERE

EXAM 715—ALPHA-NUMERIC TYPING TEST FOR MARK-UP CLERK, AUTOMATED

The Postal Service does not issue official sample questions for Exam 715.

Exam 715, the typing test for Mark-up Clerk applicants, is quite different from an ordinary typing test. You will take this test by private appointment, and all interaction will be between you and a computer. Do not be frightened. Even if you have had no experience whatsoever with computers, this is not an intimidating test. The computer is user-friendly and is very specific in spelling out directions. And, unless you are a typing whiz, the typing test itself is probably easier than a plain paper copying test.

As Exam 715 begins, the computer screen explains to you which buttons you will be using and what each does. You need to use very few buttons—letters, numbers, "return," "delete," and "lock caps." You will get a chance to use these and to become familiar with their operation as you fill in basic name and social security number types of information. A test administrator remains in the room to answer questions.

The computer then explains the typing task of the exam itself. A letter-number code appears on the upper right screen; you are to copy it, then press the return button to bring the next code to the screen. That's it. The codes all consist of four letters and three numbers, such as TYHO346 or BZIP801. The faster you type, the more codes you have an opportunity to copy. In the explanation phase of the exam, you will have 15 seconds in which to copy five codes. The computer will tell you how many you copied correctly.

After the explanation phase comes a practice session. You will be allowed five minutes to copy as many codes as you can correctly, again one at a time. The five-minute practice session does not count. This is your chance to experiment with looking at your fingers or at the screen; with memorizing each code to be typed, or with staring at the code while typing; with typing as fast as you can, not even looking at the screen to see if you are typing correctly; or with checking to make sure you are copying correctly and repairing errors before continuing.

Be aware than an error that has been corrected on the computer is not counted as an error. Since accuracy is so important and since correction is so easy on the computer, it is worthwhile to correct errors. Unless you are extremely inaccurate, you will not lose much time correcting errors and will gain valuable points through accuracy.

Here is a suggested approach:

1. Look at the code and quickly memorize it; four letters and three numbers should pose no problem for such a short-term task.
2. Type in the code, looking at the center of the screen where the letters and numbers that you are typing appear.
3. Delete and retype if you spot an error.
4. Hit the return button and do the same for the next code.

The five-minute practice period should allow you to establish a rhythm for this process. When the five minutes are up, your score will flash on the screen. A score of 14 is required for passing. If you have scored 14 or higher, approach the actual test with confidence. If your score is lower than 14, be reassured that it will not be counted. Remember that you used the first few minutes of the practice period to perfect your system. You now have five minutes to use the system with which you have become comfortable. Your second score, the score that does count, will be higher.

The actual test session is exactly like the practice session, with different codes of course. At the end of the five-minute test, your final score will appear on the screen. You will know instantly whether you have passed or failed; whether you are eligible or ineligible. If you are eligible, you can expect to be called for an employment interview sometime in the near future.

CLERK-TYPIST

Duties of the Job

A clerk-typist types records, letters, memorandums, reports, and other materials from handwritten and other drafts or from a dictating machine; he or she sets up the material typed in accordance with prescribed format and assembles it for initialing, signing, routing, and dispatch. The clerk-typist also cuts mimeograph stencils and masters for duplication by other processes. The miscellaneous office clerical duties of the position include: making up file folders, keeping them in the prescribed order, and filing in them; making and keeping routine office records; composing routine memorandums and letters relating to the business of the office, such as acknowledgments and transmittals; examining incoming and outgoing mail of the office, routing it to the appropriate persons, and controlling the time allowed for preparation of replies to incoming correspondence; receipting and delivering salary checks and filling out various personnel forms; acting as receptionist and furnishing routine information over the telephone; relieving other office personnel in their absence; operating office machines such as the mimeograph, comptometer, and adding machine.

The applicant for a position as clerk-typist must have had one year of office experience or four years of high school business courses or 36 weeks of business or secretarial school. The applicant must also show that he or she has enough of the skills, abilities, and knowledge to read and understand instructions; perform basic arithmetic computations; maintain accurate records; prepare reports and correspondence if required; and operate office machines such as calculators, adding machines, duplicators, and the like. The applicant for a clerk-typist position must pass a test of clerical abilities, Exam 710, and a "plain copy" typing test, Exam 712, administered on a personal computer, with a speed of 45 wpm and good accuracy.

CLERK-STENOGRAPHER

Duties of the Job

The clerk-stenographer performs all of the functions of the clerk-typist. In addition, the clerk-stenographer takes dictation, in shorthand or on a shorthand writing machine, of letters, memorandums, reports, and other materials given by the supervisor of the office and other employees. He or she then transcribes it on the typewriter, or word processor, setting up the material transcribed in accordance with prescribed format and assembling it for required initialing, signing, routing, and dispatch. In consideration of the extra training and skill required in the taking of dictation, the clerk-stenographer is rated at salary level five, rather than at the salary level four of the clerk-typist.

The applicant for the position of clerk-stenographer must meet all the requirements of the applicant for clerk-typist in terms of education or experience and in terms of skills, abilities, and knowledge. In addition to passing the test of clerical ability, Exam 710, and the computer-administered plain-copy typing test, Exam 712, the clerk-stenographer applicant must also pass the stenography test, Exam 711.

DATA CONVERSION OPERATOR

Duties of the Job

Data conversion operators use a computer terminal to prepare mail for automated sorting equipment. They read typed or handwritten addresses from a letter image on the terminal screen and then select and type essential information so that an address bar code can be applied to the letter. Depending on the quality of the address information shown on the image, the data conversion operator will be prompted to key the five-number ZIP code or an abbreviated version of the street and city address. Abbreviated addresses must conform to strict encoding rules so that the abbreviation can then be expanded to a full address by the computer so that it can find the correct ZIP + 4 code. Unlike some other types of data entry, this job is not just "key what you see."

Data conversion operators are the vital personnel in the Remote Bar Coding System (RBCS), a system designed to allow letter mail that cannot be read by a machine to be bar coded and processed in the automated mail stream. RBCS technology has created a new operation called a remote encoding center (REC). RBCS has two major elements, an input sub system (ISS) and an output sub system (OSS).

At the processing plant, ISS takes a video picture or image of each letter and then attempts to look up the address to find a ZIP + 4 code. For letters for which the ISS computer cannot find a ZIP + 4 code, corresponding images are transmitted by telephone lines to data conversion operators at the remote encoding center for further processing. At the REC, data conversion operators working at video display terminals are presented with images one at a time. Using specific rules, operators key data for each image so that the computers can find the correct ZIP + 4 code.

At the plant, the output sub system sprays letters with correct ZIP + 4 bar codes and performs initial sorting. Letters are then processed by bar code sorters. These elements are linked together by a communication system consisting of cabling and telephone or microwave telecommunications.

Working Conditions

Remote encoding centers offer a possibility for flexible scheduling. The basic work hours are between 3:00 P.M. and 1:00 A.M. Individual work schedules range between four and eight hours. RECs operate seven days a week. Persons filling data conversion operator positions as temporary or transitional employees will earn one hour of leave for every 20 hours worked but no other benefits. Career employees receive a full benefits package including health and life insurance, sick and annual leave, federal employees retirement system, and eligibility to participate in the thrift savings plan.

Qualification Requirements

All applicants are required to pass Exam 710, the test of clerical abilities, with a score of 70 or better. Names are placed on a hiring list in rank order. As an applicant reaches consideration for employment, he or she will be called for the computer-based Exam 714, a job-simulated data entry performance test. Typing or data-entry experience is a prerequisite for this position.

Applicants must have vision of 20/40 (Snellen) in one eye and the ability to read without strain printed material the size of typewritten characters. Corrective lenses are permitted. The ability to distinguish basic colors and shades is desirable. Applicants under consideration for employment are subject to urinalysis drug screening.

OFFICIAL SAMPLE QUESTIONS FOR EXAMINATION 710

This section discusses the exam of clerical abilities for clerk-typist, clerk-stenographer, and data conversion operator.

The following questions are samples of the types of questions that will be used on Examination 710. Study these questions carefully. Each question has several suggested answers. You are to decide which one is the **best answer.** Next, on the Sample Answer Sheet below, find the answer space that is numbered the same number as the question, then darken the space that is lettered the same as the answer you have selected. After you have answered all the questions, compare your answers with the ones given in the Correct Answers to Sample Questions.

Sample Questions 1 through 14—Clerical Aptitude

In Sample Questions 1 through 3, there is a name, number, or code in a box at the left and four other names, numbers, or codes in alphabetical or numerical order at the right. Find the correct space for the boxed name or number so that it will be in alphabetical and/or numerical order with the others and mark the letter of that space on your Sample Answer Sheet below.

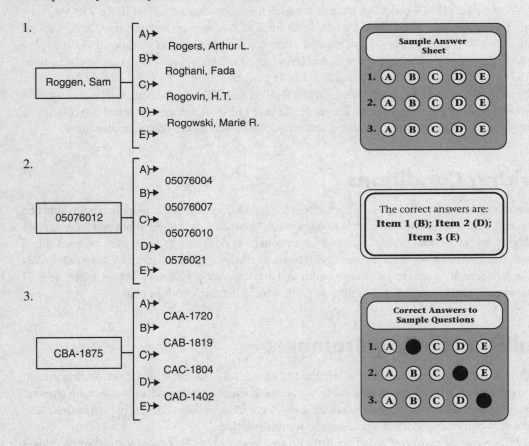

Sample Questions 4 through 8 require you to compare names, addresses, or codes. In each line across the page there are three names, addresses, or codes that are very much alike. Compare the three and decide which ones are EXACTLY alike. On the Sample Answer Sheet, mark:

A   if **ALL THREE** names, addresses, or codes are exactly **ALIKE**
B   if only the **FIRST** and **SECOND** names, addresses, or codes are exactly **ALIKE**
C   if only the **FIRST** and **THIRD** names, addresses, or codes are exactly **ALIKE**
D   if only the **SECOND** and **THIRD** names, addresses, or codes are exactly **ALIKE**
E   if **ALL THREE** names, addresses, or codes are **DIFFERENT**

4. Helene Bedell   Helene Beddell   Helene Beddell

5. F. T. Wedemeyer   F. T. Wedemeyer   F. T. Wedmeyer

6. 3214 W. Beaumont St.   3214 Beaumount St.   3214 Beaumont St.

7. BC 3105T-5   BC 3015T-5   BC 3105T-5

8. 4460327   4460327   4460327

For the next two questions, find the correct spelling of the word and darken the appropriate answer space on your Sample Answer Sheet. If none of the alternatives is correct, darken space D.

9. (A) accomodate   10. (A) manageble
    (B) acommodate   (B) manageable
    (C) accommadate   (C) manegeable
    (D) none of the above   (D) none of the above

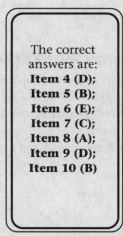

The correct answers are:
Item 4 (D);
Item 5 (B);
Item 6 (E);
Item 7 (C);
Item 8 (A);
Item 9 (D);
Item 10 (B)

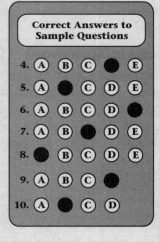

For Questions 11 through 14, perform the computation as indicated in the question and find the answer among the list of alternative responses. If the correct answer is not given among the choices, mark E.

11.   32 + 26 =
      (A) 69
      (B) 59
      (C) 58
      (D) 54
      (E) none of the above

12. 57 – 15 =
    (A) 72
    (B) 62
    (C) 54
    (D) 44
    (E) none of the above

The correct answers are:
**Item 11 (C); Item 12 (E);
Item 13 (B); Item 14 (A)**

13. 23 × 7 =
    (A) 164
    (B) 161
    (C) 154
    (D) 141
    (E) none of the above

**Correct Answers to
Sample Questions**

14. 160 / 5 =
    (A) 32
    (B) 30
    (C) 25
    (D) 21
    (E) none of the above

Sample Questions 15 through 22—Verbal Abilities

Sample Questions 15 through 17 test your ability to follow instructions. Each question directs you to mark a specific number and letter combination on your Sample Answer Sheet. The questions require your total concentration because the answers that you are instructed to mark are, for the most part, NOT in numerical sequence (i.e., you would not use Number 1 on your answer sheet to answer Question 1; Number 2 for Question 2; etc.). Instead, you must mark the number and space specifically designated in each test question.

15. Look at the letters below. Draw a circle around the middle letter. Now, on your Sample Answer Sheet, find Number 16 and darken the space for the letter you just circled.

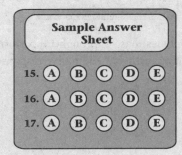

**Sample Answer
Sheet**

        R   C   H

16. Draw a line under the number shown below that is more than 10 but less than 20. Find that number on your Sample Answer Sheet, and darken Space A.

    5   9   17   22

17. Add the numbers 11 and 4 and write your answer on the blank line below. Now find this number on your Sample Answer Sheet and darken the space for the second letter in the alphabet.

    _____

Answer the remaining Sample Test Questions on the Sample Answer Sheet in numerical sequence (i.e., Number 18 on the Sample Answer Sheet for Question 18; Number 19 for Question 19, etc.).

Choose the sentence below that is most appropriate with respect to grammar, usage, and punctuation, so as to be suitable for a business letter or report and darken its letter on the Sample Answer Sheet.

18. (A) He should of responded to the letter by now.
    (B) A response to the letter by the end of the week.
    (C) The letter required his immediate response.
    (D) A response by him to the letter is necessary.

Questions 19 and 20 consist of a sentence containing a word in **boldface** type. Choose the best meaning for the word in **boldface** type and darken its letter on the Sample Answer Sheet.

The correct answers are:
Item 15 (B); Item 16 (C);
Item 17 (A)

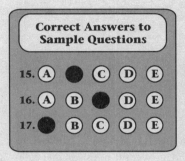

The correct answers are:
Item 18 (C); Item 19 (B);
Item 20 (D)

19. The payment was **authorized** yesterday. **Authorized** most nearly means

(A) expected
(B) approved
(C) refunded
(D) received

20. Please **delete** the second paragraph. **Delete** most nearly means

(A) type
(B) read
(C) edit
(D) omit

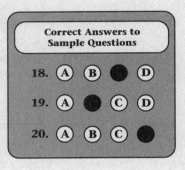

In questions 21 and 22 below, read each paragraph and answer the question that follows it by darkening the letter of the correct answer on the Sample Answer Sheet.

21. Window Clerks working for the Postal Service have direct financial responsibility for the selling of postage. In addition, they are expected to have a thorough knowledge concerning the acceptability of all material offered by customers for mailing. Any information provided to the public by these employees must be completely accurate.

The paragraph best supports the statement that Window Clerks

(A) must account for the stamps issued to them for sale
(B) have had long training in other Postal Service jobs
(C) must help sort mail to be delivered by carriers
(D) inspect the contents of all packages offered for mailing

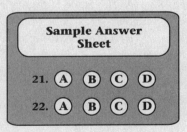

22. The most efficient method for performing a task is not always easily determined. That which is economical in terms of time must be carefully distinguished from that which is economical in terms of expended energy. In short, the quickest method may require a degree of physical effort that may be neither essential nor desirable.

The paragraph best supports the statement that

(A) it is more efficient to perform a task slowly than rapidly
(B) skill in performing a task should not be acquired at the expense of time
(C) the most efficient execution of a task is not always the one done in the shortest time
(D) energy and time cannot both be considered in the performance of a single task

The correct answers are:
Item 21 (A); Item 22 (C);

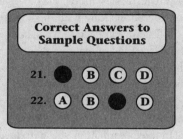

Correct Answers to Sample Questions

21. ● B C D
22. A B ● D

OFFICIAL SAMPLE QUESTIONS FOR EXAMINATION 712

This section discusses the plain copy typing test for clerk-typist, clerk-stenographer, and other positions requiring typing of text.

The plain copy typing test is administered on a personal computer, not on a typewriter. A qualifying speed is 45 words per minute, because, since corrections on the computer are quick and clean, the attitude toward errors is more relaxed than with a typing test on a typewriter. Nonetheless, accuracy is a consideration along with the 45-wpm speed required.

All stenographer and typist competitors will take this typing test (plain copy). The sample given below shows the kind of material that competitors must copy. See whether you can copy it twice in five minutes and how many errors your copy contains. Competitors will be required to meet a certain minimum in accuracy as well as in speed.

Space, paragraph, spell, punctuate, capitalize, and begin and end each line precisely as shown in the exercise.

In the examination you will have five minutes in which to make copies of the test exercise, keeping in mind that your eligibility will depend on accuracy as well as speed. When you complete the exercise, simply double space and begin again.

> This is an example of the type of material which will
> be presented to you as the actual typewriting examination.
> Each competitor will be required to typewrite the practice
> material exactly as it appears on the copy. You are to space,
> capitalize, punctuate, spell, and begin and end each line
> exactly as it is presented in the copy. Each time you reach
> the end of the paragraph you should begin again and continue
> to practice typing the practice paragraph on scratch paper
> until the examiner tells you to stop. You are advised that
> it is more important to type accurately than to type rapidly.

OFFICIAL SAMPLE QUESTIONS FOR EXAMINATION 711

This section discusses the stenography test for clerk-stenographer.

Only stenographer competitors take a stenography test. The sample below shows the length of material dictated. Sit down with your pencil and notebook, and hand this book to a friend. Have that person dictate the passage to you so that you can see how well prepared you are to take dictation at the rate of 80 words a minute. Each pair of lines is dictated in 10 seconds. Your friend should dictate periods, but not commas, and should read the exercise with the expression that the punctuation indicates.

Exactly on a minute start dictating. Finish reading each line at the number of seconds indicated below.

I realize that this practice dictation	
is not a part of the examination	10 sec.
proper and is not to be scored. (Period)	
When making a study of the private	20 sec.
pension structure and its influence on	
turnover, the most striking feature is its	30 sec.
youth. (Period) As has been shown, the time	
of greatest growth began just a few years	40 sec.
ago. (Period) The influence that this	
growth has had on the labor market and	50 sec.
worker attitudes is hard to assess,	
partly because the effects have not yet fully	1 min.
evolved and many are still in the	
growing stage. (Period) Even so, most pension	10 sec.
plans began with much more limited gains	
than they give now. (Period) For example,	20 sec.
as private plans mature they grant	
a larger profit and a greater range of gains to	30 sec.
more workers and thereby become more	
important. (Period) Plans that protect accrued pension	40 sec.
credits are rather new and are being	
revised in the light of past trends. (Period)	50 sec.
As informal and formal information on pension	
plans spreads, the workers become more	2 min.
aware of the plans and their provisions	
increase. (Period) Their impact on employee attitudes	10 sec.
and decisions will no doubt become	
stronger. (Period) Each year, more and more workers	20 sec.
will be retiring with a private pension,	
and their firsthand knowledge of the benefits to	30 sec.
be gained from private pensions will spread	
to still active workers. (Period) Thus, workers	40 sec.
may less often view pensions as just	
another part of the security package	50 sec.
based on service and more often	
see them as unique benefits. (Period)	3 min.

This transcript and word list for part of the above dictation are similar to those each competitor will receive for the dictation test. Many words have been omitted from the transcript. Compare your notes with it. When you come to a blank space in the transcript, decide what word (or words) belongs there. Look for the missing word in the word list. Notice what letter (A, B, C, or D) is printed beside the word. Write that letter in the blank. B is written in blank 1 to show how you are to record your choice. Write E if the exact answer is not in the word list. You may also write the word (or words) or the shorthand for it, if you wish. The same choice may belong in more than one blank.

ALPHABETIC WORD LIST

Write E if the answer is **not** listed.

a - D	make - A
attitudes - C	making - B
be - B	market - B
been - C	markets - D
began - D	marking - D
being - A	never - B
completely - A	not - D
examination - A	over - C
examine - B	part - C
examining - D	partly - D
feat - A	pension - C
feature - C	practical - C
full - B	practice - B
fully - D	private - D
greater - D	proper - C
grow - B	section - D
growing - C	so - B
had - D	still - A
has - C	structure - D
has been - B	structured - B
has had - A	to - D
has made - A	to be - C
in - C	trial - A
in part - B	turn - D
influence - A	turnover - B
labor - C	values - A
main - B	yet - C

TRANSCRIPT

I realize that this <u>B</u> dictation is___a
                             1   2

___of the ___ ___ and is ___
 3   4   5   6

___ scored.
 7

When ___ a ___ of the ___ ___ ___
           8   9   10 11 12

and its ___ on ___, the most striking ___
       13   14   15

is its youth. As ___ shown, the time of
               16

___ growth began just a few years ago.
 17

The ___ that this growth ___ on the
     18   19

labor ___ and worker ___ is hard to
      20   21

assess, ___ because the effects have not yet
       22

___ evolved and many are ___ in the
 23   24

___ stage. . . .
 25

(For the next sentences there would be another word list, if the entire sample dictation were transcribed.)

You will be given an answer sheet like the sample that follows, on which your answers can be scored by machine. Each number on the answer sheet stands for the blank with the same number in the transcript. Darken the space for the letter that is the same as the letter you wrote in the transcript. If you have not finished writing letters in the blanks in the transcript, or if you wish to make sure you have lettered them correctly, you may continue to use your notes after you begin marking the answer sheet.

ANSWER SHEET FOR SAMPLE TRANSCRIPT

1. Ⓐ Ⓑ Ⓒ Ⓓ Ⓔ   8. Ⓐ Ⓑ Ⓒ Ⓓ Ⓔ   14. Ⓐ Ⓑ Ⓒ Ⓓ Ⓔ   20. Ⓐ Ⓑ Ⓒ Ⓓ Ⓔ
2. Ⓐ Ⓑ Ⓒ Ⓓ Ⓔ   9. Ⓐ Ⓑ Ⓒ Ⓓ Ⓔ   15. Ⓐ Ⓑ Ⓒ Ⓓ Ⓔ   21. Ⓐ Ⓑ Ⓒ Ⓓ Ⓔ
3. Ⓐ Ⓑ Ⓒ Ⓓ Ⓔ   10. Ⓐ Ⓑ Ⓒ Ⓓ Ⓔ   16. Ⓐ Ⓑ Ⓒ Ⓓ Ⓔ   22. Ⓐ Ⓑ Ⓒ Ⓓ Ⓔ
4. Ⓐ Ⓑ Ⓒ Ⓓ Ⓔ   11. Ⓐ Ⓑ Ⓒ Ⓓ Ⓔ   17. Ⓐ Ⓑ Ⓒ Ⓓ Ⓔ   23. Ⓐ Ⓑ Ⓒ Ⓓ Ⓔ
5. Ⓐ Ⓑ Ⓒ Ⓓ Ⓔ   12. Ⓐ Ⓑ Ⓒ Ⓓ Ⓔ   18. Ⓐ Ⓑ Ⓒ Ⓓ Ⓔ   24. Ⓐ Ⓑ Ⓒ Ⓓ Ⓔ
6. Ⓐ Ⓑ Ⓒ Ⓓ Ⓔ   13. Ⓐ Ⓑ Ⓒ Ⓓ Ⓔ   19. Ⓐ Ⓑ Ⓒ Ⓓ Ⓔ   25. Ⓐ Ⓑ Ⓒ Ⓓ Ⓔ
7. Ⓐ Ⓑ Ⓒ Ⓓ Ⓔ

The correct answers for Questions 1 to 25 are:

1. **B**	6. **D**	11. **C**	16. **B**	21. **C**
2. **D**	7. **C**	12. **D**	17. **E**	22. **D**
3. **C**	8. **B**	13. **A**	18. **A**	23. **D**
4. **A**	9. **E**	14. **B**	19. **A**	24. **A**
5. **C**	10. **D**	15. **C**	20. **B**	25. **C**

OFFICIAL SAMPLE QUESTIONS FOR COMPUTER-BASED TEST 714

This section discusses the test for a remote bar coding system data conversion operator.

The CB 714 is a computer-administered and -scored exam. Applicants are assisted with the start-up of the exam and the exam instructions. You do *not* need prior experience on a computer terminal to take this test.

The exam contains a list of alpha-numeric postal data entry items just as you see in the sample items below. Applicants must demonstrate that they can type these items on the computer terminal at the following rate(s) based on the requirements of the position. The lower-level passing rate is five correct lines per minute. The higher-level passing rate is seven correct lines per minute. Credit is given only for correctly typed lines. Practice for the exam by typing the sample provided below.

Type each line as shown in the exercise, beginning with the first column. You may use lower-case or capital letters when typing the sample exercise. When you reach the end of a line, hit the space bar one time and begin typing the next line. If you reach the end of the sample items in the first column, continue with the items in the second column. If you finish both columns, simply begin again with the first column and continue to type until the five minutes have elapsed.

See whether you can copy the entire Sample Test once in five minutes. Now count the number of lines you typed correctly and divide this number by five to determine your per-minute score. Correctly typing only the items in column 1 is approximately equal to typing five correct lines per minute. Correctly typing all of the items in both columns is approximately equal to typing seven correct lines per minute.

In the exam you will have five minutes in which to type the test material. Keep in mind that in order to pass the test you must type both rapidly and accurately.

Sample Test Copy

4.90 STEERING DAMPER	JEFFERSON, W.A. 08/20/69
16.55 REAR DOOR LATCH	SPRINGFIELD 07215
23.80 TIMING CHAIN	GREENSBORO 07098
8721 8906	LEXINGTON 07540
2013 2547	FOURTH CLASS 363
5972 6841	INTN. SECTION 27
HANOVER RD. 600–699	200 BOX 10
ARKANSAS AVE. 4000–4199	18.25 DOWN SPRING
SO. MAIN ST. 1200–1299	3.10 VC GASKET
CAPITOL DR. 500–599	35.45 ROCKER ARM
L ON MAPLEWOOD PL.	4973 5261
RETRACE TO 421	6057 7382
R ON MOHICAN TO TOWER	2783 4195
4478267 LSM/LSM	GREENBRIAR DR. 1100–1399
4478271 MPLSM	MADISON ST. 3700–3799
4478289 EGR SECONDARY	BRUNSWICK AVE. 8100–8199
KNIGHT, J.R. 04/17/67	INDUSTRIAL RD. 2300–2499
CHARLES, S.M. 11/19/68	

CLEANER, CUSTODIAN, CUSTODIAL LABORER

Duties of the Job

Workers who serve as cleaners, custodians, or custodial laborers are charged with the maintenance of postal buildings. Their duties include routine and periodic heavy cleaning, routine maintenance such as replacing light bulbs, and responsibility for noticing when specialized maintenance or repair work is called for and for following through to be certain that whatever must be done is done at the proper time.

While the work of custodial laborers, cleaners, and custodians is not generally noticed by the public, their work is vital to the operation of post offices and to the health and safety of postal workers and patrons.

Qualification Requirements

The positions of cleaner, custodian, and custodial laborer are open *only* to veterans of the United States Armed Services. Applications from nonveterans will be rejected. While these positions are at the low end of the postal pay scale, they do afford the veteran an opportunity to earn a steady wage and to enjoy all the fringe benefits and security of all other postal employees. The person who starts his or her career with the Postal Service as a cleaner, custodian, or custodial laborer can advance to positions of greater responsibility within the custodial service or can prepare for examinations for other positions with the Postal Service, either more specialized jobs within building maintenance or completely different jobs such as mail handler, letter clerk, and others. People who already work for the Postal Service in any capacity need not wait for an exam that is open to the public to be announced. After being employed at their present position for a year, they may ask to take an exam at any time. Although this request may or may not be granted, this is one special advantage of postal employees that makes the Veterans-Only feature of this position so valuable. A veteran who wants a postal career can break in at the bottom and rise rapidly.

There are no educational or experience requirements for these positions and no age restrictions. Applicants must, of course, have the physical health and stamina required for the job. They must also qualify on a one-and-a-half-hour examination, Exam 911, that tests their ability to follow directions.

OFFICIAL SAMPLE QUESTIONS FOR EXAMINATION 911

This section discusses the exam for cleaner, custodian, and custodial laborer.

Directions: *The suggested answers to each question are lettered. Select the BEST answer and make a heavy pencil mark in the space on the sample answer sheet by darkening the space of the best answer to that question. Each mark must be dense black. Each mark must cover more than half of the area of the space and must not extend into neighboring spaces. If the answer to sample 1 is B, you would mark the sample answer sheet like this:*

Record your answers to each sample question. Then compare your answers with those given in the *Sample Question* instructions.

During the test, directions for answering questions will be given orally. You are to listen closely to the directions and follow them. To practice for the test you might have a friend read the directions to you while you mark your answers on the sample answer sheet.

You will be told to follow directions by writing in a test booklet and then on an answer sheet. The test booklet will have lines of material like the following four samples:

SAMPLE 1.   5 ___

SAMPLE 2.   1   6   4   3   7

SAMPLE 3.   D   B   A   E   C

SAMPLE 4.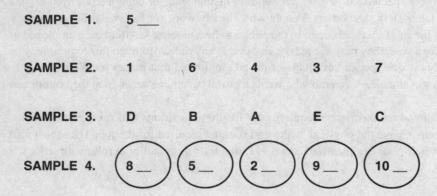

To practice this test, tear out the page of *Instructions to be read.* Then have somebody read the instructions to you, while you follow them. When the reader tells you to darken a space on the sample answer sheet, use the one on this page.

Sample Answer Sheet

1. Ⓐ Ⓑ Ⓒ Ⓓ Ⓔ   5. Ⓐ Ⓑ Ⓒ Ⓓ Ⓔ   9. Ⓐ Ⓑ Ⓒ Ⓓ Ⓔ
2. Ⓐ Ⓑ Ⓒ Ⓓ Ⓔ   6. Ⓐ Ⓑ Ⓒ Ⓓ Ⓔ   10. Ⓐ Ⓑ Ⓒ Ⓓ Ⓔ
3. Ⓐ Ⓑ Ⓒ Ⓓ Ⓔ   7. Ⓐ Ⓑ Ⓒ Ⓓ Ⓔ   11. Ⓐ Ⓑ Ⓒ Ⓓ Ⓔ
4. Ⓐ Ⓑ Ⓒ Ⓓ Ⓔ   8. Ⓐ Ⓑ Ⓒ Ⓓ Ⓔ   12. Ⓐ Ⓑ Ⓒ Ⓓ Ⓔ

Instructions to be read (the words in parentheses should not be read aloud).

You are to follow the instructions that I shall read to you. I cannot repeat them.

Look at the samples. Sample 1 has a number and a line beside it. On the line write an A. (Pause 2 seconds.) Now, on the Sample Answer Sheet, find number 5 (pause 2 seconds) and darken the space for the letter you just wrote on the line. (Pause 2 seconds.)

Look at Sample 2. (Pause slightly.) Draw a line under the third number. (Pause 2 seconds.) Now, on the Sample Answer Sheet, find the number under which you just drew a line and darken space B as in baker for that number. (Pause 5 seconds.)

Look at Sample 3. (Pause slightly.) Draw a line under the third letter in the line. (Pause 2 seconds.) Now, on your answer sheet, find number 9 (pause 2 seconds) and darken the space for the letter under which you drew a line. (Pause 5 seconds.)

Look at the five circles in Sample 4. (Pause slightly.) Each circle has a number and a line in it. Write D as in dog on the blank line in the last circle. (Pause 2 seconds.) Now, on the Sample Answer Sheet, darken the space for the number-letter combination that is in the circle you just wrote in. (Pause 5 seconds.)

Now look at the Sample Answer Sheet. (Pause slightly.) You should have darkened spaces 4B, 5A, 9A, and 10D on the Sample Answer Sheet. (If the person preparing to take the examination made any mistakes, try to help that person see why he or she made wrong marks.)

TEAR HERE

GARAGEMAN-DRIVER, TRACTOR-TRAILER OPERATOR, MOTOR VEHICLE OPERATOR

Duties of the Job

What all these jobs have in common is driving various Postal Service vehicles on the highway and within the lots and properties of the Postal Service.

Garagemen are responsible for seeing that each vehicle is in the proper place at the proper time and that each vehicle is roadworthy before it is released. (Though the official job title has historically been "garageman," this position is equally open to qualified women.) Garagemen must keep accurate records of all activity as it affects each vehicle and must follow through on what movement or maintenance is required.

Tractor-trailer operators drive huge mail rigs from city to city along superhighways, delivering large quantities of mail as quickly as possible within the bounds of safety. The work of a Postal Service tractor-trailer operator is really no different from the work of a tractor-trailer operator for private industry.

Motor vehicle operators drive various other Postal Service vehicles as needed, both within and between towns and cities. They pick up and deliver bulk quantities of mail at postal installations, mailing concerns, railroad mail facilities, and airports.

The exam for all these positions, Exam 9l, is designed to test powers of observation, ability to express oneself, accuracy in record keeping, familiarity with road signs, and ability to follow instructions. The exam is in two parts of 40 questions each. You will have sixty minutes to answer each part. The test requires concentration and careful attention to details. The sample questions that the Postal Service sends to applicants provide a good idea of what to expect from the exam itself.

Since all these positions require a Commercial Driver's License (CDL), people appointed to them must be experienced drivers over the age of 21. In addition, applicants must have good eyesight and hearing and be in excellent health and physical condition. A physical exam, drug testing, and strength and stamina tests are part of the hiring process. Candidates must also take training on the specific type of vehicle they are required to drive.

To qualify for motor vehicle operator or tractor-trailer operator, persons must have a commercial driver's license and two years of experience driving a truck with at least a seven-ton capacity or a bus carrying at least 24 passengers. One of these years must have been as a full-time professional driver. Candidates for the tractor-trailer operator position must have had six months of experience driving a tractor-trailer. All driving experience must have been gained in the United States or its territories in order to qualify. Applicants for all driving positions must have safe driving records.

OFFICIAL SAMPLE QUESTIONS FOR EXAMINATION 91 (FOR GARAGEMAN-DRIVER, TRACTOR-TRAILER OPERATOR, MOTOR VEHICLE OPERATOR)

The sample questions that follow show the kinds of questions that you will find in the written test for garageman-driver. By reading and answering these questions, you will find out how to answer the questions in the test and how hard the questions will be.

Directions: *Read the questions carefully. Be sure you know what the questions are about and then answer the questions in the way you are told to do. If you are told the answer to a question, be sure you understand why the answer is right.*

Question 1 is about Picture 1 below. Look at the picture.

Picture 1

1. How many vehicles are shown in the picture?

    . . . .
    (Write your answer for question 1 here.)

Questions 2 and 3 are about Picture 2 below. Look at the picture.

Picture 2

2. Who is sitting on the motorcycle?

    . . . .
    (Write your answer for question 2 here.)

3.   What is the policeman probably doing?

. . . .
(Write your answer for question 3 here.)

Questions 4 and 5 are about Picture 3 below. Look at the picture.

Picture 3

4.   What is happening in this picture?

. . . .
(Write your answer for question 4 here.)

5.   Show the positions of the truck and the passenger car by drawing boxes like those shown below. (Your boxes will not be in the same position as these.)

TRUCK   PASSENGER
                  CAR

Draw your boxes in the space below.

Questions 6 and 7 are about the pictures of oilcans below. Each picture has a letter. You are to tell what each picture shows by writing a short description of the picture on the answer line that goes with the question.

Now look at Picture X.

6. What does Picture X show?

. . . .

(Write your answer for question 6 here.)

Picture X shows two oilcans. So, you should have written something like "two oilcans" on the line under question 6.

Now look at Picture Y.

7. What does Picture Y show?

. . . .

(Write your answer for question 7 here.)

Question 8 requires filling in a chart. You are given the following information to put in the chart.

Truck, license number 48-7128, had its oil changed last at odometer reading 96,005.
Truck, license number 858-232, was greased last at odometer reading 89,564.

Look at the chart below. The information for the first truck has already been filled in. For question 8, fill in the information for the other truck. You are to show, in the proper columns, the license number of the truck, the kind of service, and the odometer reading when serviced.

Chart

Truck License Number	Kind of Service	Odometer Reading When Serviced
48-7128	Oil Change	96,005

Questions 9 and 10 are about words that might appear on traffic signs. In questions like these, there is one numbered line and then, just below that line, four other lines that are lettered A, B, C, and D. Read the first line. Then read the other four lines. Decide which line—A, B, C, or D—means most nearly the same as the first line in the question. Write the letter of the line that means the same as the numbered line in the answer space.

9.   Speed Limit—20 Miles
     (A) Do Not Exceed 20 Miles per Hour
     (B) Railroad Crossing
     (C) No Turns
     (D) Dangerous Intersection

. . . .

(Write letter of answer here for question 9.)

The first line says "Speed Limit—20 Miles." The line that says almost the same thing as the first line is (A), "Do Not Exceed 20 Miles per Hour." You should have marked (A) on the answer line for question 9.

10. Dead End
    (A) Merging Traffic
    (B) No U-Turns
    (C) Turn on Red
    (D) No Through Traffic

. . . .
(Write letter of answer here for question 10.)

After you answer questions like the ones you have just finished, you will be asked other questions to see how well you understand what you have written. To answer the next questions, you will use the information that you wrote for the first ten questions. Mark your answers to the next questions on the sample answer sheet on page 43.

Each of the questions in the next part is about something you should have written on your answer lines. In answering the next questions in this book, you may look back to what you have already written as often as you wish. You may look back while you are marking the sample answer sheet. In the actual test, the pictures and their questions will be taken away from you before you mark the answer sheet, but you will keep what you wrote about the pictures while marking your answer sheet. So, for this practice, try not to look at the pictures but look at what you wrote about them.

Answer each of the following questions by darkening completely space A, B, C, D, or E beside the number that you are told in the question. Mark all your answers on the sample answer sheet.

Question 11 is about question 1. Use what you wrote under question 1 to answer question 11. Mark your answer on the sample answer sheet.

11. For number 11 on the sample answer sheet, mark space

    (A) if only one vehicle is shown in the picture
    (B) if only two vehicles are shown in the picture
    (C) if only three vehicles are shown in the picture
    (D) if only four vehicles are shown in the picture
    (E) if only five vehicles are shown in the picture

If you look at the answer you gave for question 1, you will see that you wrote that three vehicles were shown in the picture. The question above tells you to mark space (C) on the sample answer sheet if only three vehicles are shown. So you should have marked space (C) for number 11 on the sample answer sheet.

Question 12 is about question 2, and question 13 is about question 3.

12. For number 12 on the sample answer sheet, mark space
    (A) if a policeman is sitting on the motorcycle
    (B) if a man in overalls is sitting on the motorcycle
    (C) if a boy in a sport shirt is sitting on the motorcycle
    (D) if a nurse is sitting on the motorcycle
    (E) if a man with a white beard is sitting on the motorcycle

13. For number 13 on the sample answer sheet, mark space

    (A) if the policeman is probably fixing a tire
    (B) if the policeman is probably using a telephone
    (C) if the policeman is probably taking off his cap
    (D) if the policeman is probably blowing a whistle
    (E) if the policeman is probably writing a ticket

Question 14 below is about question 4, and question 15 below is about question 5.

14.   For number 14 on the sample answer sheet, mark space
      (A) if a bus is passing a fire truck
      (B) if a motorcycle is hitting a fence
      (C) if a truck is backing up to a platform
      (D) if a passenger car is getting gas
      (E) if a passenger car is hitting a truck

15.   Look at the boxes you drew for question 5. For number 15 on the sample answer sheet, mark space

      (A) if a truck is on a ramp and a passenger car is on the street
      (B) if a truck is to the rear of a passenger car
      (C) if the front bumpers of a passenger car and a truck are in line
      (D) if a passenger car is to the rear of a truck
      (E) if a motorcycle is between a truck and a passenger car

Question 16 below is about question 6 under picture X, and question 17 below is about question 7 under picture Y.

16.   For number 16 on the sample answer sheet, mark space
      (A) if there is only one oilcan in picture X
      (B) if there are only two oilcans in picture X
      (C) if there are only three oilcans in picture X
      (D) if there are only four oilcans in picture X
      (E) if there are only five oilcans in picture X

17.   For number 17 on the sample answer sheet, mark space

      (A) if there is only one oilcan in picture Y
      (B) if there are only two oilcans in picture Y
      (C) if there are only three oilcans in picture Y
      (D) if there are only four oilcans in picture Y
      (E) if there are only five oilcans in picture Y

Question 18 below is about the chart you filled in. For this question, mark on the sample answer sheet the letter of the suggested answer—A, B, C, or D—that best answers the question.

18.   What is the license number of the truck that was greased? (Look at what you wrote on the chart. Don't answer from memory.)

      (A) 89,564
      (B) 48–7128
      (C) 858–232
      (D) 96,005

For number 19 on the sample answer sheet, mark the space that has the same letter as the letter you wrote on the answer line for question 9.

For number 20 on the sample answer sheet, mark the space that has the same letter as the letter you wrote on the answer line for question 10.

Now see if the answers you marked on the sample answer sheet are correct. If your answers are *not* correct, go back to the second-part questions and to the pictures and questions in the first part to see where you went wrong.

The actual exam is machine scored. Your score, therefore, will be based on the number of questions you answer correctly in the second part.

```
Sample Answer Sheet
11. Ⓐ Ⓑ Ⓒ Ⓓ Ⓔ          16. Ⓐ Ⓑ Ⓒ Ⓓ Ⓔ
12. Ⓐ Ⓑ Ⓒ Ⓓ Ⓔ          17. Ⓐ Ⓑ Ⓒ Ⓓ Ⓔ
13. Ⓐ Ⓑ Ⓒ Ⓓ Ⓔ          18. Ⓐ Ⓑ Ⓒ Ⓓ Ⓔ
14. Ⓐ Ⓑ Ⓒ Ⓓ Ⓔ          19. Ⓐ Ⓑ Ⓒ Ⓓ Ⓔ
15. Ⓐ Ⓑ Ⓒ Ⓓ Ⓔ          20. Ⓐ Ⓑ Ⓒ Ⓓ Ⓔ
```

The correct answers for questions 11 to 20 are:

| 11. **C** | 13. **E** | 15. **D** | 17. **D** | 19. **A** |
| 12. **A** | 14. **E** | 16. **B** | 18. **C** | 20. **D** |

POSTAL POLICE OFFICER

Duties of the Job

A postal police officer is essentially a security guard at post offices and at other postal installations and facilities. The postal police officer may work inside postal buildings or out of doors at loading docks and in parking lots. A postal police officer may be armed.

Qualification Requirements

An applicant for the position of postal police officer must be at least 20 years of age, and, unless a veteran, cannot be appointed until reaching the age of 21 years. The postal police officer must be physically able to perform the duties of the job, must have weight in proportion to height, must have good color vision and good distant vision (no weaker than 20/40 in one eye and 20/50 in the other eye correctable to 20/20), and must have keen hearing. Emotional and mental stability are essential for the armed officer, and drug testing and a psychological interview are part of the qualification process. The candidate must demonstrate the ability to deal with the public in a courteous and tactful manner; to work in stress situations; to collect, assemble, and act on pertinent facts; to prepare clear and accurate records; to deal effectively with individuals and groups; and to express himself or herself in both oral and written communications. A background investigation will be made on all otherwise qualified candidates. In order to be considered, each applicant must pass a written qualifying exam, Exam 630, with a score of 70 or better out of a possible 100.

OFFICIAL SAMPLE QUESTIONS FOR EXAMINATION 630 (FOR POSTAL POLICE OFFICER)

NAME AND NUMBER COMPARISONS

In each of these questions you will find listed *across* the page three names or numbers that are very similar. You should decide which ones are exactly alike. Choose the correct response from A, B, C, D, or E listed below.

A   if ALL THREE names or numbers are exactly ALIKE
B   if only the FIRST and SECOND names or numbers are exactly ALIKE
C   if only the FIRST and THIRD names or numbers are exactly ALIKE
D   if only the SECOND and THIRD names or numbers are exactly ALIKE
E   if ALL THREE names and numbers are DIFFERENT

Sample questions 1 through 10 are examples of the name and number questions in the test.

1. Davis Hazen	David Hozen	David Hazen
2. Lois Appel	Lois Appel	Lois Apfel
3. June Allan	Jane Allan	Jane Allan
4. Emily Neal Rouse	Emily Neal Rowse	Emily Neal Rowse
5. H. Merritt Audubon	H. Merriott Audubon	H. Merritt Audubon

6. 6219354	6219354	6219354
7. 2312793	2312793	2312793
8. 1065407	1065407	1065047
9. 3457988	3457986	3457986
10. 4695682	4695862	4695682

The correct responses for questions 1 through 10 are:

1.	E	6.	A
2.	B	7.	A
3.	D	8.	B
4.	D	9.	D
5.	C	10.	C

READING QUESTIONS

In each of these questions you will be given a paragraph that contains all the information necessary to infer the correct answer. Use *only* the information provided in the paragraph. Do not speculate or make assumptions that go beyond this information. Also, assume that all information given in the paragraph is true, even if it conflicts with some fact known to you. Only one correct answer can be validly inferred from the information contained in the paragraph.

Pay special attention to negated verbs (for example, "are *not*") and negative prefixes (for example, "*in*complete" or "*dis*organized"). Also pay special attention to quantifiers, such as "all," "none," and "some." For example, from a paragraph in which it is stated that "it is not true that all contracts are legal," one can validly infer that "some contracts are not legal," or that "some contracts are illegal," or that "some illegal things are contracts," but one *cannot* validly infer that "no contracts are legal," or that "some contracts are legal." Similarly, from a paragraph that states "all contracts are legal" and "all contracts are two-sided agreements," one can infer that "some two-sided agreements are legal," but one *cannot* validly infer that "all two-sided agreements are legal."

Bear in mind that in some tests, universal quantifiers such as "all" and "none" often give away incorrect response choices. That is *not* the case in this test. Some correct answers will refer to "all" or "none" of the members of a group.

Be sure to distinguish between essential information and unessential, peripheral information. That is to say, in a real test question, the example above ("all contracts are legal" and "all contracts are two-sided agreements") would appear in a longer, full-fledged paragraph. It would be up to you to separate the essential information from its context and then to realize that a response choice that states "some two-sided agreements are legal" represents a valid inference and hence the correct answer.

Sample questions 11 and 12 are examples of the reading question in the test.

11. Impressions made by the ridges on the ends of the fingers and thumbs are useful means of identification, since no two persons have the same pattern of ridges. If finger patterns from fingerprints are not decipherable, then they cannot be classified by general shape and contour or by pattern type. If they cannot be classified by these characteristics, then it is impossible to identify the person to whom the fingerprints belong.

The paragraph best supports the statement that

(A) if it is impossible to identify the person to whom fingerprints belong, then the fingerprints are not decipherable.

(B) if finger patterns from fingerprints are not decipherable, then it is impossible to identify the person to whom the fingerprints belong.

(C) if fingerprints are decipherable, then it is impossible to identify the person to whom they belong.

(D) if fingerprints can be classified by general shape and contour or by pattern type, then they are not decipherable.

(E) if it is possible to identify the person to whom fingerprints belong, then the fingerprints cannot be classified by general shape and contour or pattern.

The correct answer is response B. The essential information from which the answer can be inferred is contained in the second and third sentences. These sentences state that "if finger patterns from fingerprints are not decipherable, then they cannot be classified by general shape and contour or by pattern type. If they cannot be classified by these characteristics, then it is impossible to identify the person to whom they belong." Since response B refers to a condition in which finger patterns from fingerprints are not decipherable, we know that, in that circumstance, they cannot be classified by general shape and contour or by pattern type. From the paragraph, we can infer that since they cannot be classified by these characteristics, then it is impossible to identify the person to whom the fingerprints belong.

Response A cannot be inferred because the paragraph does not give information about all the circumstances under which it is impossible to identify the person to whom the fingerprints belong. It may be that the person is not identifiable for reasons other than the decipherability of the person's fingerprints.

Response C is incorrect because the paragraph does not provide enough information to conclude whether or not it would be possible to identify the person to whom the fingerprints belong from the mere fact of the decipherability of the fingerprints.

Response D is wrong because it contradicts the information in the second sentence of the paragraph. From that sentence, it can be concluded that if fingerprints can be classified by general shape and contour or by pattern type, then they are decipherable.

Response E is incorrect for a similar reason; it contradicts the information presented in the third sentence of the paragraph.

12. Law enforcement agencies use scientific techniques to identify suspects or to establish guilt. One obvious application of such techniques is the examination of a crime scene. Some substances found at a crime scene yield valuable clues under microscopic examination. Clothing fibers, dirt particles, and even pollen grains may reveal important information to the careful investigator. Nothing can be overlooked because all substances found at a crime scene are potential sources of evidence.

The paragraph best supports the statement that

(A) all substances that yield valuable clues under microscopic examination are substances found at a crime scene.

(B) some potential sources of evidence are substances that yield valuable clues under microscopic examination.

(C) some substances found at a crime scene are not potential sources of evidence.

(D) no potential sources of evidence are substances found at a crime scene.

(E) some substances that yield valuable clues under microscopic examination are not substances found at a crime scene.

The correct answer is response B. The essential information from which the answer can be inferred is contained in the third and fifth sentences. The third sentence tells us that "some substances found at a crime scene yield valuable clues under microscopic examination." The fifth sentence explains that ". . . all substances found at a crime scene are potential sources of evidence." Therefore, we can conclude that "some potential sources of evidence are substances that yield valuable clues under microscopic examination."

Response A cannot be inferred because the paragraph does not support the statement that all substances that yield valuable clues are found exclusively at a crime scene. It may be that valuable clues could be found elsewhere.

Responses C and D are incorrect because they contradict the fifth sentence of the paragraph, which clearly states that "all substances found at a crime scene are potential sources of evidence."

Response E is incorrect because the paragraph provides no information about the value of substances found somewhere other than at the crime scene.

ARITHMETIC REASONING QUESTIONS

In this part of the test you will have to solve problems formulated in both verbal and numeric form. You will have to analyze a paragraph in order to set up the problem, and then solve it. If the exact answer is not given as one of the response choices, you should select response E, "none of these." Sample questions 13 and 14 are examples of the arithmetic reasoning questions in this test. The use of calculators will NOT be permitted during the test; therefore, they should not be used to solve these sample questions.

13. A police department purchases badges at $16 each for all the graduates of the police training academy. The last training class graduated 10 new officers. What is the total amount of money the department will spend for badges for these new officers?

   (A) $ 70
   (B) $116
   (C) $160
   (D) $180
   (E) none of these

The correct response is C. It can be obtained by computing the following:

$$16 \times 10 = 160$$

The badges are priced at $16 each. The department must purchase 10 of them for the new officers. Multiplying the price of one badge ($16) by the number of graduates (10) gives the total price for all of the badges.
Responses A, B, and D are the result of erroneous computations.

14. An investigator rented a car for six days and was charged $450. The car rental company charged $35 per day plus $.30 per mile driven. How many miles did the investigator drive the car?

   (A)   800
   (B)   900
   (C) 1,290
   (D) 1,500
   (E) none of these

The correct answer is A. It can be obtained by computing the following:

$$6(35) + .30\,X = 450$$

The investigator rented the car for six days at $35 per day, which is $210; $210 subtracted from the total charge of $450 leaves $240, the portion of the total charge that was expended for the miles driven. This amount divided by the charge per mile ($240/.30) gives the number of miles (800) driven by the investigator.

Responses B, C, and D are the result of erroneous computations.

BUILDING AND EQUIPMENT MAINTENANCE POSITIONS

Duties of the Job

Activities of the Postal Service take place in a great number of facilities. These facilities consist not only of post offices but also of warehouses, processing centers, repair shops, garages, and office buildings. These buildings require the same maintenance services as nonpostal buildings that serve the same purposes.

Housed within the postal facilities is a myriad of machinery and equipment. Machines and equipment all require maintenance and service.

Rather than hiring maintenance workers from the private sector, the postal service retains a full staff of maintenance workers to care for its facilities and equipment.

Applicants for positions in the following titles must all qualify on the same exam. The maintenance titles are:

Area Maintenance Specialist	Maintenance Mechanic 4
Area Maintenance Technician	Maintenance Mechanic 5
Building Equipment Mechanic	Mason
Building Maintenance Custodian	Painter
Carpenter	Plumber
Machinist	Welder
Maintenance Electrician	

Qualification Requirements

Candidates for building and equipment maintenance positions must have the health and physical strength to perform the duties of the specific positions. The requirements for all positions are not alike. All candidates must take test M/N 931, which measures sixteen different Knowledge, Skills, and Abilities (KSAs) used by a variety of maintenance positions. Not all KSAs that are measured in this test are scored for every position. The qualification standard for each position lists the KSAs required for the position. Only those questions that measure KSAs required for the position(s) for which you are applying will be scored for the position(s).

Test M/N 931 covers the following Knowledge, Skills, and Abilities:

(1) *Knowledge of basic mechanics* refers to the theory of operation, terminology, usage, and characteristics of basic mechanical principles as they apply to such things as gears, pulleys, cams, pawls, power transmissions, linkages, fasteners, chains, sprockets, and belts; and includes hoisting, rigging, roping, pneumatics, and hydraulic devices.

(2) *Knowledge of basic electricity* refers to the theory, terminology, usage, and characteristics of basic electrical principles such as Ohm's Law, Kirchhoff's Law, and magnetism, as they apply to such things as AC/DC circuitry and hardware, relays, switches, and circuit breakers.

(3) *Knowledge of basic electronics* refers to the theory, terminology, usage, and characteristics of basic electronic principles concerning such things as solid-state devices, vacuum tubes, coils, capacitors, resistors, and basic logic circuitry.

(5) *Knowledge of safety procedures and equipment* refers to the knowledge of industrial hazards (e.g., mechanical, chemical, electrical, electronic) and procedures and techniques established to avoid injuries to self and others such as lock-out devices, protective clothing, and waste-disposal techniques.

(12) *Knowledge of refrigeration* refers to the theory, terminology, usage, and characteristics of refrigeration principles as they apply to such things as the refrigeration cycle, compressors, condensers, receivers, evaporators, metering devices, and refrigerant oils.

(13) *Knowledge of heating, ventilation, and air-conditioning (HVAC) equipment operation* refers to the knowledge of equipment operation such as safety considerations, start-up, shut-down, and mechanical/electrical operating characteristics of HVAC equipment (e.g., chillers, direct-expansion units, window units, heating equipment). This does not include the knowledge of refrigeration.

(19) *Ability to perform basic mathematical computations* refers to the ability to perform basic calculations such as addition, subtraction, multiplication, and division with whole numbers, fractions, and decimals.

(20) *Ability to perform more complex mathematics* refers to the ability to perform calculations such as basic algebra, geometry, scientific notation, and number conversions, as applied to mechanical, electrical, and electronic applications.

(21) *Ability to apply theoretical knowledge to practical applications* refers to mechanical, electrical, and electronic maintenance applications such as inspection, trouble-shooting equipment repair and modification, preventive maintenance, and installation of electrical equipment.

(22) *Ability to detect patterns* refers to the ability to observe and analyze qualitative factors such as number progressions, spatial relationships, and auditory and visual patterns. This includes combining information and determining how a given set of numbers, objects, or sounds are related to each other.

(23) *Ability to use written reference materials* refers to the ability to locate, read, and comprehend text material such as handbooks, manuals, bulletins, directives, checklists, and route sheets.

(26) *Ability to follow instructions* refers to the ability to comprehend and execute written and oral instructions such as work orders, checklists, route sheets, and verbal directions and instructions.

(31) *Ability to use hand tools* refers to knowledge of, and proficiency with, various hand tools. This ability involves the safe and efficient use and maintenance of such tools as screwdrivers, wrenches, hammers, pliers, chisels, punches, taps, dies, rules, gauges, and alignment tools.

(35) *Ability to use technical drawings* refers to the ability to read and comprehend technical materials such as diagrams, schematics, flow charts, and blueprints.

(36) *Ability to use test equipment* refers to the knowledge of, and proficiency with, various types of mechanical, electrical, and electronic test equipment such as VOMS, oscilloscopes, circuit tracers, amprobes, and tachometers.

(37) *Ability to solder* refers to the knowledge of the appropriate soldering techniques, and the ability to apply them safely and effectively.

The full-length Examination M/N 931 consists of 170 items. Part I takes about 20 minutes to administer. Candidates are permitted 3 hours in which to answer Part II questions. All scoring is based upon right answers only.

OFFICIAL SAMPLE QUESTIONS FOR EXAMINATION M/N 931 (FOR BUILDING AND EQUIPMENT MAINTENANCE POSITIONS)

Directions: The suggested answers to each question are lettered A, B, C, D, and E. Select the BEST answer and make a heavy pencil mark in the corresponding space on the sample answer sheet. Each mark must be dense black. Each mark must cover more than half the space and must not extend into neighboring spaces. If the answer to Sample 1 is B, you should mark the sample answer sheet like this:

1. Ⓐ ● Ⓒ Ⓓ Ⓔ

After recording your answers, compare them with the correct answers. If they do not agree, carefully reread the questions that were missed to get a clear understanding of what each question is asking.

During the test, directions for answering questions in Part I will be given orally, either by a cassette tape or by the examiner. You are to listen closely to the directions and follow them. To practice for this part of the test you might have a friend read the directions to you while you mark your answers on the sample answer sheet. Directions for answering questions in Part II will be completely described in the test booklet [not shown here]. Use the sample answer sheet on page 61 to mark your answers to the Part II sample questions.

Part I

In Part I of the test, you will be told to follow directions by writing in a test booklet and then on an answer sheet. The test booklet will have lines of material like the following five samples:

SAMPLE 1. 5_____

SAMPLE 2. 1 6 4 3 7

SAMPLE 3. D B A E C

SAMPLE 4. ⑧__ ⑤__ ②__ ⑨__ ⑩__

SAMPLE 5. ⑦__ [6__] ①__ [12__]

To practice this test, tear out the page of *Instructions to be read*. Then have somebody read the instructions to you, while you follow them. When the reader tells you to darken the space on the sample answer sheet, use the one on this page.

Sample Answer Sheet

1. Ⓐ Ⓑ Ⓒ Ⓓ Ⓔ	5. Ⓐ Ⓑ Ⓒ Ⓓ Ⓔ	9. Ⓐ Ⓑ Ⓒ Ⓓ Ⓔ
2. Ⓐ Ⓑ Ⓒ Ⓓ Ⓔ	6. Ⓐ Ⓑ Ⓒ Ⓓ Ⓔ	10. Ⓐ Ⓑ Ⓒ Ⓓ Ⓔ
3. Ⓐ Ⓑ Ⓒ Ⓓ Ⓔ	7. Ⓐ Ⓑ Ⓒ Ⓓ Ⓔ	11. Ⓐ Ⓑ Ⓒ Ⓓ Ⓔ
4. Ⓐ Ⓑ Ⓒ Ⓓ Ⓔ	8. Ⓐ Ⓑ Ⓒ Ⓓ Ⓔ	12. Ⓐ Ⓑ Ⓒ Ⓓ Ⓔ

Instructions to be read. (*The words in parentheses should not be read aloud.*)

You are to follow the instructions that I shall read to you. I cannot repeat them.

Look at the samples. Sample 1 has a number and a line beside it. On the line write an A. (Pause 2 seconds.) Now, on the sample answer sheet, find number 5 (pause 2 seconds) and darken the space for the letter you just wrote on the line. (Pause 2 seconds.)

Look at Sample 2. (Pause slightly.) Draw a line under the third number. (Pause 2 seconds.) Now, on the sample answer sheet, find the number under which you just drew a line, and darken space B as in baker for that number. (Pause 5 seconds.)

Look at Sample 3. (Pause slightly.) Draw a line under the third letter in the line. (Pause 2 seconds.) Now, on your sample answer sheet, find number 9 (pause 2 seconds) and darken the space for the letter under which you drew a line. (Pause 5 seconds.)

Look at the five circles in Sample 4. (Pause slightly.) Each circle has a number and a line in it. Write D as in dog on the blank in the last circle. (Pause 2 seconds.) Now, on the sample answer sheet, darken the space for the number-letter combination that is in the circle in which you just wrote. (Pause 5 seconds.)

Look at Sample 5. (Pause slightly.) There are two circles and two boxes of different sizes with numbers in them. **(Pause slightly.)** If 4 is more than 2 and if 5 is less than 3, write A in the smaller circle. (Pause slightly.) Otherwise write C in the larger box. (Pause 2 seconds.) Now, on the sample answer sheet, darken the space for the number-letter combination in the circle or box in which you just wrote. (Pause 5 seconds.)

Now look at the sample answer sheet. (Pause slightly.) You should have darkened spaces 4B, 5A, 9A, 10D, and 12C on the sample answer sheet. **(If the person preparing to take the examination made any mistakes, try to help him or her understand why the mistakes are wrong.)**

TEAR HERE

Part II

1. Which device is used to transfer power and rotary mechanical motion from one shaft to another?

   (A) bearing
   (B) lever
   (C) idler roller
   (D) gear
   (E) bushing

2. Lead anchors are usually mounted in

   (A) steel paneling
   (B) drywall construction
   (C) masonry construction
   (D) wood construction
   (E) gypsum board

3. Which of the following circuits is shown in Figure III-A-22?

   (A) series circuit
   (B) parallel circuit
   (C) series, parallel circuit
   (D) solid state circuit
   (E) none of the above

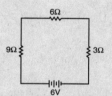

Figure III-A-22

4. Which component would BEST simulate the actions of the photocell in Figure 24-3-1?

   (A) variable resistor
   (B) variable capacitor
   (C) variable inductor
   (D) autotransformer
   (E) battery

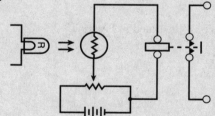

Figure 24-3-1

5. The semiconductor materials contained in a transistor are designated by the letter(s)

   (A) Q
   (B) N, P
   (C) CR
   (D) M, P, M
   (E) none of the above

6. Which of the following circuits or devices always has inductance?

(A) rectifier
(B) coil
(C) current limiter
(D) condenser
(E) filter

7. Crowbars, light bulbs, and vacuum bags are to be stored in the cabinet shown in Figure 75-25-1. Considering the balance of weight, what would be the safest arrangement?

(A) top drawer—crowbars
middle drawer—light bulbs
bottom drawer—vacuum bags
(B) top drawer—crowbars
middle drawer—vacuum bags
bottom drawer—light bulbs
(C) top drawer— vacuum bags
middle drawer—crowbars
bottom drawer—light bulbs
(D) top drawer—vacuum bags
middle drawer—light bulbs
bottom drawer—crowbars
(E) top drawer—light bulbs
middle drawer—vacuum bags
bottom drawer—crowbars

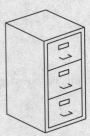

Figure 75-25-1

8. Which is most appropriate for pulling a heavy load?

(A) electric lift
(B) fork lift
(C) tow conveyor
(D) dolly
(E) pallet truck

9. What measuring device is illustrated in Figure 75-26-1?

(A) screw pitch gage
(B) vernier calipers
(C) inside calipers
(D) outside calipers
(E) outside micrometer

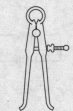

Figure 75-26-1

10. A screw pitch gage can be used for

(A) determining the pitch and number of internal threads
(B) measuring the number of gages available for use
(C) measuring the depth of a screw hole
(D) checking the thread angle
(E) cleaning the external threads

11.   What measuring device is illustrated in Figure 75-20-17?

    (A) screw pitch gage
    (B) vernier calipers
    (C) inside calipers
    (D) outside calipers
    (E) outside micrometer

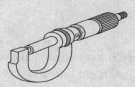

Figure 75-20-17

12.   One characteristic of the breast drill is that it

    (A) is gearless
    (B) is hand operated
    (C) has a $3^{1}/_{4}$ hp motor
    (D) has 4 speeds
    (E) is steam powered

13.   In Figure 3-8-6, what is the measurement of dimension F?

    (A) $1^{3}/_{4}$ inches
    (B) $2^{1}/_{4}$ inches
    (C) $2^{1}/_{2}$ inches
    (D) $3^{3}/_{4}$ inches
    (E) None of the above

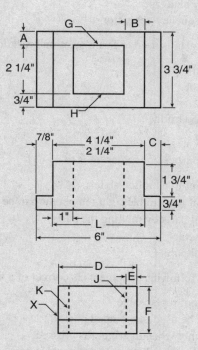

Figure 3-8-6

14. The device pictured in Figure 36 is in a rest position. Which position, if any, is the normal closed?

    (A) A
    (B) B
    (C) C
    (D) Devices of this sort have no normal closed position.
    (E) The normal closed is not shown in this diagram.

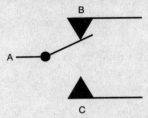

Figure 36

15. Which of the following test equipment would most likely be used in determining amplifier band width?

    (A) clamp-on ammeter
    (B) tube tester
    (C) watt meter
    (D) frequency analyzer
    (E) sweep frequency generator

16. Which instrument is used to test insulation breakdown of a conductor?

    (A) ohmmeter
    (B) ammeter
    (C) megger
    (D) wheatstone bridge
    (E) voltmeter

17. The primary purpose of soldering is to

    (A) melt solder to a molten state
    (B) heat metal parts to the right temperature to be joined
    (C) join metal parts by melting the parts
    (D) harden metal
    (E) join metal parts

18. Which of the following statements is correct of a soldering gun?

    (A) Its tip is not replaceable.
    (B) It cannot be used in cramped places.
    (C) It heats only when its trigger is pressed.
    (D) It is not rated by the number of watts it uses.
    (E) It has no light.

19. Contaminants have caused bearings to fail prematurely. Which pair of the items listed below should be kept away from bearings?

    (A) dirt and oil
    (B) grease and water
    (C) oil and grease
    (D) dirt and moisture
    (E) water and oil

20. The electrical circuit term "open circuit" refers to a closed loop being opened. When an ohmmeter is connected into this type of circuit, one can expect the meter to

    (A) read infinity
    (B) read infinity and slowly return to ZERO
    (C) read ZERO
    (D) read ZERO and slowly return to infinity
    (E) none of the above

21. A change from refrigerant vapor to liquid while the temperature stays constant results in a

    (A) latent pressure loss
    (B) sensible heat loss
    (C) sensible pressure loss
    (D) latent heat loss
    (E) super heat loss

22. The mediums normally used in condensing refrigerants are

    (A) air and water
    (B) air and vapor
    (C) water and gas
    (D) liquid and vapor
    (E) vapor and gas

23. Most condenser problems are caused by

    (A) high head pressure
    (B) high suction pressure
    (C) low head pressure
    (D) low suction pressure
    (E) line leaks

24. Most air conditioners with motors of 1 horsepower, or less, operate on which type of source?

    (A) 110-volt, single-phase
    (B) 110-volt, three-phase
    (C) 220-volt, single-phase
    (D) 220-volt, three-phase
    (E) 220–440-volt, three-phase

25. $2.6 - .5 =$

    (A) 2.0
    (B) 2.1
    (C) 3.1
    (D) 3.3
    (E) None of the above

26. $1/2$ of $1/4$ is

    (A) $1/12$
    (B) $1/8$
    (C) $1/4$
    (D) $1/2$
    (E) 8

27. A drawing of a certain large building is 10 inches by 15 inches. On this drawing, 1 inch represents 5 feet. If the same drawing had been made 20 inches by 30 inches, 1 inch on the drawing would represent

    (A) $2^{1}/_{2}$ feet
    (B) $3^{1}/_{3}$ feet
    (C) 5 feet
    (D) $7^{1}/_{2}$ feet
    (E) 10 feet

28. In a shipment of bearings, 51 were defective. This is 30 percent of the total number of bearings ordered. What was the total number of bearings ordered?

    (A) 125
    (B) 130
    (C) 153
    (D) 171
    (E) None of the above

In sample question 29 below, select the statement that is most nearly correct according to the paragraph.

Without accurate position descriptions, it is difficult to have proper understanding of who is to do what and when. As the organization obtains newer and different equipment, and as more and more data are accumulated to help establish proper preventive maintenance routines, the organization will change. When changes occur, it is important that the organization chart and the position descriptions are updated to reflect them.

29. *According to the above paragraph,* which of the following statements is most nearly correct?
    (A) Job descriptions should be general in nature to encourage job flexibility.
    (B) The organizational structure is not dependent on changes in preventive maintenance routines.
    (C) As long as supervisory personnel are aware of organizational changes, there is no need to update the organization chart constantly.
    (D) Organization changes can result from procurement of new, advanced equipment.
    (E) Formal job descriptions are not needed for an office to function on a day-to-day basis. The supervisor knows who is to do what and when.

30. A small crane was used to *raise* the heavy part. *Raise* most nearly means

    (A) lift
    (B) drag
    (C) drop
    (D) deliver
    (E) guide

31. *Short* most nearly means

    (A) tall
    (B) wide
    (C) brief
    (D) heavy
    (E) dark

In each of the sample questions below, look at the symbols in the first two boxes. Something about the three symbols in the first box makes them alike; something about the two symbols in the other box with the question mark makes them alike. Look for some characteristic that is common to all symbols in the same box, yet makes them different from the symbols in the other box. Among the five answer choices, find the symbol that can best be substituted for the question mark, because it is *like* the symbols in the second box, and, *for the same reason,* different from those in the first box.

32.

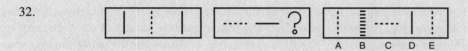

In the sample question above, all the symbols in the first box are vertical lines. The second box has two lines, one broken and one solid. Their *likeness* to each other consists in their being horizontal; and their being horizontal makes them *different* from the vertical lines in the other box. The answer must be the only one of the five lettered choices that is a horizontal line, either broken or solid. NOTE: There is not supposed to be a series or progression in these symbol questions. If you look for a progression in the first box and the second box, you will be wasting time. Remember, look for a *likeness* within each box and a *difference* between the two boxes. Now do sample question 33.

33.

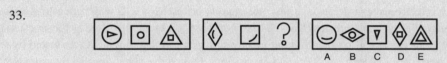

In sample question 34 below, there is at the left a drawing of a flat piece of paper and at the right, four figures labeled A, B, C, and D. When the paper is rolled, it will form one of the figures at its right. Decide which figure can be formed from the flat piece. Then on the sample answer sheet darken the space that has the same letter as your answer.

34.

Sample Answer Sheet

1. Ⓐ Ⓑ Ⓒ Ⓓ Ⓔ   8. Ⓐ Ⓑ Ⓒ Ⓓ Ⓔ   15. Ⓐ Ⓑ Ⓒ Ⓓ Ⓔ   22. Ⓐ Ⓑ Ⓒ Ⓓ Ⓔ   29. Ⓐ Ⓑ Ⓒ Ⓓ Ⓔ
2. Ⓐ Ⓑ Ⓒ Ⓓ Ⓔ   9. Ⓐ Ⓑ Ⓒ Ⓓ Ⓔ   16. Ⓐ Ⓑ Ⓒ Ⓓ Ⓔ   23. Ⓐ Ⓑ Ⓒ Ⓓ Ⓔ   30. Ⓐ Ⓑ Ⓒ Ⓓ Ⓔ
3. Ⓐ Ⓑ Ⓒ Ⓓ Ⓔ   10. Ⓐ Ⓑ Ⓒ Ⓓ Ⓔ   17. Ⓐ Ⓑ Ⓒ Ⓓ Ⓔ   24. Ⓐ Ⓑ Ⓒ Ⓓ Ⓔ   31. Ⓐ Ⓑ Ⓒ Ⓓ Ⓔ
4. Ⓐ Ⓑ Ⓒ Ⓓ Ⓔ   11. Ⓐ Ⓑ Ⓒ Ⓓ Ⓔ   18. Ⓐ Ⓑ Ⓒ Ⓓ Ⓔ   25. Ⓐ Ⓑ Ⓒ Ⓓ Ⓔ   32. Ⓐ Ⓑ Ⓒ Ⓓ Ⓔ
5. Ⓐ Ⓑ Ⓒ Ⓓ Ⓔ   12. Ⓐ Ⓑ Ⓒ Ⓓ Ⓔ   19. Ⓐ Ⓑ Ⓒ Ⓓ Ⓔ   26. Ⓐ Ⓑ Ⓒ Ⓓ Ⓔ   33. Ⓐ Ⓑ Ⓒ Ⓓ Ⓔ
6. Ⓐ Ⓑ Ⓒ Ⓓ Ⓔ   13. Ⓐ Ⓑ Ⓒ Ⓓ Ⓔ   20. Ⓐ Ⓑ Ⓒ Ⓓ Ⓔ   27. Ⓐ Ⓑ Ⓒ Ⓓ Ⓔ   34. Ⓐ Ⓑ Ⓒ Ⓓ Ⓔ
7. Ⓐ Ⓑ Ⓒ Ⓓ Ⓔ   14. Ⓐ Ⓑ Ⓒ Ⓓ Ⓔ   21. Ⓐ Ⓑ Ⓒ Ⓓ Ⓔ   28. Ⓐ Ⓑ Ⓒ Ⓓ Ⓔ

The correct answers for the questions in Part II are:

1. D	6. B	11. E	16. C	21. D	26. B	31. C
2. C	7. E	12. B	17. E	22. A	27. A	32. C
3. A	8. E	13. C	18. C	23. E	28. E	33. A
4. A	9. C	14. B	19. D	24. A	29. D	34. B
5. B	10. A	15. D	20. A	25. B	30. A	

ELECTRONIC EQUIPMENT MAINTENANCE POSITIONS

Duties of the Job

As the Postal Service moves into the twenty-first century, more and more postal operations are being handled automatically by highly sophisticated electronic equipment. The variety of sorting, stamping, coding, and routing machines is expanding rapidly, and as more post offices join the switch to automation the sheer number of these machines is also growing dramatically. Needless to say, all this electronic equipment requires regular maintenance and repair as needed.

The Postal Service retains its own teams of electronic technicians to care for its electronic equipment. These electronic technicians are hired at two levels, Electronic Technician 9 and Electronic Technician 10. The duties and responsibilities are similar, but there are some differences.

Qualification Requirements

Candidates for both electronic technician positions must qualify on test M/N 932, which measures sixteen different Knowledge, Skills, and Abilities (KSAs). Many of these KSAs are the same as those tested by test M/N 321, but some are specific to the field of electronics. And, in fact, not all KSAs tested by test M/N 932 are required for both Electronic Technician positions. Only those questions that measure KSAs required for the specific position are scored for applicants for that position.

Test M/N 932 covers the following Knowledge, Skills, and Abilities:

(1) *Knowledge of basic mechanics* refers to the theory of operation, terminology, usage, and characteristics of basic mechanical principles as they apply to such things as gears, pulleys, cams, pawls, power transmissions, linkages, fasteners, chains, sprockets, and belts; and includes hoisting, rigging, roping, pneumatics, and hydraulic devices.

(2) *Knowledge of basic electricity* refers to the theory, terminology, usage, and characteristics of basic electrical principles such as Ohm's Law, Kirchhoff's Law, and magnetism, as they apply to such things as AC/DC circuitry and hardware, relays, switches, and circuit breakers.

(3) *Knowledge of basic electronics* refers to the theory, terminology, usage, and characteristics of basic electronic principles concerning such things as solid state devices, vacuum tubes, coils, capacitors, resistors, and basic logic circuitry.

(4) *Knowledge of digital electronics* refers to the terminology, characteristics, symbology, and operation of digital components as used in such things as logic gates, registers, adders, counters, memories, encoders, and decoders.

(5) *Knowledge of safety procedures and equipment* refers to the knowledge of industrial hazards (e.g., mechanical, chemical, electrical, electronic) and procedures and techniques established to avoid injuries to self and others such as lock-out devices, protective clothing, and waste disposal techniques.

(6) *Knowledge of basic computer concepts* refers to the terminology, usage, and characteristics of digital memory storage/processing devices such as internal memory, input-output peripherals, and familiarity with programming concepts.

(19) *Ability to perform basic mathematical computations* refers to the ability to perform basic calculations such as addition, subtraction, multiplication, and division with whole numbers, fractions, and decimals.

(20) *Ability to perform more complex mathematics* refers to the ability to perform calculations such as basic algebra, geometry, scientific notation, and number conversions, as applied to mechanical, electrical, and electronic applications.

(21) *Ability to apply theoretical knowledge to practical applications* refers to mechanical, electrical, and electronic maintenance applications such as inspection, troubleshooting equipment repair and modification, preventive maintenance, and installation of electrical equipment.

(22) *Ability to detect patterns* refers to the ability to observe and analyze qualitative factors such as number progressions, spatial relationships, and auditory and visual patterns. This includes combining information and determining how a given set of numbers, objects, or sounds are related to each other.

(23) *Ability to use written reference materials* refers to the ability to locate, read, and comprehend text material such as handbooks, manuals, bulletins, directives, checklists, and route sheets.

(26) *Ability to follow instructions* refers to the ability to comprehend and execute written and oral instructions such as work orders, checklists, route sheets, and verbal directions and instructions.

(31) *Ability to use hand tools* refers to knowledge of, and proficiency with, various hand tools. This ability involves the safe and efficient use and maintenance of such tools as screwdrivers, wrenches, hammers, pliers, chisels, punches, taps, dies, rules, gauges, and alignment tools.

(35) *Ability to use technical drawings* refers to the ability to read and comprehend technical materials such as diagrams, schematics, flow charts, and blueprints.

(36) *Ability to use test equipment* refers to the knowledge of, and proficiency with, various types of mechanical, electrical, and electronic test equipment such as VOMS, oscilloscopes, circuit tracers, amprobes, and tachometers.

(37) *Ability to solder* refers to the knowledge of the appropriate soldering techniques, and the ability to apply them safely and effectively.

Because of the overlap of KSAs tested by tests M/N 931 and M/N 932, many of the same questions appear on both exams. Part I is identical on the two exams, so it will not be repeated here. Part II sample questions are presented here in their entirety despite the duplication of some questions. The actual, full-length exam consists of 170 items. Three hours are permitted to answer questions in Part II. The exam is scored "rights only."

OFFICIAL SAMPLE QUESTIONS FOR EXAMINATION M/N 932 (FOR ELECTRONIC TECHNICIAN POSITIONS)

(Part I is identical to Part I of test M/N 931)

Part II

1.   The primary function of a take-up pulley in a belt conveyor is to

   (A) carry the belt on the return trip.
   (B) track the belt.
   (C) maintain proper belt tension.
   (D) change the direction of the belt.

2.   Which device is used to transfer power and rotary mechanical motion from one shaft to another?

   (A) bearing
   (B) lever
   (C) idler roller
   (D) gear
   (E) bushing

3.   Which of the following circuits is shown in Figure III-A-22?

   (A) series circuit
   (B) parallel circuit
   (C) series, parallel circuit
   (D) solid state circuit
   (E) none of the above

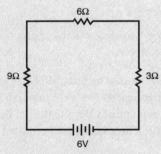

Figure III-A-22

4.   A circuit has two resistors of equal value in series. The voltage and current in the circuit are 20 volts and 2 amps respectively. What is the value of EACH resistor?

   (A)   5 ohms
   (B) 10 ohms
   (C) 20 ohms
   (D) not enough information given

5. What is the total net capacitance of two 60-farad capacitors connected in series?

    (A) 30 farads
    (B) 60 farads
    (C) 90 farads
    (D) 120 farads
    (E) 360 farads

6. Select the Boolean equation that matches the circuit diagram in Figure 79-4-17B.

    (A) Z = AB+CD+EF
    (B) Z = (A+B) (C+D) (E+F)
    (C) Z = A+B+C+D+EF
    (D) Z = ABCD(E+F)

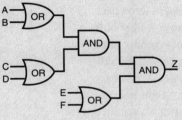

Figure 79-4-17B

7. If two 30-mH inductors are connected in series, what is the total net inductance of the combination?

    (A) 15 mH
    (B) 20 mH
    (C) 30 mH
    (D) 45 mH
    (E) 60 mH

8. In pure binary the decimal number 6 would be expressed as
    (A) 001
    (B) 011
    (C) 110
    (D) 111

9. In Figure 75-8-11, which of the following scores will be printed?

    (A) all scores > 90 and < 60
    (B) all scores < 90
    (C) all scores ≤ 90 and ≥ 60
    (D) all scores < 60

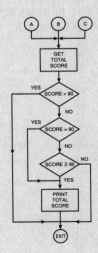

Figure 75-8-11

10. Crowbars, light bulbs, and vacuum bags are to be stored in the cabinet shown in Figure 75-25-1. Considering the balance of weight, what would be the safest arrangement?

    (A) top drawer—crowbars
    middle drawer—light bulbs
    bottom drawer—vacuum bags
    (B) top drawer—crowbars
    middle drawer—vacuum bags
    bottom drawer—light bulbs
    (C) top drawer—vacuum bags
    middle drawer—crowbars
    bottom drawer—light bulbs
    (D) top drawer—vacuum bags
    middle drawer—light bulbs
    bottom drawer—crowbars
    (E) top drawer—light bulbs
    middle drawer—vacuum bags
    bottom drawer—crowbars

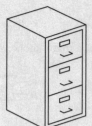

Figure 75-25-1

11. Which is most appropriate for pulling a heavy load?

    (A) electric lift
    (B) fork lift
    (C) tow conveyor
    (D) dolly
    (E) pallet truck

12. The electrical circuit term "open circuit" refers to a closed loop being opened. When an ohmmeter is connected into this type of circuit, one can expect the meter to

    (A) read infinity
    (B) read infinity and slowly return to ZERO
    (C) read ZERO
    (D) read ZERO and slowly return to infinity
    (E) none of the above

13. Contaminants have caused bearings to fail prematurely. Which pair of the items listed below should be kept away from bearings?

    (A) dirt and oil
    (B) grease and water
    (C) oil and grease
    (D) dirt and moisture
    (E) water and oil

14. In order to operate a breast drill, which direction should you turn it?

    (A) clockwise
    (B) counterclockwise
    (C) up and down
    (D) back and forth
    (E) right, then left

15. Which is the correct tool for tightening or loosening a water pipe?

    (A) slip joint pliers
    (B) household pliers
    (C) monkey wrench
    (D) water pump pliers
    (E) pipe wrench

16. What is one purpose of a chuck key?

    (A) open doors
    (B) remove drill bits
    (C) remove screws
    (D) remove set screws
    (E) unlock chucks

17. When smoke is generated as a result of using a portable electric drill for cutting holes into a piece of angle iron, one should

    (A) use a fire watch.
    (B) cease the drilling operation.
    (C) use an exhaust fan to remove smoke.
    (D) use a prescribed coolant solution to reduce friction.
    (E) call the Fire Department.

18. The primary purpose of soldering is to

    (A) melt solder to a molten state.
    (B) heat metal parts to the right temperature to be joined.
    (C) join metal parts by melting the parts.
    (D) harden metal.
    (E) join metal parts.

19. Which of the following statements is correct of a soldering gun?

    (A) Its tip is not replaceable.
    (B) It cannot be used in cramped places.
    (C) It heats only when trigger is pressed.
    (D) It is not rated by the number of watts it uses.
    (E) It has no light.

20. What unit of measurement is read on a dial torque wrench?

    (A) pounds
    (B) inches
    (C) centimeters
    (D) foot-pounds
    (E) degrees

21. Which instrument is used to test insulation breakdown of a conductor?

    (A) ohmmeter
    (B) ammeter
    (C) megger
    (D) wheatstone bridge
    (E) voltmeter

22. $^1/_2$ of $^1/_4$ =

    (A) $^1/_{12}$
    (B) $^1/_8$
    (C) $^1/_4$
    (D) $^1/_2$
    (E) 8

23. 2.6 − .5 =

    (A) 2.0
    (B) 2.1
    (C) 3.1
    (D) 3.3
    (E) None of the above

24. Simplify the following expression in terms of amps: 563×10^{-6}

    (A) 563,000,000 amps
    (B)   563,000 amps
    (C)   .563 amps
    (D)   .000563 amps
    (E) .000000563 amps

25. Solve the power equation
    $P = I^2R$ for R

    (A) $R = EI$
    (B) $R = I^2P$
    (C) $R = PI$
    (D) $R = P/I^2$
    (E) $R = E/I$

26. The product of 3 kilo ohms × 3 micro ohms is

    (A) 6×10^{-9} ohms
    (B) 6×10^{-3} ohms
    (C) 9×10^{3} ohms
    (D) 9×10^{-6} ohms
    (E) 9×10^{-3} ohms

In sample question 27 below, select the statement that is most nearly correct according to the paragraph.

Prior to 1870, a conveyor that made use of rollers was developed for transporting clay. This construction substituted rolling friction at the idler bearing points for the sliding friction of the slider bed. A primitive type of troughing belt conveyor was developed about the same time for the handling of grain. This design was improved during the latter part of the century when the troughing idler was developed.

27. *According to the above paragraph,* which of the following statements is most nearly correct?

    (A) The troughing belt conveyor was developed in about 1870 to handle clay and grain.
    (B) Rolling friction construction was replaced by sliding friction construction prior to 1870.
    (C) In the late nineteenth century, conveyors were improved with the development of the troughing idler.
    (D) The troughing idler, a significant design improvement for conveyors, was developed in the early nineteenth century.
    (E) Conveyor belts were invented and developed in the 1800s.

For sample question 28 below, select from the drawings of objects on the right labeled A, B, C, and D, the one that would have the TOP, FRONT, and RIGHT views shown in the drawing at the left.

28.

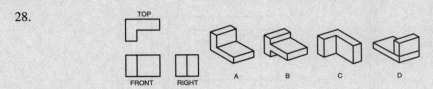

In sample question 29 below, there is, on the left, a drawing of a flat piece of paper and, on the right, four figures labeled A, B, C, and D. When the paper is bent on the dotted lines it will form one of the figures on the right. Decide which alternative can be formed from the flat piece.

29.

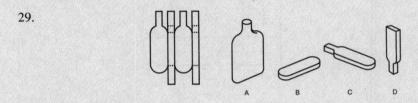

In each of the sample questions below, look at the symbols in the first two boxes. Something about the three symbols in the first box makes them alike; something about the two symbols in the other box with the question mark makes them alike. Look for some characteristic that is common to all symbols in the same box, yet makes them different from the symbols in the other box. Among the five answer choices, find the symbol that can best be substituted for the question mark, because it is *like* the symbols in the second box, and, *for the same reason,* different from those in the first box.

30.

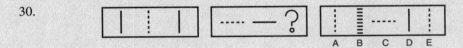

In the sample question above, all the symbols in the first box are vertical lines. The second box has two lines, one broken and one solid. Their *likeness* to each other consists in their being horizontal; and their being horizontal makes them *different* from the vertical lines in the other box. The answer must be the only one of the five lettered choices that is a horizontal line, either broken or solid. NOTE: There is not supposed to be a series or progression in these symbol questions. If you look for a progression in the first box and the second box, you will be wasting time. Remember, look for a *likeness* within each box and a *difference* between the two boxes.

Now do sample questions 31 and 32.

31.

32.

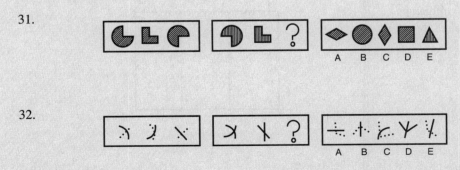

33. In Figure 3-8-6 below, what is the measurement of Dimension F? Drawing is not actual size.

(A) $1^3/_4$ inches
(B) $2^1/_4$ inches
(C) $2^1/_2$ inches
(D) $3^3/_4$ inches
(E) None of the above

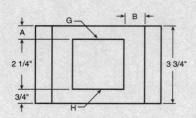

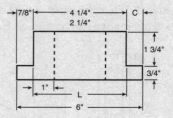

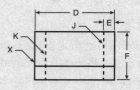

Figure 3-8-6

34. In Figure 160-57 below, what is the current flow through R_3 when:

V = 50 volts

R_1 = 25 ohms

R_2 = 25 ohms

R_3 = 50 ohms

R_4 = 50 ohms

R_5 = 50 ohms

and the current through the entire circuit totals one amp?

(A) 0.5 amp
(B) 5.0 amps
(C) 5.0 milliamps
(D) 50.0 milliamps
(E) None of the above

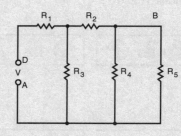

Figure 160-57

Sample Answer Sheet

1. Ⓐ Ⓑ Ⓒ Ⓓ Ⓔ   8. Ⓐ Ⓑ Ⓒ Ⓓ Ⓔ   15. Ⓐ Ⓑ Ⓒ Ⓓ Ⓔ   22. Ⓐ Ⓑ Ⓒ Ⓓ Ⓔ   29. Ⓐ Ⓑ Ⓒ Ⓓ Ⓔ
2. Ⓐ Ⓑ Ⓒ Ⓓ Ⓔ   9. Ⓐ Ⓑ Ⓒ Ⓓ Ⓔ   16. Ⓐ Ⓑ Ⓒ Ⓓ Ⓔ   23. Ⓐ Ⓑ Ⓒ Ⓓ Ⓔ   30. Ⓐ Ⓑ Ⓒ Ⓓ Ⓔ
3. Ⓐ Ⓑ Ⓒ Ⓓ Ⓔ   10. Ⓐ Ⓑ Ⓒ Ⓓ Ⓔ   17. Ⓐ Ⓑ Ⓒ Ⓓ Ⓔ   24. Ⓐ Ⓑ Ⓒ Ⓓ Ⓔ   31. Ⓐ Ⓑ Ⓒ Ⓓ Ⓔ
4. Ⓐ Ⓑ Ⓒ Ⓓ Ⓔ   11. Ⓐ Ⓑ Ⓒ Ⓓ Ⓔ   18. Ⓐ Ⓑ Ⓒ Ⓓ Ⓔ   25. Ⓐ Ⓑ Ⓒ Ⓓ Ⓔ   32. Ⓐ Ⓑ Ⓒ Ⓓ Ⓔ
5. Ⓐ Ⓑ Ⓒ Ⓓ Ⓔ   12. Ⓐ Ⓑ Ⓒ Ⓓ Ⓔ   19. Ⓐ Ⓑ Ⓒ Ⓓ Ⓔ   26. Ⓐ Ⓑ Ⓒ Ⓓ Ⓔ   33. Ⓐ Ⓑ Ⓒ Ⓓ Ⓔ
6. Ⓐ Ⓑ Ⓒ Ⓓ Ⓔ   13. Ⓐ Ⓑ Ⓒ Ⓓ Ⓔ   20. Ⓐ Ⓑ Ⓒ Ⓓ Ⓔ   27. Ⓐ Ⓑ Ⓒ Ⓓ Ⓔ   34. Ⓐ Ⓑ Ⓒ Ⓓ Ⓔ
7. Ⓐ Ⓑ Ⓒ Ⓓ Ⓔ   14. Ⓐ Ⓑ Ⓒ Ⓓ Ⓔ   21. Ⓐ Ⓑ Ⓒ Ⓓ Ⓔ   28. Ⓐ Ⓑ Ⓒ Ⓓ Ⓔ

The correct answers for the questions in Part II are:

1. C	6. B	11. E	16. B	21. C	26. E	31. E
2. D	7. E	12. A	17. D	22. B	27. C	32. D
3. A	8. C	13. D	18. E	23. B	28. C	33. C
4. A	9. C	14. A	19. C	24. D	29. C	34. A
5. A	10. E	15. E	20. D	25. D	30. C	

MAINTENANCE MECHANIC AND OVERHAUL SPECIALIST

These last two titles in the maintenance selection system represent specialized, higher-level positions within the building and equipment maintenance areas. In this group are the titles Maintenance Mechanic 7 and Overhaul Specialist 8. Exam M/N 933 covers the KSAs (Knowledge, Skills, and Abilities) necessary for performance of these jobs. As with other maintenance positions, not all KSAs are needed for performance of duties in both job titles; only questions that measure relevant KSAs for the job enter into score calculations.

Test M/N 933 covers the following Knowledge, Skills, and Abilities:

(1) *Knowledge of basic mechanics* refers to the theory of operation, terminology, usage, and characteristics of basic mechanical principles as they apply to such things as gears, pulleys, cams, pawls, power transmissions, linkages, fasteners, chains, sprockets, and belts; and includes hoisting, rigging, roping, pneumatics, and hydraulic devices.

(2) *Knowledge of basic electricity* refers to the theory, terminology, usage, and characteristics of basic electrical principles such as Ohm's Law, Kirchhoff's Law, and magnetism, as they apply to such things as AC/DC circuitry and hardware, relays, switches, and circuit breakers.

(3) *Knowledge of basic electronics* refers to the theory, terminology, usage, and characteristics of basic electronic principles concerning such things as solid state devices, vacuum tubes, coils, capacitors, resistors, and basic logic circuitry.

(5) *Knowledge of safety procedures and equipment* refers to the knowledge of industrial hazards (e.g., mechanical, chemical, electrical, electronic) and procedures and techniques established to avoid injuries to self and others such as lock-out devices, protective clothing, and waste disposal techniques.

(8) *Knowledge of lubrication materials and procedures* refers to the terminology, characteristics, storage, preparation, disposal, and usage techniques involved with lubrication materials such as oils, greases, and other types of lubricants.

(19) *Ability to perform basic mathematical computations* refers to the ability to perform basic calculations such as addition, subtraction, multiplication, and division with whole numbers, fractions, and decimals.

(20) *Ability to perform more complex mathematics* refers to the ability to perform calculations such as basic algebra, geometry, scientific notation, and number conversions, as applied to mechanical, electrical, and electronic applications.

(21) *Ability to apply theoretical knowledge to practical applications* refers to mechanical, electrical, and electronic maintenance applications such as inspection, trouble-shooting equipment repair and modification, preventive maintenance, and installation of electrical equipment.

(22) *Ability to detect patterns* refers to the ability to observe and analyze qualitative factors such as number progressions, spatial relationships, and auditory and visual patterns. This includes combining information and determining how a given set of numbers, objects, or sounds are related to each other.

(23) *Ability to use written reference materials* refers to the ability to locate, read, and comprehend text material such as handbooks, manuals, bulletins, directives, checklists, and route sheets.

(26) *Ability to follow instructions* refers to the ability to comprehend and execute written and oral instructions such as work orders, checklists, route sheets, and verbal directions and instructions.

(31) *Ability to use hand tools* refers to knowledge of, and proficiency with, various hand tools. This ability involves the safe and efficient use and maintenance of such tools as screwdrivers, wrenches, hammers, pliers, chisels, punches, taps, dies, rules, gauges, and alignment tools.

(32) *Ability to use portable power tools* refers to the knowledge of, and proficiency with, various power tools. This ability involves the safe and efficient use and maintenance of power tools such as drills, saws, sanders, and grinders.

(35) *Ability to use technical drawings* refers to the ability to read and comprehend technical materials such as diagrams, schematics, flow charts, and blueprints.

(36) *Ability to use test equipment* refers to the knowledge of, and proficiency with, various types of mechanical, electrical, and electronic test equipment such as VOMS, oscilloscopes, circuit tracers, amprobes, and tachometers.

(37) *Ability to solder* refers to the knowledge of the appropriate soldering techniques, and the ability to apply them safely and effectively.

Again, there is much overlap of KSAs and of test questions between this exam and the two previously discussed exams. Part I, Oral Instructions, is identical to Part I of Exams M/N 931 and M/N 932, so the sample questions will not be repeated here. Part II has some unique features, so the next pages will introduce you to the official sample questions distributed by the Postal Service. As with the other two exams in the maintenance series there are 170 items, and you are permitted three hours to answer Part II questions. The exam is scored "rights only."

OFFICIAL SAMPLE QUESTIONS FOR EXAMINATION M/N 933 (FOR MAINTENANCE MECHANIC 7 AND OVERHAUL SPECIALIST)

(Part I is identical to Part I of Examination M/N 931)

Part II

1. The primary function of a take-up pulley in a belt conveyor is to

   (A) carry the belt on the return trip.
   (B) track the belt.
   (C) maintain proper belt tension.
   (D) change the direction of the belt.
   (E) regulate the speed of the belt.

2. Which device is used to transfer power and rotary mechanical motion from one shaft to another?

   (A) bearing
   (B) lever
   (C) idler roller
   (D) gear
   (E) bushing

3. What special care is required in the storage of hard steel roller bearings? They should be

   (A) cleaned and spun dry with compressed air.
   (B) oiled once a month.
   (C) stored in a humid place.
   (D) wrapped in oiled paper.
   (E) stored at temperatures below 90 degrees Fahrenheit.

4. Which is the correct method to lubricate a roller chain?

   (A) Use brush to apply lubricant while chain is in motion.
   (B) Use squirt can to apply lubricant while chain is in motion.
   (C) Use brush to apply lubricant while chain is not in motion.
   (D) Soak chain in pan of lubricant and hang to allow excess to drain.
   (E) Chains do not need lubrication.

5. A circuit has two resistors of equal value in series. The voltage and current in the circuit are 20 volts and 2 amps respectively. What is the value of EACH resistor?

   (A) 5 ohms
   (B) 10 ohms
   (C) 15 ohms

(D) 20 ohms

(E) Not enough information given

6. Which of the following circuits is shown in Figure III-A-22?

(A) series circuit

(B) parallel circuit

(C) series, parallel circuit

(D) solid state circuit

(E) none of the above

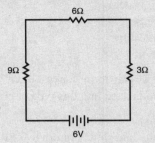

Figure III-A-22

7. What is the total net capacitance of two 60-farad capacitors connected in series?

(A)   30 F

(B)   60 F

(C)   90 F

(D) 120 F

(E) 360 F

8. If two 30-mH inductors are connected in series, what is the total net inductance of the combination?

(A) 15 mH

(B) 20 mH

(C) 30 mH

(D) 45 mH

(E) 60 mH

9. Crowbars, light bulbs, and vacuum bags are to be stored in the cabinet shown in Figure 75-25-1. Considering the balance of weight, what would be the safest arrangement?

(A) top drawer—crowbars
      middle drawer—light bulbs
      bottom drawer—vacuum bags

(B) top drawer—crowbars
      middle drawer—vacuum bags
      bottom drawer—light bulbs

(C) top drawer—vacuum bags
      middle drawer—crowbars
      bottom drawer—light bulbs

(D) top drawer—vacuum bags
      middle drawer—light bulbs
      bottom drawer—crowbars

(E) top drawer—light bulbs
      middle drawer—vacuum bags
      bottom drawer—crowbars

Figure 75-25-1

10. Contaminants have caused bearings to fail prematurely. Which pair of items listed below should be kept away from bearings?

    (A) dirt and oil
    (B) grease and water
    (C) oil and grease
    (D) dirt and moisture
    (E) water and oil

11. The electrical circuit term "open circuit" refers to a closed loop being opened. When an ohmmeter is connected into this type of circuit, one can expect the meter to

    (A) read infinity.
    (B) read infinity and slowly return to ZERO.
    (C) read ZERO.
    (D) read ZERO and slowly return to infinity.
    (E) None of the above

12. Which is most appropriate for pulling a heavy load?

    (A) electric lift
    (B) fork lift
    (C) tow conveyor
    (D) dolly
    (E) pallet truck

13. In order to operate a breast drill, which direction should you turn it?

    (A) clockwise
    (B) counterclockwise
    (C) up and down
    (D) back and forth
    (E) right, then left

14. Which is the correct tool for tightening or loosening a water pipe?

    (A) slip joint pliers
    (B) household pliers
    (C) monkey wrench
    (D) water pump pliers
    (E) pipe wrench

15. What is one purpose of a chuck key?

    (A) open doors
    (B) remove drill bits
    (C) remove screws
    (D) remove set screws
    (E) unlock chucks

16. When smoke is generated as a result of using a portable electric drill for cutting holes into a piece of angle iron, one should

    (A) use a fire watch.
    (B) cease the drilling operation.

(C) use an exhaust fan to remove smoke.

(D) use a prescribed coolant solution to reduce friction.

(E) call the Fire Department.

17. The primary purpose of soldering is to

(A) melt solder to a molten state.
(B) heat metal parts to the right temperature to be joined.
(C) join metal parts by melting the parts.
(D) harden metal.
(E) join metal parts.

18. Which of the following statements is correct concerning a soldering gun?

(A) Its tip is not replaceable.
(B) It cannot be used in cramped places.
(C) It heats only when trigger is pressed.
(D) It is not rated by the number of watts it use.
(E) It has no light.

19. What unit of measurement is read on a dial torque wrench?

(A) pounds
(B) inches
(C) centimeters
(D) foot-pounds
(E) degrees

20. Which instrument is used to test insulation breakdown of a conductor?

(A) ohmmeter
(B) ammeter
(C) megger
(D) wheatstone bridge
(E) voltmeter

21. $1/2$ of $1/4 =$

(A) $1/12$
(B) $1/8$
(C) $1/4$
(D) $1/2$
(E) 8

22. $2.6 - .5 =$

(A) 2.0
(B) 2.1
(C) 3.1
(D) 3.3
(E) none of the above

23. Solve the power equation $P = I^2R$ for R

   (A) $R = EI$
   (B) $R = I^2P$
   (C) $R = PI$
   (D) $R = P/I^2$
   (E) $R = E/I$

24. The product of 3 kilo ohms $\times$ 3 micro ohms is:

   (A) 6×10^{-9} ohms
   (B) 6×10^{-3} ohms
   (C) 9×10^3 ohms
   (D) 9×10^{-6} ohms
   (E) 9×10^{-3} ohms

In sample question 25 below, select the statement that is most nearly correct according to the paragraph.

Prior to 1870, a conveyor that made use of rollers was developed for transporting clay. This construction substituted rolling friction at the idler bearing points for the sliding friction of the slider bed. A primitive type of troughing belt conveyor was developed about the same time for the handling of grain. This design was improved during the latter part of the century when the troughing idler was developed.

25. *According to the above paragraph,* which of the following statements is most nearly correct?

   (A) The troughing belt conveyor was developed in about 1870 to handle clay and grain.
   (B) Rolling friction construction was replaced by sliding friction construction prior to 1870.
   (C) In the late nineteenth century, conveyors were improved with the development of the troughing idler.
   (D) The troughing idler, a significant design improvement for conveyors, was developed in the early nineteenth century.
   (E) Conveyor belts were invented and developed in the 1800s.

26. A small crane was used to *raise* the heavy part. *Raise* most nearly means

   (A) lift
   (B) drag
   (C) drop
   (D) deliver
   (E) guide

27. *Short* most nearly means

   (A) tall
   (B) wide
   (C) brief
   (D) heavy
   (E) dark

For sample question 28 below, select from the drawings of objects on the right labeled A, B, C, and D, the one that would have the TOP, FRONT, and RIGHT views shown in the drawing at the left.

28.

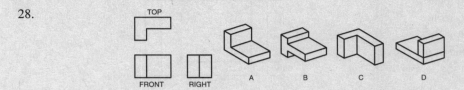

In sample question 29 below, there is, on the left, a drawing of a flat piece of paper and, on the right, four figures labeled A, B, C, and D. When the paper is bent on the dotted lines it will form one of the figures on the right. Decide which alternative can be formed from the flat piece.

29.

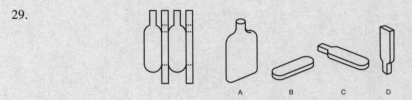

In each of the sample questions below, look at the symbols in the first two boxes. Something about the three symbols in the first box makes them alike; something about the two symbols in the other box with the question mark makes them alike. Look for some characteristic that is common to all symbols in the same box, yet makes them different from the symbols in the other box. Among the five answer choices, find the symbol that can best be substituted for the question mark, because it is *like* the symbols in the second box, and, *for the same reason,* different from those in the first box.

30.

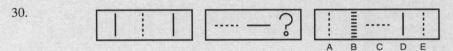

In the sample question above, all the symbols in the first box are vertical lines. The second box has two lines, one broken and one solid. Their *likeness* to each other consists in their being horizontal; and their being horizontal makes them *different* from the vertical lines in the other box. The answer must be the only one of the five lettered choices that is a horizontal line, either broken or solid. NOTE: There is not supposed to be a series or progression in these symbol questions. If you look for a progression in the first box and the second box, you will be wasting time. Remember, look for a *likeness* within each box and a *difference* between the two boxes.

Now do sample questions 31 and 32.

31.

32.

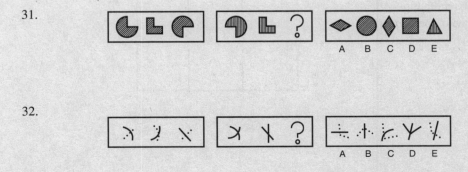

33. In Figure 3-8-6 below, what is the measurement of Dimension F? Drawing is not actual size.

   (A) $1^3/_4$ inches
   (B) $2^1/_4$ inches
   (C) $2^1/_2$ inches
   (D) $3^3/_4$ inches
   (E) none of the above

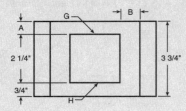
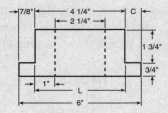
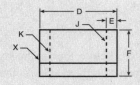

Figure 3-8-6

34. In Figure 160-57 below, what is the current flow through R_3 when:

   V   =   50 volts

   R_1 =   25 ohms

   R_2 =   25 ohms

   R_3 =   50 ohms

   R_4 =   50 ohms

   R_5 =   50 ohms

   and the current through the entire circuit totals one amp?

   (A)   0.5 amp
   (B)   5.0 amps
   (C)   5.0 milliamps
   (D) 50.0 milliamps
   (E)   none of the above

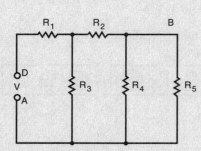

Figure 160-57

Sample Answer Sheet

1. Ⓐ Ⓑ Ⓒ Ⓓ Ⓔ	8. Ⓐ Ⓑ Ⓒ Ⓓ Ⓔ	15. Ⓐ Ⓑ Ⓒ Ⓓ Ⓔ	22. Ⓐ Ⓑ Ⓒ Ⓓ Ⓔ	29. Ⓐ Ⓑ Ⓒ Ⓓ Ⓔ
2. Ⓐ Ⓑ Ⓒ Ⓓ Ⓔ	9. Ⓐ Ⓑ Ⓒ Ⓓ Ⓔ	16. Ⓐ Ⓑ Ⓒ Ⓓ Ⓔ	23. Ⓐ Ⓑ Ⓒ Ⓓ Ⓔ	30. Ⓐ Ⓑ Ⓒ Ⓓ Ⓔ
3. Ⓐ Ⓑ Ⓒ Ⓓ Ⓔ	10. Ⓐ Ⓑ Ⓒ Ⓓ Ⓔ	17. Ⓐ Ⓑ Ⓒ Ⓓ Ⓔ	24. Ⓐ Ⓑ Ⓒ Ⓓ Ⓔ	31. Ⓐ Ⓑ Ⓒ Ⓓ Ⓔ
4. Ⓐ Ⓑ Ⓒ Ⓓ Ⓔ	11. Ⓐ Ⓑ Ⓒ Ⓓ Ⓔ	18. Ⓐ Ⓑ Ⓒ Ⓓ Ⓔ	25. Ⓐ Ⓑ Ⓒ Ⓓ Ⓔ	32. Ⓐ Ⓑ Ⓒ Ⓓ Ⓔ
5. Ⓐ Ⓑ Ⓒ Ⓓ Ⓔ	12. Ⓐ Ⓑ Ⓒ Ⓓ Ⓔ	19. Ⓐ Ⓑ Ⓒ Ⓓ Ⓔ	26. Ⓐ Ⓑ Ⓒ Ⓓ Ⓔ	33. Ⓐ Ⓑ Ⓒ Ⓓ Ⓔ
6. Ⓐ Ⓑ Ⓒ Ⓓ Ⓔ	13. Ⓐ Ⓑ Ⓒ Ⓓ Ⓔ	20. Ⓐ Ⓑ Ⓒ Ⓓ Ⓔ	27. Ⓐ Ⓑ Ⓒ Ⓓ Ⓔ	34. Ⓐ Ⓑ Ⓒ Ⓓ Ⓔ
7. Ⓐ Ⓑ Ⓒ Ⓓ Ⓔ	14. Ⓐ Ⓑ Ⓒ Ⓓ Ⓔ	21. Ⓐ Ⓑ Ⓒ Ⓓ Ⓔ	28. Ⓐ Ⓑ Ⓒ Ⓓ Ⓔ	

The correct answers for the questions in Part II are:

1. C	6. A	11. A	16. D	21. B	26. A	31. E
2. D	7. A	12. E	17. E	22. B	27. C	32. D
3. D	8. E	13. A	18. C	23. D	28. C	33. C
4. D	9. E	14. E	19. D	24. E	29. C	34. A
5. A	10. D	15. B	20. C	25. C	30. C	

SUPERVISORY POSITIONS

Supervisory positions are never filled by open competitive examinations. In order to become a supervisor, you must first prove yourself as a worker in the department or function that you would like to supervise. The person who wishes to grow into a supervisory position must first prove his or her reliability, efficiency, and initiative on the job over a period of time. Then that person must take a test of supervisory aptitude to demonstrate promise of success in a supervisory role. The test of supervisory aptitude includes questions on understanding human behavior, judgment in social situations, and judgment in business situations.

POSTAL INSPECTOR

Near the top of the postal pay schedule is the position of postal inspector. Postal inspectors are law enforcement officers within the Postal Service. They perform varied, highly responsible duties that lead to the detection, prosecution, and conviction of people committing mail fraud and other crimes related to the Postal Service. Their work is exciting, difficult, dangerous, and well paid. No one may become a postal inspector without previous Postal Service experience. All postal inspectors have risen from the ranks of postal employees. In addition, postal inspectors have passed a four-hour examination consisting of 118 questions, mostly reading comprehension and vocabulary, and have undergone and passed a rigorous eleven-week training program.

The duties and qualification requirements for postal inspectors are given in the Postal Inspector Vacancy Notice that follows.

U.S. Postal Service

Postal Inspector Vacancy Notice

Position Number:
ISSUE DATE:
CLOSING DATE:

TITLE: Postal Inspector (A)
GRADE: EAS-17
FLSA DESIGNATION: Exempt
OCCUPATION CODE: 2335-2002
SALARY RANGE:
PERSONS ELIGIBLE TO APPLY: ALL QUALIFIED POSTAL CAREER EMPLOYEES WITH AT LEAST ONE YEAR OF CAREER SERVICE MAY APPLY FOR THIS POSITION

LOCATION: Any duty station nationwide, as directed by the Regional Chief Inspector to whom assigned.

The Postal Inspection Service is recruiting for Postal Inspectors. The entry level for Inspectors is EAS-17, with promotions over the next four years based on satisfactory performance to EAS-19, 21, and 23.

Those applicants ultimately selected will be temporarily promoted to EAS-17 and enter an eleven-week basic training program at Potomac, MD. Successful completion of the training will result in permanent assignment as a Postal Inspector and relocation to the initial duty assignment. (Those not completing basic training will be returned to their former or similar positions.)

DUTIES: Conduct criminal investigations and audits; interview witnesses and complainants; obtain and evaluate information; provide testimony; prepare reports; carry firearms; arrest, search, or restrain suspects. The position requires frequent and extended travel and absences from home. Inspectors must relocate according to the needs of the Service. Relocation to a new area is required upon completion of initial training. Inspectors will normally be required to relocate at least one additional time during their careers. Many times they are required to work in undesirable areas with irregular work schedules and hours. Inspectors are FLSA-exempt and do not receive overtime compensation.

QUALIFICATIONS: All qualifications must be met by the closing date of this announcement.

1. Postal employee with at least one (1) year of career service.
2. U.S. citizen.
3. Minimum age 21, maximum age 37. (Public law 93-350 provides for mandatory retirement at age 55 with twenty years' service for certain law enforcement personnel. Therefore, persons who are over age 37 may not be appointed as Postal Inspectors.)
4. Baccalaureate degree (any major) from an accredited college or university.
5. Good physical condition.
6. Have possessed a valid state motor vehicle license for over two years.
7. No felony conviction.

8. Ability to:
   a. Communicate clearly and effectively (in English) orally and in writing
   b. Gather, interpret, and evaluate information, extract details, and draw logical conclusions
   c. Follow instructions
   d. Set priorities
   e. Deal effectively with people

SELECTION PROCEDURES: The basic selection procedure includes six steps:

1. Written examination (approximately four hours)
2. Medical examination
3. Submission of a structured resumé prepared by the candidate and an evaluation by the candidate's supervisor
4. Background suitability investigation
5. Assessment by a panel of inspectors
6. Successful completion of the Inspector Basic Training in Potomac, MD

APPLICATION PROCEDURES: All qualified (see Qualifications) career employees are eligible to apply for the examination by submitting a facsimile of the attached Questionnaire/Application form to their personnel office. Applicants who recently took the examination and were rated ineligible may retake the examination. The application forms will be available at your personnel office.

Inspector/Applicants who received a qualifying (70.0+) test score from the last vacancy announcement need not reapply.

You will receive sample questions with notification of the date and time that the examination is scheduled.

HOW TO APPLY: Individuals should complete PS Form 991, *Application for Promotion or Assignment*. PS Form 991 should include under "Postal Positions" the date, locations, grades, and titles of each assignment of more than three (3) months duration since joining the Postal Service. Included should also be experience as Security Liaison Officer, Recruitment Specialist, Acting Team Leader or AIC, Fraud, EC, IC, or Audit Specialist, etc. The supervisor will complete Page 4 of PS Form 991.

ATTENTION: WHEN SUBMITTING A PS FORM 991, EMPLOYEES ARE ENCOURAGED TO INCLUDE THE ZIP + 4 IN THEIR MAILING ADDRESS.

Applying for Postal Positions

Post office exams are not regularly scheduled exams given on the same date all over the country. Rather, each postal exam is separately scheduled in each postal geographic area. An area may comprise a number of states or, in densely populated regions, may consist of only a portion of one county. The frequency of administration also varies, though generally most exams are offered every two or three years.

When an exam is about to open in a postal area, the postal examiner for the area sends notices to all the post offices serviced by that area. The examiner also places ads in local newspapers and commercials over local radio stations. State employment offices receive and post copies of the announcement, and civil service newspapers carry the information as well. The announcement that you can pick up at your post office may look similar to this:

THE OPPORTUNITY: Applications are now being accepted, and examinations will be given to establish a register of eligibles or to expand the current register of eligibles from which future _____ vacancies in this post office will be filled. All interested persons who meet the requirements described in this announcement are urged to apply.

QUALIFICATION REQUIREMENTS: No experience is required. All applicants will be required to take a written examination designed to test aptitude for learning and performing the duties of the position. The test will consist of _____.
The test and completion of the forms will require approximately _____ hours.

DUTIES: Clerks work indoors. Clerks have to handle sacks of mail weighing as much as seventy pounds. They sort mail and distribute it by using a complicated scheme that must be memorized. Some clerks work at a public counter or window doing such jobs as selling stamps and weighing parcels and are personally responsible for all money and stamps. Clerks may be on their feet all day. They also have to stretch, reach, and throw mail. Assignments to preferred positions, such as window clerks, are filled by open bid and by reassignment of the senior qualified clerk.

City carriers have to collect and deliver mail. Some carriers walk, other carriers drive. Carriers must be out in all kinds of weather. Almost all carriers have to carry mail bags on their shoulders; loads weigh as much as thirty-five pounds. Carriers sometimes have to load and unload sacks of mail weighing as much as seventy pounds.

The duties of newly appointed clerks and carriers are at times interchangeable. As representatives of the Postal Service, they must maintain pleasant and effective public relations with patrons and others, requiring general familiarity with postal laws, regulations, and procedures commonly used.

Employees may be assigned to work in places exposed to public view. Their appearance influences the general public's confidence and attitude toward the entire Postal Service.

Employees appointed under this standard are, therefore, expected to maintain neat and proper personal attire and grooming appropriate to conducting public business, including the wearing of a uniform when required.

CARRIER POSITIONS REQUIRING DRIVING: Before eligibles may be appointed to carrier positions that require driving, they must demonstrate a safe driving record and must pass the Road Test to show they can safely drive a vehicle of the type used on the job.

Eligibles who fail to qualify in the Road Test will not be given the test again in the same group of hires. Those who fail the test a second time will not again be considered as a result of the same examination for appointment to a position that requires driving.

A valid driver's license from the state in which this post office is located must be presented at the time of appointment. Persons who do not have the license will not be appointed but their names will be restored to the register. They may not again be considered for carrier positions until they have obtained the required driver's license. After hire, individuals also must be able to obtain the required type of government operator's permit.

PHYSICAL REQUIREMENTS: Applicants must be physically able to perform the duties described elsewhere in this announcement. Any physical condition that would cause the applicant to be a hazard to himself or herself or to others will be disqualifying for appointment.

The distant vision for clerk and carrier positions not involving driving duties must test at least 20/30 (Snellen) in one eye, glasses permitted, and applicants generally must be able to hear ordinary conversation with or without a hearing aid, but some clerk positions may be filled by the hearing impaired.

For carrier positions that require driving, applicants must have at least 20/30 (Snellen) in one eye and 20/50 (Snellen) in the other with or without a corrective device for unlimited operation of motor vehicles. Hearing must be at least 15/20 with or without a hearing aid.

A physical examination, drug screen, and psychological interview will be required before appointment.

AGE REQUIREMENT: The general age requirement is eighteen years or sixteen years for high school graduates, except for those for whom age limits are waived. For carrier positions that require driving, applicants must be eighteen years of age or over. In general, there is no maximum age limit.

CITIZENSHIP: All applicants must be citizens of or owe allegiance to the United States of America or have been granted permanent resident alien status in the United States. Verification is required.

SELECTIVE SERVICE REGISTRATION REQUIREMENT: To be eligible for appointment to a position in the Postal Service, males born after December 31, 1959, must (subject to certain exceptions) be registered with the Selective Service System in accordance with Section 3 of the Military Selective Service Act. Males between 18 and 26 years of age (have not reached their 26th birthday) can register with the Selective Service System at any U.S. Post Office or consular office if outside the United States. Your registration status can be verified with the Selective Service by calling (708) 688-6888 for information.

SALARY: Results from collective bargaining.

CONSIDERATION: Consideration to fill these positions will be made of the highest eligibles on the register who are available.

VETERAN PREFERENCE: Veteran preference is granted for employment in the Postal Service. Those with a 10-point or greater compensable service-connected disability are placed at the top of the hiring list, in the order of their scores. Other eligibles are listed below this group in rank order.

HOW TO APPLY: Submit application Form 2479-AB to the postmaster of this office or place designated by him or her.

Opening date for application: _____
                                                Month   Day   Year

Closing date for application: _____
                                                Month   Day   Year

WRITTEN EXAMINATION: Applicants will be notified of date, time, and place of examination and will be sent sample questions.

POST OFFICE JOBS OFFER:

Job Security	Liberal Retirement	Cash for Suggestions
Paid Vacations	Sick Leave with Pay	Promotion Opportunities
On-the-Job Training	Low-Cost Life Insurance	Paid Holidays
	Low-Cost Health Insurance	

Ask for an application card at your local post office. The card is bright yellow and in two sections joined at a perforation. Do NOT separate the two sections. The section on the left is called the Application Card, that on the right the Admission Card. Instructions for filling out both sections are printed on the back of the card. Follow these directions precisely, and carefully fill out both sections of the card. Hand in or mail the completed application as instructed.

The application and admission card look like those below and on the next page.

(We have had to separate the sections to fit the book page. You must NOT separate the sections.)

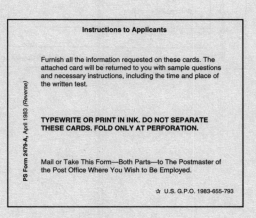

(Front)   (Back)

You will be notified by mail when the examination date, time, and place are set. You will receive instructions as to where and when to report for the exam. You will also receive the admission-card portion of the application card. Be sure to bring the admission card with you when you report for the exam. Along with the admission card and exam information, you will receive a set of sample questions for your examination.

(Front)

ADMISSION CARD

Title of Examination	Social Security No.	Do Not Write In This Space

Date of Birth	Today's Date	Post Office Applied For

If you have performed active duty in the Armed Forces of the United States and were separated under honorable conditions indicate periods of service

From (Mo., Day, Yr.)_____to (Mo., Day, Yr.)

DO YOU CLAIM VETERAN PREFERENCE?   NO   YES   IF YES, BASED ON
(1) Active duty in the Armed Forces of the U.S. during World War I or the period December 7, 1941, through July 1, 1955
(2) More than 180 consecutive days of active duty (other than for training) in the Armed Forces of the U.S. any part of which occurred between Jan. 31, 1955 and Oct. 14, 1976, or (3) Award of a campaign badge or service medal
Your status as (1) a disabled veteran or a veteran who was awarded the purple heart for wounds or injuries received in action, (2) a veteran's widow who has not remarried, (3) the wife of an ex serviceman who has a service connected disability which disqualifies him for civil service appointment, or (4) the widowed, divorced or separated mother of an ex-service son or daughter who died in action or who is totally and permanently disabled

Print or Type Your Name and Address	Name (First, Middle, Last)	
	Address (House, Apt. No. & Street)	This card will be returned to you. Bring it, along with personal identification bearing your picture or description, with you when you report for the test. ID's will be checked, and a fingerprint or signature specimen may be required.
➤	City, State, ZIP Code (ZIP Code must be included)	

(Back)

Final Eligibility in This Examination is Subject to Suitability Determination

The collection of information on this form is authorized by 39 U.S.C. 401.1001; completion of this form is voluntary. This information will be used to determine qualification, suitability, and availability of applicants for USPS employment, and may be disclosed to relevant Federal Agencies regarding eligibility and suitability for employment, law enforcement activities when there is an indication of a potential violation of law, in connection with private relief legislation (to Office of Management and Budget)/ to a congressional office at your request, to a labor organization as required by the NLRA, and where pertinent, in a legal proceeding to which the Postal Service is a party. If this information is not provided, you may not receive full consideration for a position.

Disclosure by you of your Social Security Nmber (SSN) is mandatory to obtain the services, benefits, or processes that you are seeking. Solicitation of the SSN by the United States Postal Service is authorized under provisions of Executive Order 9397, dated November 22, 1943. The information gathered through the use of the number will be used only as necessary in authorized personnel administration processes.

PS Form 2479-B, April 1983 (Reverse)

Applicant	Fingerprint
Make no marks on this side of the card unless so instructed by examiner.	
Signature of Applicant	

Political Recommendations Prohibited

The law (39 U.S. Code 1002) prohibits political and certain other recommendations for appointments, promotions, assignments, transfers, or designations of persons in the Postal Service. Statements relating solely to character and residence are permitted, but every other kind of statement or recommendation is prohibited unless it either is requested by the Postal Service and consists solely of an evaluation of the work performance, ability, aptitude, and general qualifications of an individual or is requested by a Government representative investigating the individual's loyalty, suitability, and character. Anyone who requests or solicits a prohibited statement or recommendation is subject to disqualification from the Postal Service and anyone in the Postal Service who accepts such a statement may be suspended or removed from office.

Have You Answered All Questions on the Reverse of This Form?

Test-Taking Techniques

Many factors enter into a test score. The most important factor should be ability to answer the questions, which in turn indicates ability to learn and perform the duties of the job. Assuming that you have this ability, knowing what to expect on the exam and familiarity with techniques of effective test taking should give you the confidence you need to do your best on the exam.

On the examination day assigned to you, allow the test itself to be the main attraction of the day. Do not squeeze it in between other activities. Arrive rested, relaxed, and on time. In fact, plan to arrive a little bit early. Leave plenty of time for traffic tie-ups or other complications that might upset you and interfere with your test performance. Remember to bring your admission card, identification with your picture and signature, and two number 2 pencils, sharpened, with clean erasers.

In the test room, the examiner will hand out forms for you to fill out. He or she will give you the instructions that you must follow in taking the examination. The examiner may distribute the pencils to be used for marking the answer sheet and will tell you how to fill in the grids on the forms. Time limits and timing signals will be explained. If you do not understand any of the examiner's instructions, ASK QUESTIONS. It would be ridiculous to score less than your best because of poor communication.

During the testing session for most exams, you will answer both sample questions and actual test questions. If you have sample questions in the testing room, you will see the answers to the sample questions. You will not be given the answers to the actual test questions, even after the test is over.

At the examination, you must follow instructions exactly. Fill in the grids on the forms carefully and accurately. Misgridding may lead to loss of veterans' credits to which you may be entitled or to misaddressing of your test results. Do not begin until you are told to begin. Stop as soon as the examiner tells you to stop. Do not turn pages until you are told to do so. Do not go back to parts you have already completed. Any infraction of the rules is considered cheating. If you cheat, your test paper will not be scored, and you will not be eligible for appointment.

The answer sheet for your postal exam is machine scored. You cannot give any explanations to the machine, so you must fill out the answer sheet clearly and correctly.

HOW TO MARK YOUR ANSWER SHEET

1. Blacken your answer space firmly and completely. ● is the only correct way to mark the answer sheet. ◑, ⊗, ⊘, and ∅ are all unacceptable. The machine might not read them at all.
2. Mark only one answer for each question. If you mark more than one answer you will be considered wrong even if one of the answers is correct.
3. If you change your mind, you must erase your mark. Attempting to cross out an incorrect answer like this ✖ will not work. You must erase any incorrect answer completely. An incomplete erasure might be read as a second answer.
4. All of your answering should be in the form of blackened spaces. The machine cannot read English. Do not write any notes in the margins.
5. MOST IMPORTANT: Answer each question in the right place. Question 1 must be answered in space 1; question 52 in space 52. If you should skip an answer space and mark a series of answers in the wrong places, you must erase all those answers and do the questions over, marking your answers in the proper places. You cannot afford to use the limited time in this way. Therefore, as you answer *each* question, look at its number and check that you are marking your answer in the space with the same number.

SHOULD YOU GUESS?

You may be wondering whether it is wise to guess when you are not sure of an answer or whether it is better to skip the question when you are not certain. The wisdom of guessing depends on the scoring method for the particular examination part. If the scoring is "rights only," that is, one point for each correct answer and no subtraction for wrong answers, then by all means you should guess. Read the question and all the answer choices carefully. Eliminate those answer choices that you are certain are wrong. Then guess from among the remaining choices. You cannot gain a point if you leave the answer space blank; you may gain a point with an educated guess or even with a lucky guess. In fact, it is foolish to leave any spaces blank on a test that counts "rights only." If it appears that you are about to run out of time before completing such an exam, mark all the remaining blanks with the same letter. According to the law of averages, you should get some portion of those questions right.

If the scoring method is rights minus wrongs, such as on an Address Checking part, DO NOT GUESS. A wrong answer counts heavily against you. On this type of test, do not rush to fill answer spaces randomly at the end. Work as quickly as possible while concentrating on accuracy. Keep working carefully until time is called. Then stop and leave the remaining answer spaces blank.

There are other question styles in which the decision to guess or not to guess is really up to you and your personality. These are the sections in which you lose a fraction of a point for each wrong answer. Examples of these questions are Memory for Addresses and the Stenography Test. A correct answer gives you one point; a skipped space gives you nothing at all, but costs you nothing except the chance of getting the answer right; a wrong answer costs you a quarter of a point. Your best bet is to first answer every question of which you are certain. You need every point you can count on. Just be VERY careful to mark each answer in the correct place. Then return to the unanswered questions and make educated guesses if you can and random guesses if you wish.

One of the questions you should ask in the testing room is what scoring method will be used on your particular exam. You can then guide your guessing procedure accordingly.

GUESSING GUIDE FOR POSTAL EXAMS

Type of Exam	Whether or Not to Guess

Exam 470 and Exam 460
   Clerk
   City Carrier
   Distribution Clerk, Machine
     (LSM Operator)
   Flat Sorting Machine Operator
   Mail Handler
   Mail Processor
   Mark-up Clerk, Automated
   Rural Carrier
	Part
	A. Address Checking, rights minus wrongs; do NOT guess
	B. Memory for Addresses, $\frac{1}{4}$ off; your choice
	C. Number Series, rights only; GUESS
	D. Following Oral Instructions, rights only; GUESS

Exam 710
   Clerk-Typist
   Clerk-Stenographer
   Data Conversion Operator
	Both parts rights only; GUESS

Exam 711 Stenography Test	¹/₄ off for each error; your choice

Exam 911
    Cleaner
    Custodian
    Custodial Laborer
	Rights only; GUESS

Exam 630
    Postal Police Officer
	Part
	1. Name and Number Comparisons,
	    1/4 off for each error; your choice
	2 and 3. Reading and Arithmetic
	    Reasoning, rights only; GUESS

Exam 91
    Garageman-Driver
    Tractor-Trailer Operator
    Motor Vehicle Operator
	Both parts rights only; GUESS

Exams M/N 931, 932, 933 Maintenance positions	Both parts rights only; GUESS

SCORING THE EXAM

When the exam is over, the examiner will collect the test booklets and answer sheets. The answer sheets will be sent to the test center in Virginia where a machine will scan your answers and mark them right or wrong. Then your raw score will be calculated. Your raw score is the score you get according to the scoring formula used for each exam.

However, your raw score is *not* your final score. The Postal Service takes the raw scores on all parts of an exam, combines them according to a formula of its own, and converts them to a scaled score, on a scale of 1 to 100. The entire process of conversion from raw to scaled score is confidential information. The score you receive is not your number right, is not your raw score, and is not a percent. The score you receive is a *scaled score*. Before reporting any scaled scores, the Postal Service adds any veterans' service points or any other advantages to which the applicant might be entitled. Veterans' service points are added only to passing scaled scores of 70 or more. A failing score cannot be brought to passing level by adding veterans' points. The score earned plus veterans' service points results in the final scaled score that finds its place on the eligibility list.

A total scaled score of 70 is a passing score. The names of all persons with scaled scores of 70 or more are placed on the list sent to the local post office. Those names are placed on the list in order, with the highest score at the top of the list. Hiring then takes place from the top of the list as vacancies occur.

The scoring process may take six or ten weeks or even longer. Be patient. If you pass the exam, you will receive notice of your scaled score. Applicants who fail the exam are not told their scores. They are simply notified that they will not be considered for the position.

TEST-TAKING TIPS

1. READ. Read every word of the instructions. Read every word of every question. Read all of the answer choices before you mark your answer. It is statistically true that most errors are made when the correct answer is the last choice. Too many people mark the first answer that seems correct without reading through all the choices to find out which answer is BEST.

2. Mark your answers by completely blackening the answer space of your choice.

3. Mark only ONE answer for each question, even if you think that more than one answer is correct. You must choose only one. If you mark more than one answer, the scoring machine will consider you wrong.

4. If you change your mind, erase completely. Leave no doubt as to which answer you mean.

5. If your exam permits you to use scratch paper or the margins of the test booklet for figuring, don't forget to mark the answer on the answer sheet. Only the answer sheet is scored.

6. Check often to be sure that the question number matches the answer space and that you have not skipped a space by mistake.

7. Guess according to the Guessing Guide.

8. Stay alert. Be careful not to mark a wrong answer just because you were not concentrating.

9. Do not panic. If you cannot finish any part before time is up, do not worry. If you are accurate, you can do well even without finishing. At any rate, do not let your performance on any one part affect your performance on any other part.

10. Check and recheck, time permitting. If you finish any part before time is up, use the remaining time to check that each question is answered in the right space and that there is only one answer for each question. Return to the difficult questions and rethink them.

Good luck!

PART

TWO

Five Model Examinations

Model Examination 1
Answer Sheet

Exam 470

Clerk
City Carrier
Distribution Clerk, Machine (Letter-Sorting Machine Operator)
Flat Sorting Machine Operator
Mail Handler
Mail Processor
Mark-up Clerk, Automated

Exam 460

Rural Carrier

PART A—ADDRESS CHECKING

1. Ⓐ Ⓓ	20. Ⓐ Ⓓ	39. Ⓐ Ⓓ	58. Ⓐ Ⓓ	77. Ⓐ Ⓓ
2. Ⓐ Ⓓ	21. Ⓐ Ⓓ	40. Ⓐ Ⓓ	59. Ⓐ Ⓓ	78. Ⓐ Ⓓ
3. Ⓐ Ⓓ	22. Ⓐ Ⓓ	41. Ⓐ Ⓓ	60. Ⓐ Ⓓ	79. Ⓐ Ⓓ
4. Ⓐ Ⓓ	23. Ⓐ Ⓓ	42. Ⓐ Ⓓ	61. Ⓐ Ⓓ	80. Ⓐ Ⓓ
5. Ⓐ Ⓓ	24. Ⓐ Ⓓ	43. Ⓐ Ⓓ	62. Ⓐ Ⓓ	81. Ⓐ Ⓓ
6. Ⓐ Ⓓ	25. Ⓐ Ⓓ	44. Ⓐ Ⓓ	63. Ⓐ Ⓓ	82. Ⓐ Ⓓ
7. Ⓐ Ⓓ	26. Ⓐ Ⓓ	45. Ⓐ Ⓓ	64. Ⓐ Ⓓ	83. Ⓐ Ⓓ
8. Ⓐ Ⓓ	27. Ⓐ Ⓓ	46. Ⓐ Ⓓ	65. Ⓐ Ⓓ	84. Ⓐ Ⓓ
9. Ⓐ Ⓓ	28. Ⓐ Ⓓ	47. Ⓐ Ⓓ	66. Ⓐ Ⓓ	85. Ⓐ Ⓓ
10. Ⓐ Ⓓ	29. Ⓐ Ⓓ	48. Ⓐ Ⓓ	67. Ⓐ Ⓓ	86. Ⓐ Ⓓ
11. Ⓐ Ⓓ	30. Ⓐ Ⓓ	49. Ⓐ Ⓓ	68. Ⓐ Ⓓ	87. Ⓐ Ⓓ
12. Ⓐ Ⓓ	31. Ⓐ Ⓓ	50. Ⓐ Ⓓ	69. Ⓐ Ⓓ	88. Ⓐ Ⓓ
13. Ⓐ Ⓓ	32. Ⓐ Ⓓ	51. Ⓐ Ⓓ	70. Ⓐ Ⓓ	89. Ⓐ Ⓓ
14. Ⓐ Ⓓ	33. Ⓐ Ⓓ	52. Ⓐ Ⓓ	71. Ⓐ Ⓓ	90. Ⓐ Ⓓ
15. Ⓐ Ⓓ	34. Ⓐ Ⓓ	53. Ⓐ Ⓓ	72. Ⓐ Ⓓ	91. Ⓐ Ⓓ
16. Ⓐ Ⓓ	35. Ⓐ Ⓓ	54. Ⓐ Ⓓ	73. Ⓐ Ⓓ	92. Ⓐ Ⓓ
17. Ⓐ Ⓓ	36. Ⓐ Ⓓ	55. Ⓐ Ⓓ	74. Ⓐ Ⓓ	93. Ⓐ Ⓓ
18. Ⓐ Ⓓ	37. Ⓐ Ⓓ	56. Ⓐ Ⓓ	75. Ⓐ Ⓓ	94. Ⓐ Ⓓ
19. Ⓐ Ⓓ	38. Ⓐ Ⓓ	57. Ⓐ Ⓓ	76. Ⓐ Ⓓ	95. Ⓐ Ⓓ

PART B—MEMORY FOR ADDRESSES

1 Ⓐ Ⓑ Ⓒ Ⓓ Ⓔ   23 Ⓐ Ⓑ Ⓒ Ⓓ Ⓔ   45 Ⓐ Ⓑ Ⓒ Ⓓ Ⓔ   67 Ⓐ Ⓑ Ⓒ Ⓓ Ⓔ

2 Ⓐ Ⓑ Ⓒ Ⓓ Ⓔ   24 Ⓐ Ⓑ Ⓒ Ⓓ Ⓔ   46 Ⓐ Ⓑ Ⓒ Ⓓ Ⓔ   68 Ⓐ Ⓑ Ⓒ Ⓓ Ⓔ

3 Ⓐ Ⓑ Ⓒ Ⓓ Ⓔ   25 Ⓐ Ⓑ Ⓒ Ⓓ Ⓔ   47 Ⓐ Ⓑ Ⓒ Ⓓ Ⓔ   69 Ⓐ Ⓑ Ⓒ Ⓓ Ⓔ

4 Ⓐ Ⓑ Ⓒ Ⓓ Ⓔ   26 Ⓐ Ⓑ Ⓒ Ⓓ Ⓔ   48 Ⓐ Ⓑ Ⓒ Ⓓ Ⓔ   70 Ⓐ Ⓑ Ⓒ Ⓓ Ⓔ

5 Ⓐ Ⓑ Ⓒ Ⓓ Ⓔ   27 Ⓐ Ⓑ Ⓒ Ⓓ Ⓔ   49 Ⓐ Ⓑ Ⓒ Ⓓ Ⓔ   71 Ⓐ Ⓑ Ⓒ Ⓓ Ⓔ

6 Ⓐ Ⓑ Ⓒ Ⓓ Ⓔ   28 Ⓐ Ⓑ Ⓒ Ⓓ Ⓔ   50 Ⓐ Ⓑ Ⓒ Ⓓ Ⓔ   72 Ⓐ Ⓑ Ⓒ Ⓓ Ⓔ

7 Ⓐ Ⓑ Ⓒ Ⓓ Ⓔ   29 Ⓐ Ⓑ Ⓒ Ⓓ Ⓔ   51 Ⓐ Ⓑ Ⓒ Ⓓ Ⓔ   73 Ⓐ Ⓑ Ⓒ Ⓓ Ⓔ

8 Ⓐ Ⓑ Ⓒ Ⓓ Ⓔ   30 Ⓐ Ⓑ Ⓒ Ⓓ Ⓔ   52 Ⓐ Ⓑ Ⓒ Ⓓ Ⓔ   74 Ⓐ Ⓑ Ⓒ Ⓓ Ⓔ

9 Ⓐ Ⓑ Ⓒ Ⓓ Ⓔ   31 Ⓐ Ⓑ Ⓒ Ⓓ Ⓔ   53 Ⓐ Ⓑ Ⓒ Ⓓ Ⓔ   75 Ⓐ Ⓑ Ⓒ Ⓓ Ⓔ

10 Ⓐ Ⓑ Ⓒ Ⓓ Ⓔ   32 Ⓐ Ⓑ Ⓒ Ⓓ Ⓔ   54 Ⓐ Ⓑ Ⓒ Ⓓ Ⓔ   76 Ⓐ Ⓑ Ⓒ Ⓓ Ⓔ

11 Ⓐ Ⓑ Ⓒ Ⓓ Ⓔ   33 Ⓐ Ⓑ Ⓒ Ⓓ Ⓔ   55 Ⓐ Ⓑ Ⓒ Ⓓ Ⓔ   77 Ⓐ Ⓑ Ⓒ Ⓓ Ⓔ

12 Ⓐ Ⓑ Ⓒ Ⓓ Ⓔ   34 Ⓐ Ⓑ Ⓒ Ⓓ Ⓔ   56 Ⓐ Ⓑ Ⓒ Ⓓ Ⓔ   78 Ⓐ Ⓑ Ⓒ Ⓓ Ⓔ

13 Ⓐ Ⓑ Ⓒ Ⓓ Ⓔ   35 Ⓐ Ⓑ Ⓒ Ⓓ Ⓔ   57 Ⓐ Ⓑ Ⓒ Ⓓ Ⓔ   79 Ⓐ Ⓑ Ⓒ Ⓓ Ⓔ

14 Ⓐ Ⓑ Ⓒ Ⓓ Ⓔ   36 Ⓐ Ⓑ Ⓒ Ⓓ Ⓔ   58 Ⓐ Ⓑ Ⓒ Ⓓ Ⓔ   80 Ⓐ Ⓑ Ⓒ Ⓓ Ⓔ

15 Ⓐ Ⓑ Ⓒ Ⓓ Ⓔ   37 Ⓐ Ⓑ Ⓒ Ⓓ Ⓔ   59 Ⓐ Ⓑ Ⓒ Ⓓ Ⓔ   81 Ⓐ Ⓑ Ⓒ Ⓓ Ⓔ

16 Ⓐ Ⓑ Ⓒ Ⓓ Ⓔ   38 Ⓐ Ⓑ Ⓒ Ⓓ Ⓔ   60 Ⓐ Ⓑ Ⓒ Ⓓ Ⓔ   82 Ⓐ Ⓑ Ⓒ Ⓓ Ⓔ

17 Ⓐ Ⓑ Ⓒ Ⓓ Ⓔ   39 Ⓐ Ⓑ Ⓒ Ⓓ Ⓔ   61 Ⓐ Ⓑ Ⓒ Ⓓ Ⓔ   83 Ⓐ Ⓑ Ⓒ Ⓓ Ⓔ

18 Ⓐ Ⓑ Ⓒ Ⓓ Ⓔ   40 Ⓐ Ⓑ Ⓒ Ⓓ Ⓔ   62 Ⓐ Ⓑ Ⓒ Ⓓ Ⓔ   84 Ⓐ Ⓑ Ⓒ Ⓓ Ⓔ

19 Ⓐ Ⓑ Ⓒ Ⓓ Ⓔ   41 Ⓐ Ⓑ Ⓒ Ⓓ Ⓔ   63 Ⓐ Ⓑ Ⓒ Ⓓ Ⓔ   85 Ⓐ Ⓑ Ⓒ Ⓓ Ⓔ

20 Ⓐ Ⓑ Ⓒ Ⓓ Ⓔ   42 Ⓐ Ⓑ Ⓒ Ⓓ Ⓔ   64 Ⓐ Ⓑ Ⓒ Ⓓ Ⓔ   86 Ⓐ Ⓑ Ⓒ Ⓓ Ⓔ

21 Ⓐ Ⓑ Ⓒ Ⓓ Ⓔ   43 Ⓐ Ⓑ Ⓒ Ⓓ Ⓔ   65 Ⓐ Ⓑ Ⓒ Ⓓ Ⓔ   87 Ⓐ Ⓑ Ⓒ Ⓓ Ⓔ

22 Ⓐ Ⓑ Ⓒ Ⓓ Ⓔ   44 Ⓐ Ⓑ Ⓒ Ⓓ Ⓔ   66 Ⓐ Ⓑ Ⓒ Ⓓ Ⓔ   88 Ⓐ Ⓑ Ⓒ Ⓓ Ⓔ

PART C—NUMBER SERIES

1. Ⓐ Ⓑ Ⓒ Ⓓ Ⓔ   7. Ⓐ Ⓑ Ⓒ Ⓓ Ⓔ   13. Ⓐ Ⓑ Ⓒ Ⓓ Ⓔ   19. Ⓐ Ⓑ Ⓒ Ⓓ Ⓔ

2. Ⓐ Ⓑ Ⓒ Ⓓ Ⓔ   8. Ⓐ Ⓑ Ⓒ Ⓓ Ⓔ   14. Ⓐ Ⓑ Ⓒ Ⓓ Ⓔ   20. Ⓐ Ⓑ Ⓒ Ⓓ Ⓔ

3. Ⓐ Ⓑ Ⓒ Ⓓ Ⓔ   9. Ⓐ Ⓑ Ⓒ Ⓓ Ⓔ   15. Ⓐ Ⓑ Ⓒ Ⓓ Ⓔ   21. Ⓐ Ⓑ Ⓒ Ⓓ Ⓔ

4. Ⓐ Ⓑ Ⓒ Ⓓ Ⓔ   10. Ⓐ Ⓑ Ⓒ Ⓓ Ⓔ   16. Ⓐ Ⓑ Ⓒ Ⓓ Ⓔ   22. Ⓐ Ⓑ Ⓒ Ⓓ Ⓔ

5. Ⓐ Ⓑ Ⓒ Ⓓ Ⓔ   11. Ⓐ Ⓑ Ⓒ Ⓓ Ⓔ   17. Ⓐ Ⓑ Ⓒ Ⓓ Ⓔ   23. Ⓐ Ⓑ Ⓒ Ⓓ Ⓔ

6. Ⓐ Ⓑ Ⓒ Ⓓ Ⓔ   12. Ⓐ Ⓑ Ⓒ Ⓓ Ⓔ   18. Ⓐ Ⓑ Ⓒ Ⓓ Ⓔ   24. Ⓐ Ⓑ Ⓒ Ⓓ Ⓔ

PART D—FOLLOWING ORAL INSTRUCTIONS

1 Ⓐ Ⓑ Ⓒ Ⓓ Ⓔ   23 Ⓐ Ⓑ Ⓒ Ⓓ Ⓔ   45 Ⓐ Ⓑ Ⓒ Ⓓ Ⓔ   67 Ⓐ Ⓑ Ⓒ Ⓓ Ⓔ
2 Ⓐ Ⓑ Ⓒ Ⓓ Ⓔ   24 Ⓐ Ⓑ Ⓒ Ⓓ Ⓔ   46 Ⓐ Ⓑ Ⓒ Ⓓ Ⓔ   68 Ⓐ Ⓑ Ⓒ Ⓓ Ⓔ
3 Ⓐ Ⓑ Ⓒ Ⓓ Ⓔ   25 Ⓐ Ⓑ Ⓒ Ⓓ Ⓔ   47 Ⓐ Ⓑ Ⓒ Ⓓ Ⓔ   69 Ⓐ Ⓑ Ⓒ Ⓓ Ⓔ
4 Ⓐ Ⓑ Ⓒ Ⓓ Ⓔ   26 Ⓐ Ⓑ Ⓒ Ⓓ Ⓔ   48 Ⓐ Ⓑ Ⓒ Ⓓ Ⓔ   70 Ⓐ Ⓑ Ⓒ Ⓓ Ⓔ
5 Ⓐ Ⓑ Ⓒ Ⓓ Ⓔ   27 Ⓐ Ⓑ Ⓒ Ⓓ Ⓔ   49 Ⓐ Ⓑ Ⓒ Ⓓ Ⓔ   71 Ⓐ Ⓑ Ⓒ Ⓓ Ⓔ
6 Ⓐ Ⓑ Ⓒ Ⓓ Ⓔ   28 Ⓐ Ⓑ Ⓒ Ⓓ Ⓔ   50 Ⓐ Ⓑ Ⓒ Ⓓ Ⓔ   72 Ⓐ Ⓑ Ⓒ Ⓓ Ⓔ
7 Ⓐ Ⓑ Ⓒ Ⓓ Ⓔ   29 Ⓐ Ⓑ Ⓒ Ⓓ Ⓔ   51 Ⓐ Ⓑ Ⓒ Ⓓ Ⓔ   73 Ⓐ Ⓑ Ⓒ Ⓓ Ⓔ
8 Ⓐ Ⓑ Ⓒ Ⓓ Ⓔ   30 Ⓐ Ⓑ Ⓒ Ⓓ Ⓔ   52 Ⓐ Ⓑ Ⓒ Ⓓ Ⓔ   74 Ⓐ Ⓑ Ⓒ Ⓓ Ⓔ
9 Ⓐ Ⓑ Ⓒ Ⓓ Ⓔ   31 Ⓐ Ⓑ Ⓒ Ⓓ Ⓔ   53 Ⓐ Ⓑ Ⓒ Ⓓ Ⓔ   75 Ⓐ Ⓑ Ⓒ Ⓓ Ⓔ
10 Ⓐ Ⓑ Ⓒ Ⓓ Ⓔ   32 Ⓐ Ⓑ Ⓒ Ⓓ Ⓔ   54 Ⓐ Ⓑ Ⓒ Ⓓ Ⓔ   76 Ⓐ Ⓑ Ⓒ Ⓓ Ⓔ
11 Ⓐ Ⓑ Ⓒ Ⓓ Ⓔ   33 Ⓐ Ⓑ Ⓒ Ⓓ Ⓔ   55 Ⓐ Ⓑ Ⓒ Ⓓ Ⓔ   77 Ⓐ Ⓑ Ⓒ Ⓓ Ⓔ
12 Ⓐ Ⓑ Ⓒ Ⓓ Ⓔ   34 Ⓐ Ⓑ Ⓒ Ⓓ Ⓔ   56 Ⓐ Ⓑ Ⓒ Ⓓ Ⓔ   78 Ⓐ Ⓑ Ⓒ Ⓓ Ⓔ
13 Ⓐ Ⓑ Ⓒ Ⓓ Ⓔ   35 Ⓐ Ⓑ Ⓒ Ⓓ Ⓔ   57 Ⓐ Ⓑ Ⓒ Ⓓ Ⓔ   79 Ⓐ Ⓑ Ⓒ Ⓓ Ⓔ
14 Ⓐ Ⓑ Ⓒ Ⓓ Ⓔ   36 Ⓐ Ⓑ Ⓒ Ⓓ Ⓔ   58 Ⓐ Ⓑ Ⓒ Ⓓ Ⓔ   80 Ⓐ Ⓑ Ⓒ Ⓓ Ⓔ
15 Ⓐ Ⓑ Ⓒ Ⓓ Ⓔ   37 Ⓐ Ⓑ Ⓒ Ⓓ Ⓔ   59 Ⓐ Ⓑ Ⓒ Ⓓ Ⓔ   81 Ⓐ Ⓑ Ⓒ Ⓓ Ⓔ
16 Ⓐ Ⓑ Ⓒ Ⓓ Ⓔ   38 Ⓐ Ⓑ Ⓒ Ⓓ Ⓔ   60 Ⓐ Ⓑ Ⓒ Ⓓ Ⓔ   82 Ⓐ Ⓑ Ⓒ Ⓓ Ⓔ
17 Ⓐ Ⓑ Ⓒ Ⓓ Ⓔ   39 Ⓐ Ⓑ Ⓒ Ⓓ Ⓔ   61 Ⓐ Ⓑ Ⓒ Ⓓ Ⓔ   83 Ⓔ Ⓐ Ⓒ Ⓓ Ⓔ
18 Ⓐ Ⓑ Ⓒ Ⓓ Ⓔ   40 Ⓐ Ⓑ Ⓒ Ⓓ Ⓔ   62 Ⓐ Ⓑ Ⓒ Ⓓ Ⓔ   84 Ⓐ Ⓑ Ⓒ Ⓓ Ⓔ
19 Ⓐ Ⓑ Ⓒ Ⓓ Ⓔ   41 Ⓐ Ⓑ Ⓒ Ⓓ Ⓔ   63 Ⓐ Ⓑ Ⓒ Ⓓ Ⓔ   85 Ⓐ Ⓑ Ⓒ Ⓓ Ⓔ
20 Ⓐ Ⓑ Ⓒ Ⓓ Ⓔ   42 Ⓐ Ⓑ Ⓒ Ⓓ Ⓔ   64 Ⓐ Ⓑ Ⓒ Ⓓ Ⓔ   86 Ⓐ Ⓑ Ⓒ Ⓓ Ⓔ
21 Ⓐ Ⓑ Ⓒ Ⓓ Ⓔ   43 Ⓐ Ⓑ Ⓒ Ⓓ Ⓔ   65 Ⓐ Ⓑ Ⓒ Ⓓ Ⓔ   87 Ⓐ Ⓑ Ⓒ Ⓓ Ⓔ
22 Ⓐ Ⓑ Ⓒ Ⓓ Ⓔ   44 Ⓐ Ⓑ Ⓒ Ⓓ Ⓔ   66 Ⓐ Ⓑ Ⓒ Ⓓ Ⓔ   88 Ⓐ Ⓑ Ⓒ Ⓓ Ⓔ

TEAR HERE

PART A—ADDRESS CHECKING

Sample Questions

You will be allowed three minutes to read the directions and answer the five sample questions that follow. On the actual test, however, you will have only six minutes to answer 95 questions, so see how quickly you can compare addresses and still get the correct answer.

Directions: Each question consists of two addresses. If the two addresses are alike in EVERY way, *mark A on your answer sheet. If the two addresses are* different in ANY way, *mark D on your answer sheet.*

1 ... 4836 Mineola Blvd	4386 Mineola Blvd
2 ... 3062 W 197th St	3062 W 197th Rd
3 ... Columbus OH 43210	Columbus OH 43210
4 ... 9413 Alcan Hwy So	9413 Alcan Hwy So
5 ... 4186 Carrier Ln	4186 Carreer Ln

```
┌─────────────────────────────────┐
│     SAMPLE ANSWER SHEET         │
│                                 │
│  1. Ⓐ Ⓓ      4. Ⓐ Ⓓ           │
│  2. Ⓐ Ⓓ      5. Ⓐ Ⓓ           │
│  3. Ⓐ Ⓓ                         │
└─────────────────────────────────┘
```

```
┌─────────────────────────────────┐
│       CORRECT ANSWERS           │
│                                 │
│  1. Ⓐ ●      4. ● Ⓓ            │
│  2. Ⓐ ●      5. Ⓐ ●            │
│  3. ● Ⓓ                         │
└─────────────────────────────────┘
```

Address Checking

Time: 6 Minutes. 95 Questions.

Directions: For each question, compare the address in the left column with the address in the right column. If the two addresses are ALIKE IN **EVERY** WAY, blacken space A on your answer sheet. If the two addresses are DIFFERENT IN **ANY** WAY, blacken space D on your answer sheet. Correct answers for this test are on page 123.

1 ... 462 Midland Ave	462 Midland Ave
2 ... 2319 Sherry Dr	3219 Sherry Dr
3 ... 1015 Kimball Ave	1015 Kimball Av
4 ... Wappinger Falls NY 12590	Wappinger Falls NY 12590
5 ... 1255 North Ave	1225 North Ave
6 ... 1826 Tibbets Rd	1826 Tibetts Rd
7 ... 603 N Division St	603 N Division St
8 ... 2304 Manhattan Ave	2034 Manhattan Ave
9 ... Worcester MA 01610	Worcester ME 01610
10 ... 1186 Vernon Drive	1186 Vernon Drive
11 ... 209 Peter Bont Rd	209 Peter Bent Rd
12 ... Miami Beach FL 33139	Miami Beach FL 33193
13 ... 1100 West Ave	1100 East Ave
14 ... 2063 Winyah Ter	2036 Winyah Ter
15 ... 3483 Suncrest Ave	3483 Suncrest Dr
16 ... 234 Rochambeau Rd	234 Roshambeau Rd
17 ... 306 N Terrace Blvd	306 N Terrace Blvd
18 ... 1632 Paine St	1632 Pain St
19 ... Palm Springs CA 92262	Palm Spring CA 92262
20 ... 286 Marietta Ave	286 Marrietta Ave
21 ... 2445 Pigott Rd	2445 Pigott Rd
22 ... 2204 PineBrook Blvd	2204 Pinebrook Blvd
23 ... Buffalo NY 42113	Buffulo NY 42113
24 ... 487 Warburton Ave	487 Warburton Ave
25 ... 9386 North St	9386 North Ave
26 ... 2272 Glandale Rd	2772 Glandale Rd
27 ... 9236 Puritan Dr	9236 Puritan Pl
28 ... Watertown MA 02172	Watertown MA 02172

29 ... 7803 Kimball Ave	7803 Kimbal Ave
30 ... 1362 Colonial Pkwy	1362 Colonial Pkwy
31 ... 115 Rolling Hills Rd	115 Rolling Hills Rd
32 ... 218 Rockledge Rd	2181 Rockledge Rd
33 ... 8346 N Broadway	8346 W Broadway
34 ... West Chester PA 19380	West Chester PA 19830
35 ... 9224 Highland Way	9244 Highland Way
36 ... 8383 Mamaroneck Ave	8383 Mamaroneck Ave
37 ... 276 Furnace Dock Rd	276 Furnace Dock Rd
38 ... 4137 Loockerman St	4137 Lockerman St
39 ... 532 Broadhollow Rd	532 Broadhollow Rd
40 ... Sunrise FL 33313	Sunrise FL 33133
41 ... 148 Cortlandt Rd	148 Cortland Rd
42 ... 5951 W Hartsdale Rd	5951 W Hartsdale Ave
43 ... 5231 Alta Vista Cir	5321 Alta Vista Cir
44 ... 6459 Chippewa Rd	6459 Chippewa Rd
45 ... 1171 S Highland Rd	1771 S Highland Rd
46 ... Dover DE 19901	Dover DL 19901
47 ... 2363 Old Farm Ln	2363 Old Farm Ln
48 ... 1001 Hemingway Dr	1001 Hemmingway Dr
49 ... 1555 Morningside Ave	1555 Morningslide Ave
50 ... Purchase NY 10577	Purchase NY 10577
51 ... 1189 E 9th St	1189 E 9th St
52 ... 168 Old Lyme Rd	186 Old Lyme Rd
53 ... 106 Notingham Rd	106 Nottingham Rd
54 ... 1428 Midland Ave	1428 Midland Ave
55 ... Elmhurst NY 11373	Elmherst NY 11373
56 ... 1450 West Chester Pike	1450 West Chester Pike
57 ... 3357 NW Main St	3357 NE Main St
58 ... 5062 Marietta Ave	5062 Marrietta Ave
59 ... 1890 NE 3rd Ct	1980 NE 3rd Ct
60 ... Wilmington DE 19810	Wilmington DE 19810
61 ... 1075 Central Park Av	1075 Central Park W
62 ... 672 Bacon Hill Rd	672 Beacon Hill Rd

63 ... 1725 W 17th St	1725 W 17th St
64 ... Bronxville NY 10708	Bronxville NJ 10708
65 ... 2066 Old Wilmot Rd	2066 Old Wilmont Rd
66 ... 3333 S State St	3333 S State St
67 ... 1483 Meritoria Dr	1438 Meritoria Dr
68 ... 2327 E 23rd St	2327 E 27th St
69 ... Baltimore MD 21215	Baltimore MD 21215
70 ... 137 Clarence Rd	137 Claremont Rd
71 ... 3516 N Ely Ave	3516 N Ely Ave
72 ... 111 Beechwood St	1111 Beechwood St
73 ... 143 N Highland Ave	143 N Highland Ave
74 ... Miami Beach FL 33179	Miami FL 33179
75 ... 6430 Spring Mill Rd	6340 Spring Mill Rd
76 ... 1416 87th Ave	1416 78th Ave
77 ... 4204 S Lexington Ave	4204 Lexington Ave
78 ... 3601 Clarks Lane	3601 Clark Lane
79 ... Indianapolis IN 46260	Indianapolis IN 46260
80 ... 4256 Fairfield Ave	4256 Fairfield Ave
81 ... Jamaica NY 11435	Jamiaca NY 11435
82 ... 1809 83rd St	1809 83rd St
83 ... 3288 Page Ct	3288 Paige Ct
84 ... 2436 S Broadway	2436 S Broadway
85 ... 6309 The Green	6309 The Green
86 ... Kew Gardens NY 11415	Kew Garden NY 11415
87 ... 4370 W 158th St	4370 W 158th St
88 ... 4263 3rd Ave	4623 3rd Ave
89 ... 1737 Fisher Ave	1737 Fischer Ave
90 ... Bronx NY 10475	Bronx NY 10475
91 ... 5148 West End Ave	5184 West End Ave
92 ... 1011 Ocean Ave	1011 Ocean Ave
93 ... 1593 Webster Dr	1593 Webster Dr
94 ... Darien CT 06820	Darien CT 06820
95 ... 1626 E 115th St	1662 E 115th St

END OF ADDRESS CHECKING

PART B—MEMORY FOR ADDRESSES

Sample Questions

The sample questions for this part are based on the addresses in the five boxes below. Your task is to mark on your answer sheet the letter of the box in which each address belongs. You will have five minutes now to study the locations of the addresses. Then cover the boxes and try to mark the location of the sample questions. You may look back at the boxes if you cannot yet mark the address locations from memory.

The exam itself provides three practice sessions before the question set that really counts. Practice I and Practice III supply you with the boxes and permit you to refer to them if necessary. Practice II and the Memory for Addresses Test itself do not permit you to look at the boxes. The test itself is based on memory.

A	B	C	D	E
4100–4199 Plum	1000–1399 Plum	4200–4599 Plum	1400–4099 Plum	4600–5299 Plum
Bardack	Greenhouse	Flynn	Pepper	Cedar
4200–4599 Ash	4600–5299 Ash	1400–4099 Ash	1000–1399 Ash	4100–4199 Ash
Lemon	Dalby	Race	Clown	Hawk
1000–1399 Neff	4100–4199 Neff	4600–5299 Neff	4200–4599 Neff	1400–4099 Neff

1. 1400–4099 Plum

2. 1000–1399 Neff

3. Lemon

4. Flynn

5. 4200–4599 Ash

6. 4600–5299 Ash

7. Cedar

8. Pepper

9. 4100–4199 Plum

10. 4600–5299 Neff

11. 1000–1399 Plum

12. Clown

13. Greenhouse

14. 4100–4199 Ash

SAMPLE ANSWER SHEET

1. Ⓐ Ⓑ Ⓒ Ⓓ Ⓔ   8. Ⓐ Ⓑ Ⓒ Ⓓ Ⓔ
2. Ⓐ Ⓑ Ⓒ Ⓓ Ⓔ   9. Ⓐ Ⓑ Ⓒ Ⓓ Ⓔ
3. Ⓐ Ⓑ Ⓒ Ⓓ Ⓔ 10. Ⓐ Ⓑ Ⓒ Ⓓ Ⓔ
4. Ⓐ Ⓑ Ⓒ Ⓓ Ⓔ 11. Ⓐ Ⓑ Ⓒ Ⓓ Ⓔ
5. Ⓐ Ⓑ Ⓒ Ⓓ Ⓔ 12. Ⓐ Ⓑ Ⓒ Ⓓ Ⓔ
6. Ⓐ Ⓑ Ⓒ Ⓓ Ⓔ 13. Ⓐ Ⓑ Ⓒ Ⓓ Ⓔ
7. Ⓐ Ⓑ Ⓒ Ⓓ Ⓔ 14. Ⓐ Ⓑ Ⓒ Ⓓ Ⓔ

CORRECT ANSWERS

1. Ⓐ Ⓑ Ⓒ ● Ⓔ   8. Ⓐ Ⓑ Ⓒ ● Ⓔ
2. ● Ⓑ Ⓒ Ⓓ Ⓔ   9. ● Ⓑ Ⓒ Ⓓ Ⓔ
3. ● Ⓑ Ⓒ Ⓓ Ⓔ 10. Ⓐ Ⓑ ● Ⓓ Ⓔ
4. Ⓐ Ⓑ ● Ⓓ Ⓔ 11. Ⓐ ● Ⓒ Ⓓ Ⓔ
5. ● Ⓑ Ⓒ Ⓓ Ⓔ 12. Ⓐ Ⓑ Ⓒ ● Ⓔ
6. Ⓐ ● Ⓒ Ⓓ Ⓔ 13. Ⓐ ● Ⓒ Ⓓ Ⓔ
7. Ⓐ Ⓑ Ⓒ Ⓓ ● 14. Ⓐ Ⓑ Ⓒ Ⓓ ●

Practice for Memory for Addresses

DIRECTIONS: The five boxes below are labeled A, B, C, D, and E. In each box are three sets of number spans with names and two names that are not associated with numbers. In the next THREE MINUTES, you must try to memorize the box location of each name and number span. The position of a name or number span within its box is not important. You need only remember the letter of the box in which the item is to be found. You will use these names and numbers to answer three sets of practice questions that are NOT scored and one actual test that is scored. Correct answers are on pages 124 and 125.

A	B	C	D	E
4100–4199 Plum	1000–1399 Plum	4200–4599 Plum	1400–4099 Plum	4600–5299 Plum
Bardack	Greenhouse	Flynn	Pepper	Cedar
4200–4599 Ash	4600–5299 Ash	1400–4099 Ash	1000–1399 Ash	4100–4199 Ash
Lemon	Dalby	Race	Clown	Hawk
1000–1399 Neff	4100–4199 Neff	4600–5299 Neff	4200–4599 Neff	1400–4099 Neff

Practice I

DIRECTIONS: Use the next THREE MINUTES to mark on your answer sheet the letter of the box in which each item that follows is to be found. Try to mark each item without looking back at the boxes. If, however, you get stuck, you may refer to the boxes during this practice exercise. If you find that you must look at the boxes, try to memorize as you do so. This test is for practice only. It will not be scored.

1. 4600–5299 Ash
2. 4600–5299 Neff
3. 1400–4099 Plum
4. Cedar
5. Bardack
6. 1400–4099 Neff
7. 1400–4099 Ash
8. 1000–1399 Plum
9. Greenhouse
10. Lemon
11. 4600–5299 Plum
12. 4200–4599 Ash
13. 4600–5299 Neff
14. Dalby
15. Hawk
16. 4100–4199 Plum
17. 4200–4599 Plum
18. 4600–5299 Ash
19. 4200–4599 Neff

20. Race
21. Pepper
22. 4100–4199 Ash
23. 1000–1399 Neff
24. 1000–1399 Plum
25. Cedar
26. Dalby
27. 4600–5299 Plum
28. 1400–4099 Plum
29. Bardack
30. 4200–4599 Ash
31. 1400–4099 Neff
32. 4600–5299 Neff
33. 1400–4099 Ash
34. Flynn
35. Lemon
36. Clown
37. 4100–4199 Plum
38. 1000–1399 Ash

39. 4100–4199 Neff
40. Greenhouse
41. Hawk
42. 4600–5299 Plum
43. 1000–1399 Neff
44. 1400–4099 Ash
45. 4600–5299 Ash
46. Cedar
47. Greenhouse
48. 1400–4099 Plum
49. 4200–4599 Neff
50. 1000-1399 Ash
51. Race
52. Flynn
53. 4600–5299 Ash
54. 4600–5299 Plum
55. 4600–5299 Neff
56. Pepper
57. Lemon

58. 1000–1399 Plum
59. 4100–4199 Plum
60. 1000–1399 Neff
61. 4100–4199 Ash
62. Bardack
63. Dalby
64. Clown
65. 4200–4599 Ash
66. 1400–4099 Ash
67. 4200–4599 Plum

68. Hawk
69. 4100–4199 Neff
70. 1400–4099 Neff
71. 1000–1399 Plum
72. Pepper
73. 1000–1399 Neff
74. 4100–4199 Ash
75. Dalby
76. Cedar
77. 4100–4199 Plum
78. 1400–4099 Ash

79. 1400–4099 Plum
80. 1400–4099 Neff
81. Pepper
82. Hawk
83. 4600–5299 Ash
84. 4600–5299 Plum
85. 1000–1399 Ash
86. 1000–1399 Neff
87. Cedar
88. Greenhouse

Practice I Answer Sheet

1 Ⓐ Ⓑ Ⓒ Ⓓ Ⓔ	23 Ⓐ Ⓑ Ⓒ Ⓓ Ⓔ	45 Ⓐ Ⓑ Ⓒ Ⓓ Ⓔ	67 Ⓐ Ⓑ Ⓒ Ⓓ Ⓔ
2 Ⓐ Ⓑ Ⓒ Ⓓ Ⓔ	24 Ⓐ Ⓑ Ⓒ Ⓓ Ⓔ	46 Ⓐ Ⓑ Ⓒ Ⓓ Ⓔ	68 Ⓐ Ⓑ Ⓒ Ⓓ Ⓔ
3 Ⓐ Ⓑ Ⓒ Ⓓ Ⓔ	25 Ⓐ Ⓑ Ⓒ Ⓓ Ⓔ	47 Ⓐ Ⓑ Ⓒ Ⓓ Ⓔ	69 Ⓐ Ⓑ Ⓒ Ⓓ Ⓔ
4 Ⓐ Ⓑ Ⓒ Ⓓ Ⓔ	26 Ⓐ Ⓑ Ⓒ Ⓓ Ⓔ	48 Ⓐ Ⓑ Ⓒ Ⓓ Ⓔ	70 Ⓐ Ⓑ Ⓒ Ⓓ Ⓔ
5 Ⓐ Ⓑ Ⓒ Ⓓ Ⓔ	27 Ⓐ Ⓑ Ⓒ Ⓓ Ⓔ	49 Ⓐ Ⓑ Ⓒ Ⓓ Ⓔ	71 Ⓐ Ⓑ Ⓒ Ⓓ Ⓔ
6 Ⓐ Ⓑ Ⓒ Ⓓ Ⓔ	28 Ⓐ Ⓑ Ⓒ Ⓓ Ⓔ	50 Ⓐ Ⓑ Ⓒ Ⓓ Ⓔ	72 Ⓐ Ⓑ Ⓒ Ⓓ Ⓔ
7 Ⓐ Ⓑ Ⓒ Ⓓ Ⓔ	29 Ⓐ Ⓑ Ⓒ Ⓓ Ⓔ	51 Ⓐ Ⓑ Ⓒ Ⓓ Ⓔ	73 Ⓐ Ⓑ Ⓒ Ⓓ Ⓔ
8 Ⓐ Ⓑ Ⓒ Ⓓ Ⓔ	30 Ⓐ Ⓑ Ⓒ Ⓓ Ⓔ	52 Ⓐ Ⓑ Ⓒ Ⓓ Ⓔ	74 Ⓐ Ⓑ Ⓒ Ⓓ Ⓔ
9 Ⓐ Ⓑ Ⓒ Ⓓ Ⓔ	31 Ⓐ Ⓑ Ⓒ Ⓓ Ⓔ	53 Ⓐ Ⓑ Ⓒ Ⓓ Ⓔ	75 Ⓐ Ⓑ Ⓒ Ⓓ Ⓔ
10 Ⓐ Ⓑ Ⓒ Ⓓ Ⓔ	32 Ⓐ Ⓑ Ⓒ Ⓓ Ⓔ	54 Ⓐ Ⓑ Ⓒ Ⓓ Ⓔ	76 Ⓐ Ⓑ Ⓒ Ⓓ Ⓔ
11 Ⓐ Ⓑ Ⓒ Ⓓ Ⓔ	33 Ⓐ Ⓑ Ⓒ Ⓓ Ⓔ	55 Ⓐ Ⓑ Ⓒ Ⓓ Ⓔ	77 Ⓐ Ⓑ Ⓒ Ⓓ Ⓔ
12 Ⓐ Ⓑ Ⓒ Ⓓ Ⓔ	34 Ⓐ Ⓑ Ⓒ Ⓓ Ⓔ	56 Ⓐ Ⓑ Ⓒ Ⓓ Ⓔ	78 Ⓐ Ⓑ Ⓒ Ⓓ Ⓔ
13 Ⓐ Ⓑ Ⓒ Ⓓ Ⓔ	35 Ⓐ Ⓑ Ⓒ Ⓓ Ⓔ	57 Ⓐ Ⓑ Ⓒ Ⓓ Ⓔ	79 Ⓐ Ⓑ Ⓒ Ⓓ Ⓔ
14 Ⓐ Ⓑ Ⓒ Ⓓ Ⓔ	36 Ⓐ Ⓑ Ⓒ Ⓓ Ⓔ	58 Ⓐ Ⓑ Ⓒ Ⓓ Ⓔ	80 Ⓐ Ⓑ Ⓒ Ⓓ Ⓔ
15 Ⓐ Ⓑ Ⓒ Ⓓ Ⓔ	37 Ⓐ Ⓑ Ⓒ Ⓓ Ⓔ	59 Ⓐ Ⓑ Ⓒ Ⓓ Ⓔ	81 Ⓐ Ⓑ Ⓒ Ⓓ Ⓔ
16 Ⓐ Ⓑ Ⓒ Ⓓ Ⓔ	38 Ⓐ Ⓑ Ⓒ Ⓓ Ⓔ	60 Ⓐ Ⓑ Ⓒ Ⓓ Ⓔ	82 Ⓐ Ⓑ Ⓒ Ⓓ Ⓔ
17 Ⓐ Ⓑ Ⓒ Ⓓ Ⓔ	39 Ⓐ Ⓑ Ⓒ Ⓓ Ⓔ	61 Ⓐ Ⓑ Ⓒ Ⓓ Ⓔ	83 Ⓐ Ⓑ Ⓒ Ⓓ Ⓔ
18 Ⓐ Ⓑ Ⓒ Ⓓ Ⓔ	40 Ⓐ Ⓑ Ⓒ Ⓓ Ⓔ	62 Ⓐ Ⓑ Ⓒ Ⓓ Ⓔ	84 Ⓐ Ⓑ Ⓒ Ⓓ Ⓔ
19 Ⓐ Ⓑ Ⓒ Ⓓ Ⓔ	41 Ⓐ Ⓑ Ⓒ Ⓓ Ⓔ	63 Ⓐ Ⓑ Ⓒ Ⓓ Ⓔ	85 Ⓐ Ⓑ Ⓒ Ⓓ Ⓔ
20 Ⓐ Ⓑ Ⓒ Ⓓ Ⓔ	42 Ⓐ Ⓑ Ⓒ Ⓓ Ⓔ	64 Ⓐ Ⓑ Ⓒ Ⓓ Ⓔ	86 Ⓐ Ⓑ Ⓒ Ⓓ Ⓔ
21 Ⓐ Ⓑ Ⓒ Ⓓ Ⓔ	43 Ⓐ Ⓑ Ⓒ Ⓓ Ⓔ	65 Ⓐ Ⓑ Ⓒ Ⓓ Ⓔ	87 Ⓐ Ⓑ Ⓒ Ⓓ Ⓔ
22 Ⓐ Ⓑ Ⓒ Ⓓ Ⓔ	44 Ⓐ Ⓑ Ⓒ Ⓓ Ⓔ	66 Ⓐ Ⓑ Ⓒ Ⓓ Ⓔ	88 Ⓐ Ⓑ Ⓒ Ⓓ Ⓔ

Practice II

DIRECTIONS: *The next 88 questions constitute another practice exercise. Again, you should mark your answers on your answer sheet. Again, the time limit is THREE MINUTES. This time, however, you must NOT look at the boxes while answering the questions. You must rely on your memory in marking the box location of each item. This practice test will not be scored.*

1. 4100–4199 Plum
2. 1400–4099 Neff
3. 1400–4099 Ash
4. Clown
5. Greenhouse
6. 4100–4199 Neff
7. 1000–1399 Ash
8. 4100–4199 Ash
9. Race
10. Flynn
11. 4600–5299 Plum
12. 1000–1399 Neff
13. 4200–4599 Ash
14. 1000–1399 Plum
15. Cedar
16. Dalby
17. Pepper
18. 4600–5299 Neff
19. 4200–4599 Neff
20. 1400–4099 Plum
21. Bardack
22. Lemon
23. Hawk
24. 4200–4599 Plum
25. 4600–5299 Ash
26. 4200–4599 Plum
27. 4600–5299 Neff
28. 1400–4099 Ash
29. Lemon
30. Pepper

31. 4100–4199 Neff
32. 1400–4099 Plum
33. 4200–4599 Neff
34. Dalby
35. Flynn
36. 4200–4599 Ash
37. 4600–5299 Plum
38. 4100–4199 Plum
39. Bardack
40. Hawk
41. 1000–1399 Plum
42. 1000–1399 Neff
43. 1000–1399 Ash
44. Greenhouse
45. Clown
46. 4600–5299 Ash
47. 4100–4199 Ash
48. 1400–4099 Neff
49. Race
50. Cedar
`51. Flynn
52. Hawk
53. 4100–4199 Neff
54. 1000–1399 Ash
55. 4100–4199 Plum
56. 1400–4099 Plum
57. 4200–4599 Plum
58. Bardack
59. 4600–5299 Neff
60. 4200–4599 Neff

61. 4200–4599 Ash
62. Pepper
63. Clown
64. 4600–5299 Ash
65. 1000–1399 Neff
66. 1000–1399 Plum
67. Race
68. Dalby
69. 1400–4099 Ash
70. 4100–4199 Ash
71. 4600–5299 Plum
72. 4600–5299 Neff
73. Cedar
74. 1400–4099 Neff
75. Greenhouse
76. 4100–4199 Plum
77. 4200–4599 Neff
78. 4200–4599 Ash
79. Clown
80. Dalby
81. 4200–4599 Plum
82. 1400–4099 Ash
83. 1000–1399 Neff
84. Pepper
85. Bardack
86. 4100–4199 Plum
87. 1400–4099 Neff
88. 4100–4199 Ash

Practice II Answer Sheet

1 Ⓐ Ⓑ Ⓒ Ⓓ Ⓔ	23 Ⓐ Ⓑ Ⓒ Ⓓ Ⓔ	45 Ⓐ Ⓑ Ⓒ Ⓓ Ⓔ	67 Ⓐ Ⓑ Ⓒ Ⓓ Ⓔ
2 Ⓐ Ⓑ Ⓒ Ⓓ Ⓔ	24 Ⓐ Ⓑ Ⓒ Ⓓ Ⓔ	46 Ⓐ Ⓑ Ⓒ Ⓓ Ⓔ	68 Ⓐ Ⓑ Ⓒ Ⓓ Ⓔ
3 Ⓐ Ⓑ Ⓒ Ⓓ Ⓔ	25 Ⓐ Ⓑ Ⓒ Ⓓ Ⓔ	47 Ⓐ Ⓑ Ⓒ Ⓓ Ⓔ	69 Ⓐ Ⓑ Ⓒ Ⓓ Ⓔ
4 Ⓐ Ⓑ Ⓒ Ⓓ Ⓔ	26 Ⓐ Ⓑ Ⓒ Ⓓ Ⓔ	48 Ⓐ Ⓑ Ⓒ Ⓓ Ⓔ	70 Ⓐ Ⓑ Ⓒ Ⓓ Ⓔ
5 Ⓐ Ⓑ Ⓒ Ⓓ Ⓔ	27 Ⓐ Ⓑ Ⓒ Ⓓ Ⓔ	49 Ⓐ Ⓑ Ⓒ Ⓓ Ⓔ	71 Ⓐ Ⓑ Ⓒ Ⓓ Ⓔ
6 Ⓐ Ⓑ Ⓒ Ⓓ Ⓔ	28 Ⓐ Ⓑ Ⓒ Ⓓ Ⓔ	50 Ⓐ Ⓑ Ⓒ Ⓓ Ⓔ	72 Ⓐ Ⓑ Ⓒ Ⓓ Ⓔ
7 Ⓐ Ⓑ Ⓒ Ⓓ Ⓔ	29 Ⓐ Ⓑ Ⓒ Ⓓ Ⓔ	51 Ⓐ Ⓑ Ⓒ Ⓓ Ⓔ	73 Ⓐ Ⓑ Ⓒ Ⓓ Ⓔ
8 Ⓐ Ⓑ Ⓒ Ⓓ Ⓔ	30 Ⓐ Ⓑ Ⓒ Ⓓ Ⓔ	52 Ⓐ Ⓑ Ⓒ Ⓓ Ⓔ	74 Ⓐ Ⓑ Ⓒ Ⓓ Ⓔ
9 Ⓐ Ⓑ Ⓒ Ⓓ Ⓔ	31 Ⓐ Ⓑ Ⓒ Ⓓ Ⓔ	53 Ⓐ Ⓑ Ⓒ Ⓓ Ⓔ	75 Ⓐ Ⓑ Ⓒ Ⓓ Ⓔ
10 Ⓐ Ⓑ Ⓒ Ⓓ Ⓔ	32 Ⓐ Ⓑ Ⓒ Ⓓ Ⓔ	54 Ⓐ Ⓑ Ⓒ Ⓓ Ⓔ	76 Ⓐ Ⓑ Ⓒ Ⓓ Ⓔ
11 Ⓐ Ⓑ Ⓒ Ⓓ Ⓔ	33 Ⓐ Ⓑ Ⓒ Ⓓ Ⓔ	55 Ⓐ Ⓑ Ⓒ Ⓓ Ⓔ	77 Ⓐ Ⓑ Ⓒ Ⓓ Ⓔ
12 Ⓐ Ⓑ Ⓒ Ⓓ Ⓔ	34 Ⓐ Ⓑ Ⓒ Ⓓ Ⓔ	56 Ⓐ Ⓑ Ⓒ Ⓓ Ⓔ	78 Ⓐ Ⓑ Ⓒ Ⓓ Ⓔ
13 Ⓐ Ⓑ Ⓒ Ⓓ Ⓔ	35 Ⓐ Ⓑ Ⓒ Ⓓ Ⓔ	57 Ⓐ Ⓑ Ⓒ Ⓓ Ⓔ	79 Ⓐ Ⓑ Ⓒ Ⓓ Ⓔ
14 Ⓐ Ⓑ Ⓒ Ⓓ Ⓔ	36 Ⓐ Ⓑ Ⓒ Ⓓ Ⓔ	58 Ⓐ Ⓑ Ⓒ Ⓓ Ⓔ	80 Ⓐ Ⓑ Ⓒ Ⓓ Ⓔ
15 Ⓐ Ⓑ Ⓒ Ⓓ Ⓔ	37 Ⓐ Ⓑ Ⓒ Ⓓ Ⓔ	59 Ⓐ Ⓑ Ⓒ Ⓓ Ⓔ	81 Ⓐ Ⓑ Ⓒ Ⓓ Ⓔ
16 Ⓐ Ⓑ Ⓒ Ⓓ Ⓔ	38 Ⓐ Ⓑ Ⓒ Ⓓ Ⓔ	60 Ⓐ Ⓑ Ⓒ Ⓓ Ⓔ	82 Ⓐ Ⓑ Ⓒ Ⓓ Ⓔ
17 Ⓐ Ⓑ Ⓒ Ⓓ Ⓔ	39 Ⓐ Ⓑ Ⓒ Ⓓ Ⓔ	61 Ⓐ Ⓑ Ⓒ Ⓓ Ⓔ	83 Ⓐ Ⓑ Ⓒ Ⓓ Ⓔ
18 Ⓐ Ⓑ Ⓒ Ⓓ Ⓔ	40 Ⓐ Ⓑ Ⓒ Ⓓ Ⓔ	62 Ⓐ Ⓑ Ⓒ Ⓓ Ⓔ	84 Ⓐ Ⓑ Ⓒ Ⓓ Ⓔ
19 Ⓐ Ⓑ Ⓒ Ⓓ Ⓔ	41 Ⓐ Ⓑ Ⓒ Ⓓ Ⓔ	63 Ⓐ Ⓑ Ⓒ Ⓓ Ⓔ	85 Ⓐ Ⓑ Ⓒ Ⓓ Ⓔ
20 Ⓐ Ⓑ Ⓒ Ⓓ Ⓔ	42 Ⓐ Ⓑ Ⓒ Ⓓ Ⓔ	64 Ⓐ Ⓑ Ⓒ Ⓓ Ⓔ	86 Ⓐ Ⓑ Ⓒ Ⓓ Ⓔ
21 Ⓐ Ⓑ Ⓒ Ⓓ Ⓔ	43 Ⓐ Ⓑ Ⓒ Ⓓ Ⓔ	65 Ⓐ Ⓑ Ⓒ Ⓓ Ⓔ	87 Ⓐ Ⓑ Ⓒ Ⓓ Ⓔ
22 Ⓐ Ⓑ Ⓒ Ⓓ Ⓔ	44 Ⓐ Ⓑ Ⓒ Ⓓ Ⓔ	66 Ⓐ Ⓑ Ⓒ Ⓓ Ⓔ	88 Ⓐ Ⓑ Ⓒ Ⓓ Ⓔ

Practice III

DIRECTIONS: *The names and address are repeated for you in the boxes below. Each name and each number span is in the same box in which you found it in the original set. You will now be allowed FIVE MINUTES to study the locations again. Do your best to memorize the letter of the box in which each item is located. This is your last chance to see the boxes.*

A	B	C	D	E
4100–4199 Plum	1000–1399 Plum	4200–4599 Plum	1400–4099 Plum	4600–5299 Plum
Bardack	Greenhouse	Flynn	Pepper	Cedar
4200–4599 Ash	4600–5299 Ash	1400–4099 Ash	1000–1399 Ash	4100–4199 Ash
Lemon	Dalby	Race	Clown	Hawk
1000–1399 Neff	4100–4199 Neff	4600–5299 Neff	4200–4599 Neff	1400–4099 Neff

DIRECTIONS: *This is your last practice test. Mark the location of each of the 88 items on your answer sheet. You will have FIVE MINUTES to answer these questions. Do NOT look back at the boxes. This practice test will not be scored.*

1. 1400–4099 Ash
2. 4600–5299 Plum
3. 1000–1399 Neff
4. Pepper
5. Greenhouse
6. 4100–4199 Plum
7. 1400–4099 Neff
8. 4600–5299 Ash
9. 1000–1399 Ash
10. Bardack
11. Lemon
12. Hawk
13. 1000–1399 Plum
14. 4200–4599 Neff
15. 4200–4599 Ash
16. 4100–4199 Neff
17. 1400–4099 Plum
18. 4100–4199 Ash
19. Clown
20. Flynn
21. 4600–5299 Ash
22. 1000–1399 Plum

23. 4200–4599 Ash
24. Lemon
25. Race
26. 4600–5299 Neff
27. 4600–5299 Plum
28. Dalby
29. Cedar
30. 4200–4599 Neff
31. 1000–1399 Plum
32. 1400–4099 Ash
33. 4200–4599 Neff
34. 1400–4099 Plum
35. 4100–4199 Neff
36. Ceda
37. Clown
38. Dalby
39. 4200–4599 Ash
40. 4100–4199 Ash
41. 4600–5299 Plum
42. 1000–1399 Neff
43. Greenhouse
44. Pepper

45. 4100–4199 Plum
46. 1400–4099 Neff
47. 4600–5299 Ash
48. 1000–1399 Ash
49. Clown
50. Bardack
51. Lemon
52. 4200–4599 Plum
53. 4600–5299 Neff
54. Hawk
55. Flynn
56. Race
57. 1400–4099 Plum
58. 1000–1399 Neff
59. 4100–4199 Ash
60. 1400–4099 Ash
61. 1400–4099 Plum
62. 4100–4199 Neff
63. 1400–4099 Neff
64. Hawk
65. Lemon
66. 1000–1399 Plum

67. 4100–4199 Neff
68. 4600–5299 Ash
69. Pepper
70. Dalby
71. 1000–1399 Neff
72. 4600–5299 Plum
73. 4100–4199 Ash
74. Greenhouse

75. Race
76. 4200–4599 Neff
77. 1000–1399 Ash
78. 4200–4599 Plum
79. Bardack
80. Cedar
81. 4200–4599 Ash
82. 4100–4199 Plum

83. 4600–5299 Neff
84. Flynn
85. Clown
86. 1400–4099 Ash
87. 4600–5299 Plum
88. 4100–4199 Plum

Practice III Answer Sheet

1 Ⓐ Ⓑ Ⓒ Ⓓ Ⓔ   23 Ⓐ Ⓑ Ⓒ Ⓓ Ⓔ   45 Ⓐ Ⓑ Ⓒ Ⓓ Ⓔ   67 Ⓐ Ⓑ Ⓒ Ⓓ Ⓔ
2 Ⓐ Ⓑ Ⓒ Ⓓ Ⓔ   24 Ⓐ Ⓑ Ⓒ Ⓓ Ⓔ   46 Ⓐ Ⓑ Ⓒ Ⓓ Ⓔ   68 Ⓐ Ⓑ Ⓒ Ⓓ Ⓔ
3 Ⓐ Ⓑ Ⓒ Ⓓ Ⓔ   25 Ⓐ Ⓑ Ⓒ Ⓓ Ⓔ   47 Ⓐ Ⓑ Ⓒ Ⓓ Ⓔ   69 Ⓐ Ⓑ Ⓒ Ⓓ Ⓔ
4 Ⓐ Ⓑ Ⓒ Ⓓ Ⓔ   26 Ⓐ Ⓑ Ⓒ Ⓓ Ⓔ   48 Ⓐ Ⓑ Ⓒ Ⓓ Ⓔ   70 Ⓐ Ⓑ Ⓒ Ⓓ Ⓔ
5 Ⓐ Ⓑ Ⓒ Ⓓ Ⓔ   27 Ⓐ Ⓑ Ⓒ Ⓓ Ⓔ   49 Ⓐ Ⓑ Ⓒ Ⓓ Ⓔ   71 Ⓐ Ⓑ Ⓒ Ⓓ Ⓔ
6 Ⓐ Ⓑ Ⓒ Ⓓ Ⓔ   28 Ⓐ Ⓑ Ⓒ Ⓓ Ⓔ   50 Ⓐ Ⓑ Ⓒ Ⓓ Ⓔ   72 Ⓐ Ⓑ Ⓒ Ⓓ Ⓔ
7 Ⓐ Ⓑ Ⓒ Ⓓ Ⓔ   29 Ⓐ Ⓑ Ⓒ Ⓓ Ⓔ   51 Ⓐ Ⓑ Ⓒ Ⓓ Ⓔ   73 Ⓐ Ⓑ Ⓒ Ⓓ Ⓔ
8 Ⓐ Ⓑ Ⓒ Ⓓ Ⓔ   30 Ⓐ Ⓑ Ⓒ Ⓓ Ⓔ   52 Ⓐ Ⓑ Ⓒ Ⓓ Ⓔ   74 Ⓐ Ⓑ Ⓒ Ⓓ Ⓔ
9 Ⓐ Ⓑ Ⓒ Ⓓ Ⓔ   31 Ⓐ Ⓑ Ⓒ Ⓓ Ⓔ   53 Ⓐ Ⓑ Ⓒ Ⓓ Ⓔ   75 Ⓐ Ⓑ Ⓒ Ⓓ Ⓔ
10 Ⓐ Ⓑ Ⓒ Ⓓ Ⓔ 32 Ⓐ Ⓑ Ⓒ Ⓓ Ⓔ   54 Ⓐ Ⓑ Ⓒ Ⓓ Ⓔ   76 Ⓐ Ⓑ Ⓒ Ⓓ Ⓔ
11 Ⓐ Ⓑ Ⓒ Ⓓ Ⓔ 33 Ⓐ Ⓑ Ⓒ Ⓓ Ⓔ   55 Ⓐ Ⓑ Ⓒ Ⓓ Ⓔ   77 Ⓐ Ⓑ Ⓒ Ⓓ Ⓔ
12 Ⓐ Ⓑ Ⓒ Ⓓ Ⓔ 34 Ⓐ Ⓑ Ⓒ Ⓓ Ⓔ   56 Ⓐ Ⓑ Ⓒ Ⓓ Ⓔ   78 Ⓐ Ⓑ Ⓒ Ⓓ Ⓔ
13 Ⓐ Ⓑ Ⓒ Ⓓ Ⓔ 35 Ⓐ Ⓑ Ⓒ Ⓓ Ⓔ   57 Ⓐ Ⓑ Ⓒ Ⓓ Ⓔ   79 Ⓐ Ⓑ Ⓒ Ⓓ Ⓔ
14 Ⓐ Ⓑ Ⓒ Ⓓ Ⓔ 36 Ⓐ Ⓑ Ⓒ Ⓓ Ⓔ   58 Ⓐ Ⓑ Ⓒ Ⓓ Ⓔ   80 Ⓐ Ⓑ Ⓒ Ⓓ Ⓔ
15 Ⓐ Ⓑ Ⓒ Ⓓ Ⓔ 37 Ⓐ Ⓑ Ⓒ Ⓓ Ⓔ   59 Ⓐ Ⓑ Ⓒ Ⓓ Ⓔ   81 Ⓐ Ⓑ Ⓒ Ⓓ Ⓔ
16 Ⓐ Ⓑ Ⓒ Ⓓ Ⓔ 38 Ⓐ Ⓑ Ⓒ Ⓓ Ⓔ   60 Ⓐ Ⓑ Ⓒ Ⓓ Ⓔ   82 Ⓐ Ⓑ Ⓒ Ⓓ Ⓔ
17 Ⓐ Ⓑ Ⓒ Ⓓ Ⓔ 39 Ⓐ Ⓑ Ⓒ Ⓓ Ⓔ   61 Ⓐ Ⓑ Ⓒ Ⓓ Ⓔ   83 Ⓐ Ⓑ Ⓒ Ⓓ Ⓔ
18 Ⓐ Ⓑ Ⓒ Ⓓ Ⓔ 40 Ⓐ Ⓑ Ⓒ Ⓓ Ⓔ   62 Ⓐ Ⓑ Ⓒ Ⓓ Ⓔ   84 Ⓐ Ⓑ Ⓒ Ⓓ Ⓔ
19 Ⓐ Ⓑ Ⓒ Ⓓ Ⓔ 41 Ⓐ Ⓑ Ⓒ Ⓓ Ⓔ   63 Ⓐ Ⓑ Ⓒ Ⓓ Ⓔ   85 Ⓐ Ⓑ Ⓒ Ⓓ Ⓔ
20 Ⓐ Ⓑ Ⓒ Ⓓ Ⓔ 42 Ⓐ Ⓑ Ⓒ Ⓓ Ⓔ   64 Ⓐ Ⓑ Ⓒ Ⓓ Ⓔ   86 Ⓐ Ⓑ Ⓒ Ⓓ Ⓔ
21 Ⓐ Ⓑ Ⓒ Ⓓ Ⓔ 43 Ⓐ Ⓑ Ⓒ Ⓓ Ⓔ   65 Ⓐ Ⓑ Ⓒ Ⓓ Ⓔ   87 Ⓐ Ⓑ Ⓒ Ⓓ Ⓔ
22 Ⓐ Ⓑ Ⓒ Ⓓ Ⓔ 44 Ⓐ Ⓑ Ⓒ Ⓓ Ⓔ   66 Ⓐ Ⓑ Ⓒ Ⓓ Ⓔ   88 Ⓐ Ⓑ Ⓒ Ⓓ Ⓔ

Memory for Addresses

Time: 5 Minutes. 88 Questions.

DIRECTIONS: Mark your answers on the answer sheet in the section headed "MEMORY FOR ADDRESSES." This test will be scored. You are NOT permitted to look at the boxes. Work from memory, as quickly and as accurately as you can. Correct answers are on page 125.

1. 1400–4099 Neff
2. 4100–4199 Plum
3. 1400–4099 Ash
4. Pepper
5. Dalby
6. 4200–4599 Plum
7. 4600–5299 Neff
8. 4100–4199 Ash
9. 4200–4599 Ash
10. Bardack
11. Hawk
12. 4600–5299 Plum
13. 1000–1399 Neff
14. 1000–1399 Ash
15. Clown
16. Flynn
17. 4600–5299 Ash
18. 1400–4099 Plum
19. 1000–1399 Plum
20. Cedar
21. Race
22. Lemon
23. 4100–4199 Neff
24. Greenhouse
25. 4200–4599 Neff
26. 1000–1399 Plum
27. 1400–4099 Neff
28. 4200–4599 Ash
29. Hawk
30. Flynn
31. 4100–4199 Plum
32. 4200–4599 Neff
33. 1400–4099 Ash
34. Clown
35. Dalby
36. 4100–4199 Ash
37. 4100–4199 Neff
38. 1400–4099 Plum
39. Cedar
40. Bardack
41. 1000–1399 Plum
42. 4600–5299 Neff
43. 1400–4099 Plum
44. Lemon
45. Cedar
46. 4200–4599 Ash
47. 4100–4199 Ash
48. 4100–4199 Plum
49. 1000–1399 Neff
50. 4100–4199 Neff
51. Hawk
52. Greenhouse
53. Dalby
54. 1400–4099 Ash
55. 4600–5299 Ash
56. 4200–4599 Plum
57. Clown
58. Race
59. 1000–1399 Ash
60. 4600–5299 Plum
61. Bardack
62. 4200–4599 Neff
63. Flynn
64. Pepper
65. 1400–4099 Neff
66. 4100–4199 Ash
67. 4600–5299 Neff
68. 1000–1399 Plum
69. 4100–4199 Plum
70. 4600–5299 Ash
71. 4600–5299 Neff
72. Lemon
73. Pepper
74. Cedar
75. 1400–4099 Ash
76. 1400–4099 Neff
77. 4100–4199 Ash
78. 4600–5299 Plum
79. Greenhouse
80. Dalby
81. 1000–1399 Plum
82. 1000–1399 Ash
83. 4100–4199 Neff
84. 4200–4599 Plum
85. Flynn
86. Clown
87. 4200–4599 Ash
88. 4100–4199 Ash

END OF MEMORY FOR ADDRESSES

PART C—NUMBER SERIES

Sample Questions

The following sample questions show you the type of question that will be used in Part C. You will have three minutes to answer the sample questions below and to study the explanations.

Directions: *Each number series question consists of a series of numbers that follows some definite order. The numbers progress from left to right according to some rule. One pair of numbers to the right of the series comprises the next two numbers in the series. Study each series to try to find a pattern to the series and to figure out the rule that governs the progression. Choose the answer pair that continues the series according to the pattern established and mark its letter on your answer sheet.*

   1. 23 25 27 29 31 33 35 .... (A) 35 36 (B) 35 37 (C) 36 37 (D) 37 38 (E) 37 39

The answer (**E**) should be easy to see. This series progresses by adding 2. 35 + 2 = 37 + 2 = 39.

   2. 3 3 6 6 12 12 24 .... (A) 24 36 (B) 36 36 (C) 24 24 (D) 24 48 (E) 48 48

The answer is (**D**) because the series requires you to repeat a number, then multiply it by 2.

   3. 11 13 16 20 25 31 38 .... (A) 46 55 (B) 45 55 (C) 40 42 (D) 47 58 (E) 42 46

The easiest way to solve this problem is to write the degree and direction of change between the numbers. By doing this, you see that the pattern is +2, +3, +4, +5, +6, +7. Continue the series by continuing the pattern: 38 + 8 = 46 + 9 = 55. The answer is (**A**).

   4. 76 72 72 68 64 64 60 .... (A) 60 56 (B) 60 60 (C) 56 56 (D) 56 52 (E) 56 54

Here the pattern is: –4, repeat the number, –4; –4, repeat the number, –4. To find that (**C**) is the answer you must realize that you are at the beginning of the pattern. 60 – 4=56, then repeat the number 56.

   5. 92 94 96 92 94 96 92 .... (A) 92 94 (B) 94 96 (C) 96 92 (D) 96 94 (E) 96 98

The series consists of the sequence 92 94 96 repeated over and over again. (**B**) is the answer because 94 96 continues the sequence after 92.

SAMPLE ANSWER SHEET	CORRECT ANSWERS
1. Ⓐ Ⓑ Ⓒ Ⓓ Ⓔ	1. Ⓐ Ⓑ Ⓒ Ⓓ ●
2. Ⓐ Ⓑ Ⓒ Ⓓ Ⓔ	2. Ⓐ Ⓑ Ⓒ ● Ⓔ
3. Ⓐ Ⓑ Ⓒ Ⓓ Ⓔ	3. ● Ⓑ Ⓒ Ⓓ Ⓔ
4. Ⓐ Ⓑ Ⓒ Ⓓ Ⓔ	4. Ⓐ Ⓑ ● Ⓓ Ⓔ
5. Ⓐ Ⓑ Ⓒ Ⓓ Ⓔ	5. Ⓐ ● Ⓒ Ⓓ Ⓔ

Number Series

Time: 20 Minutes. 24 Questions.

Directions: *Each number series question consists of a series of numbers that follows some definite order. The numbers progress from left to right according to some rule. One lettered pair of numbers comprises the next two numbers in the series. Study each series to try to find a pattern to the series and to figure out the rule that governs the progression. Choose the answer pair that continues the series according to the pattern established and mark its letter on your answer sheet. Correct answers are on page 126.*

1. 8 9 9 8 10 10 8 .... (A) 11 8   (B) 8 13   (C) 8 11   (D) 11 11   (E) 8 8
2. 10 10 11 11 12 12 13 .... (A) 15 15   (B) 13 13   (C) 14 14   (D) 13 14   (E) 14 15
3. 6 6 10 6 6 12 6 .... (A) 6 14   (B) 13 6   (C) 14 6   (D) 6 13   (E) 6 6
4. 17 11 5 16 10 4 15 .... (A) 13 9   (B) 13 11   (C) 8 5   (D) 9 5   (E) 9 3
5. 1 3 2 4 3 5 4 .... (A) 6 8   (B) 5 6   (C) 6 5   (D) 3 4   (E) 3 5
6. 11 11 10 12 12 11 13 .... (A) 12 14   (B) 14 12   (C) 14 14   (D) 13 14   (E) 13 12
7. 18 5 6 18 7 8 18 .... (A) 9 9   (B) 9 10   (C) 18 9   (D) 8 9   (E) 18 7
8. 8 1 9 3 10 5 11 .... (A) 7 12   (B) 6 12   (C) 12 6   (D) 7 8   (E) 6 7
9. 14 12 10 20 18 16 32 30 .... (A) 60 18   (B) 32 64   (C) 30 28   (D) 28 56   (E) 28 28
10. 67 59 52 44 37 29 22 .... (A) 15 7   (B) 14 8   (C) 14 7   (D) 15 8   (E) 16 11
11. 17 79 20 74 23 69 26 .... (A) 64 29   (B) 65 30   (C) 29 64   (D) 23 75   (E) 26 64
12. 3 5 10 8 4 6 12 10 5 .... (A) 8 16   (B) 7 14   (C) 10 20   (D) 10 5   (E) 7 9
13. 58 52 52 46 46 40 40 .... (A) 34 28   (B) 28 28   (C) 40 34   (D) 35 35   (E) 34 34
14. 32 37 33 33 38 34 34 .... (A) 38 43   (B) 34 39   (C) 39 35   (D) 39 39   (E) 34 40
15. 15 17 19 16 18 20 17 .... (A) 14 16   (B) 19 21   (C) 17 19   (D) 16 18   (E) 19 16
16. 5 15 7 21 13 39 31 .... (A) 93 85   (B) 62 69   (C) 39 117   (D) 93 87   (E) 31 93
17. 84 76 70 62 56 48 42 .... (A) 42 36   (B) 34 26   (C) 36 28   (D) 36 24   (E) 34 28
18. 47 23 43 27 39 31 35 .... (A) 31 27   (B) 39 43   (C) 39 35   (D) 35 31   (E) 31 35
19. 14 23 31 38 44 49 53 .... (A) 55 57   (B) 57 61   (C) 56 58   (D) 57 59   (E) 58 62
20. 5 6 8 8 9 11 11 12 .... (A) 12 13   (B) 14 14   (C) 14 15   (D) 14 16   (E) 12 14
21. 9 18 41 41 36 72 41 .... (A) 108 108   (B) 41 108   (C) 41 144   (D) 144 144   (E) 72 41
22. 13 15 17 13 15 17 13 .... (A) 17 15   (B) 13 15   (C) 17 13   (D) 15 13   (E) 15 17
23. 13 92 17 89 21 86 25 .... (A) 83 29   (B) 24 89   (C) 29 83   (D) 25 83   (E) 89 21
24. 10 20 23 13 26 29 19 .... (A) 9 12   (B) 38 41   (C) 22 44   (D) 44 33   (E) 36 39

END OF NUMBER SERIES

PART D—FOLLOWING ORAL INSTRUCTIONS

Directions and Sample Questions

LISTENING TO INSTRUCTIONS: When you are ready to try these sample questions, give the following instructions to a friend and have the friend read them aloud to you at the rate of 80 words per minute. Do not read them to yourself. Your friend will need a watch with a second hand. Listen carefully and do exactly what your friend tells you to do with the worksheet and answer sheet. Your friend will tell you some things to do with each item on the worksheet. After each set of instructions, your friend will give you time to mark your answer by darkening a circle on the sample answer sheet. Since B and D sound very much alike, your friend will say "B as in baker" when he or she means B and "D as in dog" when he or she means D.

Before proceeding further, tear out the worksheet on page 115. Then hand this book to your friend.

TO THE PERSON WHO IS TO READ THE INSTRUCTIONS: The instructions are to be read at the rate of 80 words per minute. Do not read aloud the material that is in parentheses. Do not repeat any instructions.

Read Aloud to the Candidate

Look at line 1 on your worksheet. (Pause slightly.) Draw two lines under the middle number on line 1. (Pause 2 seconds.) Now, on your answer sheet, find the number under which you just drew two lines and darken space D as in dog for that number. (Pause 5 seconds.)

Look at line 2 on your worksheet. (Pause slightly.) Write the letter A in the left-hand circle. (Pause 2 seconds.) Now, on your answer sheet, darken the space for the number-letter combination in the circle in which you just wrote. (Pause 5 seconds.)

Look at line 3 on your worksheet. (Pause slightly.) Count the number of times the letter E appears on line 3 and write the number at the end of the line. (Pause 2 seconds.) Now, on your answer sheet, darken space C for the number you just wrote. (Pause 5 seconds.)

Look at line 4 on your worksheet. (Pause slightly.) If an hour is longer than a day, write the letter B as in baker on the line next to the first number on line 4; if not, write the letter E on the line next to the third number. (Pause 5 seconds.) Now, on your answer sheet, darken the space for the number-letter combination you just wrote. (Pause 5 seconds.)

Look at line 4 again. (Pause slightly.) Write the second letter of the alphabet on the line next to the middle number. (Pause 2 seconds.) Now, on your answer sheet, darken the space for the number-letter combination you just wrote. (Pause 5 seconds.)

Sample Worksheet

DIRECTIONS: Listening carefully to each set of instructions, mark each item on this worksheet as directed. Then complete each question by marking the sample answer sheet below as directed. For each answer you will darken the answer for a number-letter combination. Should you fall behind and miss an instruction, don't become excited. Let that one go and listen for the next one. If, when you start to darken a space for a number, you find that you have already darkened another space for that number, either erase the first mark and darken the space for the new combination or let the first mark stay and do not darken a space for the new combination. Write with a pencil that has a clean eraser. When you finish, you should have no more than one space darkened for each number.

1.   9   7   12   14   1

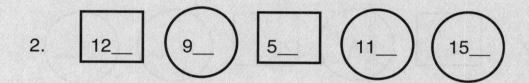

2.   12__   9__   5__   11__   15__

3.   WARNING. BEWARE OF DOG. __

4.   4___   13___   6___

TEAR HERE

CORRECT ANSWERS TO SAMPLE QUESTIONS

1. Ⓐ Ⓑ Ⓒ Ⓓ Ⓔ   6. Ⓐ Ⓑ Ⓒ Ⓓ ●   11. Ⓐ Ⓑ Ⓒ Ⓓ Ⓔ
2. Ⓐ Ⓑ ● Ⓓ Ⓔ   7. Ⓐ Ⓑ Ⓒ Ⓓ Ⓔ   12. Ⓐ Ⓑ Ⓒ ● Ⓔ
3. Ⓐ Ⓑ Ⓒ Ⓓ Ⓔ   8. Ⓐ Ⓑ Ⓒ Ⓓ Ⓔ   13. Ⓐ ● Ⓒ Ⓓ Ⓔ
4. Ⓐ Ⓑ Ⓒ Ⓓ Ⓔ   9. ● Ⓑ Ⓒ Ⓓ Ⓔ   14. Ⓐ Ⓑ Ⓒ Ⓓ Ⓔ
5. Ⓐ Ⓑ Ⓒ Ⓓ Ⓔ   10. Ⓐ Ⓑ Ⓒ Ⓓ Ⓔ   15. Ⓐ Ⓑ Ⓒ Ⓓ Ⓔ

Correctly Filled Worksheet

1.   9   7   <u>12</u>   14   1

2.   [12__]   (9Ⱥ)   [5__]   (11__)   (15__)

3.   WARNING. BEWARE OF DOG. <u>2</u>

4.   4___   13 <u>B</u>   6 <u>E</u>

Following Oral Instructions

Time: 25 Minutes.

Listening to Instructions

DIRECTIONS: When you are ready to try this test of the Model Exam, give the following instructions to a friend and have the friend read them aloud to you at the rate of 80 words per minute. Do NOT read them to yourself. Your friend will need a watch with a second hand. Listen carefully and do exactly what your friend tells you to do with the worksheet and with the answer sheet. Your friend will tell you some things to do with each item on the worksheet. After each set of instructions, you friend will give you time to mark your answer by darkening a circle on the answer sheet. Since B and D sound very much alike, your friend will say "B as in baker" when he or she means B and "D as in dog" when he or she means D.

> Before proceeding further, tear out the worksheet on page 121. Then hand this book to your friend.

TO THE PERSON WHO IS TO READ THE INSTRUCTIONS: The instructions are to be read at the rate of 80 words per minute. Do not read aloud the material that is in parentheses. Once you have begun the test itself, do not repeat any instructions. The next three paragraphs consist of approximately 120 words. Read these three paragraphs aloud to the candidate in about one and one-half minutes. You may reread these paragraphs as often as necessary to establish an 80 words-per-minute reading speed.

Read Aloud to the Candidate

On the job you will have to listen to directions and then do what you have been told to do. In this test, I will read instructions to you. Try to understand them as I read them; I cannot repeat them. Once we begin, you may not ask any questions until the end of the test.

On the job you won't have to deal with pictures, numbers, and letters like those in the test, but you will have to listen to instructions and follow them. We are using this test to see how well you can follow instructions.

You are to mark your test booklet according to the instructions that I'll read to you. After each set of instructions, I'll give you time to record your answers on the separate answer sheet.

The actual test begins now.

Look at line 1 on your worksheet. (Pause slightly.) Draw one line under the first number on line 1. (Pause 2 seconds.) Now, on your answer sheet, darken space E for the number under which you just drew one line. (Pause 5 seconds.)

Look at line 1 again. (Pause slightly.) Draw two lines under the lowest number on line 1. (Pause 2 seconds.) Now, on your answer sheet, darken space B as in baker for the number under which you just drew two lines. (Pause 5 seconds.)

Look at line 2 on your worksheet. (Pause slightly.) Write the number 38 in front of the letter that comes second in the alphabet. (Pause 2 seconds.) Now, on your answer sheet, darken the space for the number-letter combination you just wrote. (Pause 5 seconds.)

Look at line 3 on your worksheet. The numbers represent afternoon pickup times at corner mailboxes. (Pause slightly.) Draw a line under the latest pickup time. (Pause 2 seconds.) Now, on your answer sheet, darken the letter A for the last two digits, the minutes, of the time under which you just drew a line. (Pause 5 seconds.)

Look at line 3 again. (Pause slightly.) Find the earliest pickup time and add together all the digits of that time. Write the sum of the digits on the line at the end of line 3. (Pause 8 seconds.) Now, on your answer sheet, darken letter D as in dog for the number you just wrote. (Pause 5 seconds.)

Look at line 4 on your worksheet. (Pause slightly.) In the first circle, write the answer to this question: How many hours are there in a day? (Pause 2 seconds.) In the third circle write the answer to this question: How many working hours are there in a 5-day, 8-hours-per-day workweek? (Pause 5 seconds.) Now, on your answer sheet, darken the number-letter combinations that appear in both circles that you wrote in. (Pause 10 seconds.)

Look at line 5 on your worksheet. (Pause slightly.) If a yard is longer than ten inches, write the letter C in the triangle. If not, write E. (Pause 2 seconds.) Now, on your answer sheet, darken the space for the number-letter combination in the triangle. (Pause 5 seconds.)

Look at line 5 again. (Pause slightly.) If you are older than 36 months, write the letter A in the rectangle. If not, write the letter B as in baker in the square. (Pause 5 seconds.) Now, on your answer sheet, darken the space for the number-letter combination in the figure you just wrote in. (Pause 5 seconds.)

Look at line 6 on your worksheet. (Pause slightly.) Write the letter E beside the number that is second from the last on line 6. (Pause 2 seconds.) Now, on your answer sheet, darken the space for the number-letter combination you just wrote. (Pause 5 seconds.)

Look at line 7 on your worksheet. The numbers on line 7 represent a bar code. (Pause slightly.) Draw a line under each 0 in the bar code. (Pause 5 seconds.) Count the number of lines you have drawn, add 50, and write that number at the end of line 7. (Pause 5 seconds.) Now, on your answer sheet, darken space E for the number you just wrote. (Pause 5 seconds.)

Look at line 8 on your worksheet. The numbers in the mailsacks represent the weight of the mailsacks in pounds. (Pause slightly.) Write the letter D as in dog in the heaviest mailsack. (Pause 2 seconds.) Now, on your answer sheet, darken the space for the number-letter combination in the mailsack you just wrote in. (Pause 5 seconds.)

Look at line 9 on your worksheet. (Pause slightly.) Mark an X through the second number on line 9 and an X through every other number thereafter on line 9. (Pause 5 seconds.) Now, on your answer sheet, darken space A for the first number you drew an X through. (Pause 5 seconds.)

Look at line 9 again. (Pause slightly.) For all other numbers through which you drew an X, mark C on your answer sheet. (Pause 15 seconds.)

Look at line 10 on your worksheet. (Pause slightly.) Write the number 1 in the second figure in line 10. (Pause 2 seconds.) Now, on your answer sheet, darken the space for the number-letter combination in the figure you just wrote in. (Pause 5 seconds.)

Look at line 10 again. (Pause slightly.) Write the number 12 in the first circle on line 10. (Pause 2 seconds.) Now, on your answer sheet, darken the space for the number-letter combination in the figure you just wrote in. (Pause 5 seconds.)

Look at line 11 on your worksheet. (Pause slightly.) Write the letter A in the figure with fewer sides. (Pause 2 seconds.) Now, on your answer sheet, darken the space for the number-letter combination in the figure you just wrote in. (Pause 5 seconds.)

Look at line 12 on your worksheet. (Pause slightly.) If 3 is less than 5 and 10 is more than 2, write the number 79 in the first box. (Pause 5 seconds.) If not, write the number 76 in the second box. (Pause 5 seconds.) Now, on your answer sheet, darken the space for the number-letter combination in the box you just wrote in. (Pause 5 seconds.)

Look at line 13 on your worksheet. (Pause slightly.) Write the first letter of the third word in the second box. (Pause 5 seconds.) Write the third letter of the second word in the first box. (Pause 5 seconds.) Write the second letter of the first word in the third box. (Pause 5 seconds.) Now, on your answer sheet, darken the spaces for the number-letter combinations in the three boxes. (Pause 15 seconds.)

Look at line 14 on your worksheet. (Pause slightly.) If it is possible to purchase two 29¢ stamps for 55¢, write the number 72 on the second line. (Pause 5 seconds.) If not, write the number 19 on the first line. (Pause 5 seconds.) Now, on your answer sheet, darken the space for the number-letter combination you just wrote. (Pause 5 seconds.)

Look at line 15 on your worksheet. (Pause slightly.) Write the larger of these two numbers, 65 and 46, in the smaller box. (Pause 2 seconds.) Now, on your answer sheet, darken the space for the number-letter combination in the figure you just wrote in. (Pause 5 seconds.)

Look at line 15 again. (Pause slightly.) Write the sum of 10 plus 20 in the first box. (Pause 2 seconds.) Now, on your answer sheet, darken the space for the number-letter combination in the figure you just wrote in. (Pause 5 seconds.)

Look at line 16 on your worksheet. (Pause slightly.) Circle the fourth number on line 16. (Pause 2 seconds.) Now, on your answer sheet, darken the space for letter C for the number you just circled. (Pause 5 seconds.)

Look at line 17 on your worksheet. (Pause slightly.) If the number in the oval is greater than the number in the square, write the letter A in the circle. (Pause 5 seconds.) If not, write the letter B as in baker in the square. (Pause 5 seconds.) Now, on your answer sheet, darken the space for the number-letter combination in the figure you just wrote in. (Pause 5 seconds.)

Look at line 17 again. (Pause slightly.) If the number in the triangle is less than 25, write the letter D as in dog in the triangle. (Pause 2 seconds.) If not, write the letter C in the oval. (Pause 2 seconds.) Now, on your answer sheet, darken the space for the number-letter combination in the figure you just wrote in. (Pause 5 seconds.)

Look at line 18 on your worksheet. (Pause slightly.) Find the letter on line 18 that does not appear in the word GRADE and circle that letter. (Pause 2 seconds.) Now, on your answer sheet, find the number 44 and darken the space for the letter you just circled. (Pause 5 seconds.)

Look at line 19 on your worksheet. (Pause slightly.) Listen to the following numbers and write the smallest number beside the second letter: 59, 62, 49, 54, 87. (Pause 5 seconds.) Now, on your answer sheet, darken the number-letter combination you just wrote. (Pause 5 seconds.)

Following Oral Instructions
Worksheet

DIRECTIONS: Listening carefully to each set of instructions, mark each item on this worksheet as directed. Then complete each question by marking the answer sheet as directed. For each answer you will darken the answer for a number-letter combination. Should you fall behind and miss an instruction, don't become excited. Let that one go and listen for the next one. If, when you start to darken a space for a number, you find that you have already darkened another space for that number, either erase the first mark and darken the space for the new combination or let the first mark stay and do not darken a space for the new combination. Write with a pencil that has a clean eraser. When you finish, you should have no more than one space darkened for each number. Correct answers are on page 127.

1. 75   14   9   27   54   12

2. ___ B   ___ D   ___ C   ___ A   ___ E

3. 5:43   4:32   3:58   6:27

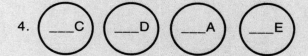

4. (___ C) (___ D) (___ A) (___ E)

5. [33 ___]   △ 81 ___   (17 ___)   [3 ___]

6. 35 ___   16 ___   10 ___   52 ___   6 ___   80 ___

7. 7 1 0 5 0 3 3 0 6 8 0 4 0

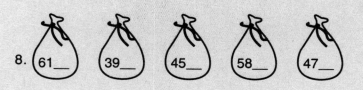

8. (61 ___) (39 ___) (45 ___) (58 ___) (47 ___)

9. 17   51   37   46   76   87   12   5

10.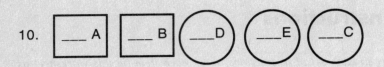

11.

12. [___ B]   [___ D]

13. [33___]   [85___]   [57___]   SACK   CODE   EXAM

14.   ___ B   ___ E

15. [___ E]   (__ A)   [__ D]   (__ C)

16.   45   19   81   22   10   76

17. [29___]   (73___)   △10__   ⬭72___

18.   D   G   E   B   R   A

19.   ___ A   ___ E   ___ C   ___ B

END OF EXAMINATION

CORRECT ANSWERS FOR MODEL EXAMINATION 1

PART A—ADDRESS CHECKING

1. A	13. D	25. D	37. A	49. D	61. D	73. A	85. A
2. D	14. D	26. D	38. D	50. A	62. D	74. D	86. D
3. D	15. D	27. D	39. A	51. A	63. A	75. D	87. A
4. A	16. D	28. A	40. D	52. D	64. D	76. D	88. D
5. D	17. A	29. D	41. D	53. D	65. D	77. D	89. D
6. D	18. D	30. A	42. D	54. A	66. A	78. D	90. A
7. A	19. D	31. A	43. D	55. D	67. D	79. A	91. D
8. D	20. D	32. D	44. A	56. A	68. D	80. A	92. A
9. D	21. A	33. D	45. D	57. D	69. A	81. D	93. A
10. A	22. D	34. D	46. D	58. D	70. D	82. A	94. A
11. D	23. D	35. D	47. A	59. D	71. A	83. D	95. D
12. D	24. A	36. A	48. D	60. A	72. D	84. A	

Analyzing Your Errors

This Address Checking Test contains 35 addresses that are exactly alike and 60 addresses that are different. The chart below shows what kind of difference occurs in each of the addresses that contains a difference. Check your answers against this chart to see which kind of difference you missed most often. Note also the questions in which you thought you saw a difference but in which there really was none. Becoming aware of your errors will help you to eliminate those errors on the actual exam.

Type of Difference	Question Numbers	Number of Questions You Missed
Difference in NUMBERS	2, 5, 8, 12, 14, 26, 32, 34, 35, 40, 43, 45, 52, 59, 67, 68, 72, 75, 76, 88, 91, 95	
Difference in ABBREVIATIONS	3, 9, 15, 25, 27, 33, 42, 46, 57, 61, 64, 77	
Difference in NAMES	6, 11, 13, 16, 18, 19, 20, 22, 23, 29, 38, 41, 48, 49, 53, 55, 58, 62, 65, 70, 74, 78, 81, 83, 86, 89	
No Difference	1, 4, 7, 10, 17, 21, 24, 28, 30, 31, 36, 37, 39, 44, 47, 50, 51, 54, 56, 60, 63, 66, 69, 71, 73, 79, 80, 82, 84, 85, 87, 90, 92, 93, 94	

PART B—MEMORY FOR ADDRESSES

Practice I

1. B	12. A	23. A	34. C	45. B	56. D	67. C	78. C
2. C	13. C	24. B	35. A	46. E	57. A	68. E	79. D
3. D	14. B	25. E	36. D	47. B	58. B	69. B	80. E
4. E	15. E	26. B	37. A	48. D	59. A	70. E	81. D
5. A	16. A	27. E	38. D	49. D	60. A	71. B	82. E
6. E	17. C	28. D	39. B	50. D	61. E	72. D	83. B
7. C	18. B	29. A	40. B	51. C	62. A	73. A	84. E
8. B	19. D	30. A	41. E	52. C	63. B	74. E	85. D
9. B	20. C	31. E	42. E	53. B	64. D	75. B	86. A
10. A	21. D	32. C	43. A	54. E	65. A	76. E	87. E
11. E	22. E	33. C	44. C	55. C	66. C	77. A	88. B

Practice II

1. A	12. A	23. E	34. B	45. D	56. D	67. C	78. A
2. E	13. A	24. C	35. C	46. B	57. C	68. B	79. D
3. C	14. B	25. B	36. A	47. E	58. A	69. C	80. B
4. D	15. E	26. C	37. E	48. E	59. C	70. E	81. C
5. B	16. B	27. C	38. A	49. C	60. D	71. E	82. C
6. B	17. D	28. C	39. A	50. E	61. A	72. C	83. A
7. D	18. C	29. A	40. E	51. C	62. D	73. E	84. D
8. E	19. D	30. D	41. B	52. E	63. D	74. E	85. A
9. C	20. D	31. B	42. A	53. B	64. B	75. B	86. A
10. C	21. A	32. D	43. D	54. D	65. A	76. A	87. E
11. E	22. A	33. D	44. B	55. A	66. B	77. D	88. E

Practice III

1. C	12. E	23. A	34. D	45. A	56. C	67. B	78. C
2. E	13. B	24. A	35. B	46. E	57. D	68. B	79. A
3. A	14. D	25. C	36. E	47. B	58. A	69. D	80. E
4. D	15. A	26. C	37. D	48. D	59. E	70. B	81. A
5. B	16. B	27. E	38. B	49. D	60. C	71. A	82. A
6. A	17. D	28. B	39. A	50. A	61. D	72. E	83. C
7. E	18. E	29. E	40. E	51. A	62. B	73. E	84. C
8. B	19. D	30. D	41. E	52. C	63. E	74. B	85. D
9. D	20. C	31. B	42. A	53. C	64. E	75. C	86. C
10. A	21. B	32. C	43. B	54. E	65. A	76. D	87. E
11. A	22. B	33. D	44. D	55. C	66. B	77. D	88. A

Memory for Addresses

1. E	12. E	23. B	34. D	45. E	56. C	67. C	78. E
2. A	13. A	24. B	35. B	46. A	57. D	68. B	79. B
3. C	14. D	25. D	36. E	47. E	58. C	69. A	80. B
4. D	15. D	26. B	37. B	48. A	59. D	70. B	81. B
5. B	16. C	27. E	38. D	49. A	60. E	71. C	82. D
6. C	17. B	28. A	39. E	50. B	61. A	72. A	83. B
7. C	18. D	29. E	40. A	51. E	62. D	73. D	84. C
8. E	19. B	30. C	41. B	52. B	63. C	74. E	85. C
9. A	20. E	31. A	42. C	53. B	64. D	75. C	86. D
10. A	21. C	32. D	43. D	54. C	65. E	76. E	87. A
11. E	22. A	33. C	44. A	55. B	66. E	77. E	88. E

PART C—NUMBER SERIES

1. D	4. E	7. B	10. C	13. E	16. A	19. C	22. E
2. D	5. C	8. A	11. A	14. C	17. E	20. B	23. A
3. A	6. E	9. D	12. B	15. B	18. D	21. C	24. B

Explanations

1. **(D)** The series really begins with <u>9</u> and consists of repeated numbers moving upward in order. The number <u>8</u> is inserted between each pair of repeated numbers in the series.

2. **(D)** The numbers repeat themselves and move up in order.

3. **(A)** <u>6 6</u> is a repetitive theme. Between each set of 6s, the numbers move up by +2.

4. **(E)** The full sequence is a number of sets of mini-series. Each mini-series consists of three numbers decreasing by –6. Each succeeding mini-series begins with a number one lower than the previous mini-series.

5. **(C)** Two alternating series each increase by +1. The first series starts at <u>1</u> and the second series starts at <u>3</u>.

6. **(E)** Two series alternate. The first series consists of repeating numbers that move up by +1. The alternating series consists of numbers that move up by +1 without repeating.

7. **(B)** The series proceeds 5 6 7 8 9 10, with the number <u>18</u> appearing between each two numbers.

8. **(A)** The first series ascends one number at a time starting from <u>8</u>. The alternating series ascends by +2 starting from <u>1</u>.

9. **(D)** The pattern is: –2, –2, ×2; –2, –2, ×2....

10. **(C)** The pattern is: –8, –7; –8, –7; –8, –7....

11. **(A)** Two series alternate. The firs series ascends by +3; the alternating series descends by –5.

12. **(B)** This is a tough one. The pattern is +2, ×2, –2, ÷2; +2, ×2, –2, ÷2....

13. **(E)** The pattern is: –6, repeat the number; –6, repeat the number....

14. **(C)** The pattern is: +5, –4, repeat the number; +5, –4, repeat the number....

15. **(B)** The pattern is: +2, +2, –3; +2, +2, –3....

16. **(A)** The pattern is: ×3, –8; ×3, –8; ×3, –8....

17. **(E)** The pattern is: –8, –6; –8, –6; –8, –6....

18. **(D)** There are two alternating series. The first series descends by –4 starting from <u>47</u>; the alternating series ascends by +4, starting from <u>23</u>.

19. **(C)** The pattern is: +9, +8, +7, +6, +5, +4, +3, +2, +1.

20. **(B)** Then pattern is: +1, +2, repeat the number; + 1, +2, repeat the number....

21. **(C)** This is really a times 2 series with the number 41 appearing twice after each two numbers in the series. Thus: $9 ^{\times 2} 18^{\times 2} 36^{\times 2} 72^{\times 2} 144$.

22. **(E)** The sequence 13 15 17 repeats itself over and over.

23. **(A)** Two series alternate. The first series ascends by +4; the alternating series descends by –3.

24. **(B)** The pattern is: ×2, +3, –10; ×2, +3, –10; ×2, +3, –10....

PART D—FOLLOWING ORAL INSTRUCTIONS

Correctly Filled Answer Grid

1 Ⓐ ● Ⓒ Ⓓ Ⓔ	23 Ⓐ Ⓑ Ⓒ Ⓓ Ⓔ	45 Ⓐ Ⓑ Ⓒ Ⓓ Ⓔ	67 Ⓐ Ⓑ Ⓒ Ⓓ Ⓔ
2 Ⓐ Ⓑ Ⓒ Ⓓ Ⓔ	24 Ⓐ Ⓑ ● Ⓓ Ⓔ	46 Ⓐ Ⓑ ● Ⓓ Ⓔ	68 ● Ⓑ Ⓒ Ⓓ Ⓔ
3 ● Ⓑ Ⓒ Ⓓ Ⓔ	25 Ⓐ Ⓑ Ⓒ Ⓓ Ⓔ	47 Ⓐ Ⓑ Ⓒ Ⓓ Ⓔ	69 Ⓐ Ⓑ Ⓒ Ⓓ Ⓔ
4 Ⓐ Ⓑ Ⓒ Ⓓ Ⓔ	26 Ⓐ Ⓑ Ⓒ Ⓓ Ⓔ	48 Ⓐ Ⓑ Ⓒ Ⓓ Ⓔ	70 Ⓐ Ⓑ Ⓒ Ⓓ Ⓔ
5 Ⓐ Ⓑ ● Ⓓ Ⓔ	27 ● Ⓑ Ⓒ Ⓓ Ⓔ	49 Ⓐ Ⓑ Ⓒ Ⓓ ●	71 Ⓐ Ⓑ Ⓒ Ⓓ Ⓔ
6 Ⓐ Ⓑ Ⓒ Ⓓ ●	28 Ⓐ Ⓑ Ⓒ Ⓓ Ⓔ	50 Ⓐ Ⓑ Ⓒ Ⓓ Ⓔ	72 Ⓐ Ⓑ Ⓒ Ⓓ Ⓔ
7 Ⓐ Ⓑ Ⓒ Ⓓ Ⓔ	29 Ⓐ Ⓑ Ⓒ Ⓓ Ⓔ	51 ● Ⓑ Ⓒ Ⓓ Ⓔ	73 ● Ⓑ Ⓒ Ⓓ Ⓔ
8 Ⓐ Ⓑ Ⓒ Ⓓ Ⓔ	30 Ⓐ Ⓑ Ⓒ Ⓓ ●	52 Ⓐ Ⓑ Ⓒ Ⓓ Ⓔ	74 Ⓐ Ⓑ Ⓒ Ⓓ Ⓔ
9 Ⓐ ● Ⓒ Ⓓ Ⓔ	31 Ⓐ Ⓑ Ⓒ Ⓓ Ⓔ	53 Ⓐ Ⓑ Ⓒ Ⓓ Ⓔ	75 Ⓐ Ⓑ Ⓒ Ⓓ ●
10 Ⓐ Ⓑ Ⓒ ● Ⓔ	32 Ⓐ Ⓑ Ⓒ Ⓓ Ⓔ	54 Ⓐ Ⓑ Ⓒ Ⓓ Ⓔ	76 Ⓐ Ⓑ Ⓒ Ⓓ Ⓔ
11 Ⓐ Ⓑ Ⓒ Ⓓ Ⓔ	33 Ⓐ Ⓑ Ⓒ ● Ⓔ	55 Ⓐ Ⓑ Ⓒ Ⓓ ●	77 Ⓐ Ⓑ Ⓒ Ⓓ Ⓔ
12 Ⓐ Ⓑ Ⓒ ● Ⓔ	34 Ⓐ Ⓑ Ⓒ Ⓓ Ⓔ	56 Ⓐ Ⓑ Ⓒ Ⓓ Ⓔ	78 Ⓐ Ⓑ Ⓒ Ⓓ Ⓔ
13 Ⓐ Ⓑ Ⓒ Ⓓ Ⓔ	35 Ⓐ Ⓑ Ⓒ Ⓓ Ⓔ	57 ● Ⓑ Ⓒ Ⓓ Ⓔ	79 Ⓐ ● Ⓒ Ⓓ Ⓔ
14 Ⓐ Ⓑ Ⓒ Ⓓ Ⓔ	36 Ⓐ Ⓑ Ⓒ Ⓓ Ⓔ	58 Ⓐ Ⓑ Ⓒ Ⓓ Ⓔ	80 Ⓐ Ⓑ Ⓒ Ⓓ Ⓔ
15 Ⓐ Ⓑ Ⓒ Ⓓ Ⓔ	37 Ⓐ Ⓑ Ⓒ Ⓓ Ⓔ	59 Ⓐ Ⓑ Ⓒ Ⓓ Ⓔ	81 Ⓐ Ⓑ ● Ⓓ Ⓔ
16 Ⓐ Ⓑ Ⓒ ● Ⓔ	38 Ⓐ ● Ⓒ Ⓓ Ⓔ	60 Ⓐ Ⓑ Ⓒ Ⓓ Ⓔ	82 Ⓐ Ⓑ Ⓒ Ⓓ Ⓔ
17 Ⓐ Ⓑ Ⓒ Ⓓ Ⓔ	39 Ⓐ Ⓑ Ⓒ Ⓓ Ⓔ	61 Ⓐ Ⓑ Ⓒ ● Ⓔ	83 Ⓐ Ⓑ Ⓒ Ⓓ Ⓔ
18 Ⓐ Ⓑ Ⓒ Ⓓ Ⓔ	40 ● Ⓑ Ⓒ Ⓓ Ⓔ	62 Ⓐ Ⓑ Ⓒ Ⓓ Ⓔ	84 Ⓐ Ⓑ Ⓒ Ⓓ Ⓔ
19 Ⓐ ● Ⓒ Ⓓ Ⓔ	41 Ⓐ Ⓑ Ⓒ Ⓓ Ⓔ	63 Ⓐ Ⓑ Ⓒ Ⓓ Ⓔ	85 Ⓐ Ⓑ Ⓒ Ⓓ ●
20 Ⓐ Ⓑ Ⓒ Ⓓ Ⓔ	42 Ⓐ Ⓑ Ⓒ Ⓓ Ⓔ	64 Ⓐ Ⓑ Ⓒ Ⓓ Ⓔ	86 Ⓐ Ⓑ Ⓒ Ⓓ Ⓔ
21 Ⓐ Ⓑ Ⓒ Ⓓ Ⓔ	43 Ⓐ Ⓑ Ⓒ Ⓓ Ⓔ	65 Ⓐ Ⓑ Ⓒ ● Ⓔ	87 Ⓐ Ⓑ ● Ⓓ Ⓔ
22 Ⓐ Ⓑ ● Ⓓ Ⓔ	44 Ⓐ ● Ⓒ Ⓓ Ⓔ	66 Ⓐ Ⓑ Ⓒ Ⓓ Ⓔ	88 Ⓐ Ⓑ Ⓒ Ⓓ Ⓔ

Correctly Filled Worksheet

1. <u>75</u>   14 <u>9</u>   27   54   12

2. <u>38</u> B   ___ D   ___ C   ___ A   ___ E

3. 5:43   4:32   3:58   <u>6:27</u>   <u>16</u>

4. (<u>24</u>C) (___D) (<u>40</u>A) (___E)

5. [33___] △81 <u>C</u> (17___) [3 <u>A</u>]

6. 35___   16 ___   10 ___   52 ___   6 <u>E</u>   80___

7. 7 1 <u>0</u> 5 <u>0</u> 3 3 <u>0</u> 6 8 <u>0</u> 4 <u>0</u> <u>55</u>

8. (61<u>D</u>) (39___) (45___) (58___) (47___)

9. 17 ✗ 37 ✗ 76 ✗ 12 ✗

10. [___ A] [_I_ B] (**12** D) (___ E) (___ C)

11. (86___) (68 _Λ_)

12. [_19_ B] [___ D]

13. [33 _D_] [85 _E_] [57 _Λ_]   SACK   CODE   EXAM

14. _19_ B   ___ E

15. [_30_ E] (__ A) [**65** D] (__ C)

16.   45   19   81   (22)   10   76

17. [29 ___] (73 _Λ_) (10 _D_) (72___)

18.   D   G   E   (B)   R   A

19. ___ A   _49_ E   ___ C   ___ B

SCORE SHEET

ADDRESS CHECKING: Your score on the Address Checking part is based upon the number of questions you answered correctly minus the number of questions you answered incorrectly. To determine your score, subtract the number of wrong answers from the number of correct answers.

Number Right − Number Wrong = Raw Score

_____ − _____ = _____

MEMORY FOR ADDRESSES: Your score on the Memory for Addresses part is based upon the number of questions you answered correctly minus one-fourth of the questions you answered incorrectly (number wrong divided by 4). Calculate this now: Number Wrong ÷ 4 = ___.

Number Right − Number Wrong ÷ 4 = Raw Score

_____ − _____ = _____

NUMBER SERIES: Your score on the Number Series part is based only on the number of questions you answered correctly. Wrong answers do not count against you.

Number Right = Raw Score

_____ = _____

FOLLOWING ORAL INSTRUCTIONS: Your score on the Following Oral Instructions part is based only upon the number of questions you marked correctly on the answer sheet. The worksheet is not scored, and wrong answers on the answer sheet do not count against you.

Number Right = Raw Score

_____ = _____

TOTAL SCORE: To find your total raw score, add together the raw scores for each section of the exam.

Address Checking Score   _____

    +

Memory for Addresses Score   _____

    +

Number Series Score   _____

    +

Following Oral Instructions Score   _____

    =   _____

Total Raw Score   _____

Self Evaluation Chart

Calculate your raw score for each test as shown above. Then check to see where your score falls on the scale from Poor to Excellent. Lightly shade in the boxes in which your scores fall.

Part	Excellent	Good	Average	Fair	Poor
Address Checking	80–95	65–79	50–64	35–49	1–34
Memory for Addresses	75–88	60–74	45–59	30–44	1–29
Number Series	21–24	18–20	14–17	11–13	1–10
Following Oral Instructions	27–32	23–26	19–22	14–18	1–13

For step-by-step instruction on how to prepare for and do well on Exam 470 and Exam 460, and for lots of practice with six additional full-length model exams, purchase Arco's Postal Clerk and Carrier.

Model Examination 2
Answer Sheet

Exam 710 (Parts A & B)

Clerk-Typist
Clerk-Stenographer
Data Conversion Operator

Exam 711 (Part C)

Clerk-Stenographer only

PART A

1. Ⓐ Ⓑ Ⓒ Ⓓ Ⓔ	23. Ⓐ Ⓑ Ⓒ Ⓓ Ⓔ	44. Ⓐ Ⓑ Ⓒ Ⓓ Ⓔ	65. Ⓐ Ⓑ Ⓒ Ⓓ Ⓔ
2. Ⓐ Ⓑ Ⓒ Ⓓ Ⓔ	24. Ⓐ Ⓑ Ⓒ Ⓓ Ⓔ	45. Ⓐ Ⓑ Ⓒ Ⓓ Ⓔ	66. Ⓐ Ⓑ Ⓒ Ⓓ Ⓔ
3. Ⓐ Ⓑ Ⓒ Ⓓ Ⓔ	25. Ⓐ Ⓑ Ⓒ Ⓓ Ⓔ	46. Ⓐ Ⓑ Ⓒ Ⓓ Ⓔ	67. Ⓐ Ⓑ Ⓒ Ⓓ Ⓔ
4. Ⓐ Ⓑ Ⓒ Ⓓ Ⓔ	26. Ⓐ Ⓑ Ⓒ Ⓓ Ⓔ	47. Ⓐ Ⓑ Ⓒ Ⓓ Ⓔ	68. Ⓐ Ⓑ Ⓒ Ⓓ Ⓔ
5. Ⓐ Ⓑ Ⓒ Ⓓ Ⓔ	27. Ⓐ Ⓑ Ⓒ Ⓓ Ⓔ	48. Ⓐ Ⓑ Ⓒ Ⓓ Ⓔ	69. Ⓐ Ⓑ Ⓒ Ⓓ Ⓔ
6. Ⓐ Ⓑ Ⓒ Ⓓ Ⓔ	28. Ⓐ Ⓑ Ⓒ Ⓓ Ⓔ	49. Ⓐ Ⓑ Ⓒ Ⓓ Ⓔ	70. Ⓐ Ⓑ Ⓒ Ⓓ Ⓔ
7. Ⓐ Ⓑ Ⓒ Ⓓ Ⓔ	29. Ⓐ Ⓑ Ⓒ Ⓓ Ⓔ	50. Ⓐ Ⓑ Ⓒ Ⓓ Ⓔ	71. Ⓐ Ⓑ Ⓒ Ⓓ Ⓔ
8. Ⓐ Ⓑ Ⓒ Ⓓ Ⓔ	30. Ⓐ Ⓑ Ⓒ Ⓓ Ⓔ	51. Ⓐ Ⓑ Ⓒ Ⓓ Ⓔ	72. Ⓐ Ⓑ Ⓒ Ⓓ Ⓔ
9. Ⓐ Ⓑ Ⓒ Ⓓ Ⓔ	31. Ⓐ Ⓑ Ⓒ Ⓓ Ⓔ	52. Ⓐ Ⓑ Ⓒ Ⓓ Ⓔ	73. Ⓐ Ⓑ Ⓒ Ⓓ Ⓔ
10. Ⓐ Ⓑ Ⓒ Ⓓ Ⓔ	32. Ⓐ Ⓑ Ⓒ Ⓓ Ⓔ	53. Ⓐ Ⓑ Ⓒ Ⓓ Ⓔ	74. Ⓐ Ⓑ Ⓒ Ⓓ Ⓔ
11. Ⓐ Ⓑ Ⓒ Ⓓ Ⓔ	33. Ⓐ Ⓑ Ⓒ Ⓓ Ⓔ	54. Ⓐ Ⓑ Ⓒ Ⓓ Ⓔ	75. Ⓐ Ⓑ Ⓒ Ⓓ Ⓔ
12. Ⓐ Ⓑ Ⓒ Ⓓ Ⓔ	34. Ⓐ Ⓑ Ⓒ Ⓓ Ⓔ	55. Ⓐ Ⓑ Ⓒ Ⓓ Ⓔ	76. Ⓐ Ⓑ Ⓒ Ⓓ Ⓔ
13. Ⓐ Ⓑ Ⓒ Ⓓ Ⓔ	35. Ⓐ Ⓑ Ⓒ Ⓓ Ⓔ	56. Ⓐ Ⓑ Ⓒ Ⓓ Ⓔ	77. Ⓐ Ⓑ Ⓒ Ⓓ Ⓔ
14. Ⓐ Ⓑ Ⓒ Ⓓ Ⓔ	36. Ⓐ Ⓑ Ⓒ Ⓓ Ⓔ	57. Ⓐ Ⓑ Ⓒ Ⓓ Ⓔ	78. Ⓐ Ⓑ Ⓒ Ⓓ Ⓔ
15. Ⓐ Ⓑ Ⓒ Ⓓ Ⓔ	37. Ⓐ Ⓑ Ⓒ Ⓓ Ⓔ	58. Ⓐ Ⓑ Ⓒ Ⓓ Ⓔ	79. Ⓐ Ⓑ Ⓒ Ⓓ Ⓔ
16. Ⓐ Ⓑ Ⓒ Ⓓ Ⓔ	38. Ⓐ Ⓑ Ⓒ Ⓓ Ⓔ	59. Ⓐ Ⓑ Ⓒ Ⓓ Ⓔ	80. Ⓐ Ⓑ Ⓒ Ⓓ Ⓔ
17. Ⓐ Ⓑ Ⓒ Ⓓ Ⓔ	39. Ⓐ Ⓑ Ⓒ Ⓓ Ⓔ	60. Ⓐ Ⓑ Ⓒ Ⓓ Ⓔ	81. Ⓐ Ⓑ Ⓒ Ⓓ Ⓔ
18. Ⓐ Ⓑ Ⓒ Ⓓ Ⓔ	40. Ⓐ Ⓑ Ⓒ Ⓓ Ⓔ	61. Ⓐ Ⓑ Ⓒ Ⓓ Ⓔ	82. Ⓐ Ⓑ Ⓒ Ⓓ Ⓔ
19. Ⓐ Ⓑ Ⓒ Ⓓ Ⓔ	41. Ⓐ Ⓑ Ⓒ Ⓓ Ⓔ	62. Ⓐ Ⓑ Ⓒ Ⓓ Ⓔ	83. Ⓐ Ⓑ Ⓒ Ⓓ Ⓔ
20. Ⓐ Ⓑ Ⓒ Ⓓ Ⓔ	42. Ⓐ Ⓑ Ⓒ Ⓓ Ⓔ	63. Ⓐ Ⓑ Ⓒ Ⓓ Ⓔ	84. Ⓐ Ⓑ Ⓒ Ⓓ Ⓔ
21. Ⓐ Ⓑ Ⓒ Ⓓ Ⓔ	43. Ⓐ Ⓑ Ⓒ Ⓓ Ⓔ	64. Ⓐ Ⓑ Ⓒ Ⓓ Ⓔ	85. Ⓐ Ⓑ Ⓒ Ⓓ Ⓔ
22. Ⓐ Ⓑ Ⓒ Ⓓ Ⓔ			

TEAR HERE

PART B

1. Ⓐ Ⓑ Ⓒ Ⓓ Ⓔ	33. Ⓐ Ⓑ Ⓒ Ⓓ Ⓔ	65. Ⓐ Ⓑ Ⓒ Ⓓ Ⓔ	97. Ⓐ Ⓑ Ⓒ Ⓓ Ⓔ
2. Ⓐ Ⓑ Ⓒ Ⓓ Ⓔ	34. Ⓐ Ⓑ Ⓒ Ⓓ Ⓔ	66. Ⓐ Ⓑ Ⓒ Ⓓ Ⓔ	98. Ⓐ Ⓑ Ⓒ Ⓓ Ⓔ
3. Ⓐ Ⓑ Ⓒ Ⓓ Ⓔ	35. Ⓐ Ⓑ Ⓒ Ⓓ Ⓔ	67. Ⓐ Ⓑ Ⓒ Ⓓ Ⓔ	99. Ⓐ Ⓑ Ⓒ Ⓓ Ⓔ
4. Ⓐ Ⓑ Ⓒ Ⓓ Ⓔ	36. Ⓐ Ⓑ Ⓒ Ⓓ Ⓔ	68. Ⓐ Ⓑ Ⓒ Ⓓ Ⓔ	100. Ⓐ Ⓑ Ⓒ Ⓓ Ⓔ
5. Ⓐ Ⓑ Ⓒ Ⓓ Ⓔ	37. Ⓐ Ⓑ Ⓒ Ⓓ Ⓔ	69. Ⓐ Ⓑ Ⓒ Ⓓ Ⓔ	101. Ⓐ Ⓑ Ⓒ Ⓓ Ⓔ
6. Ⓐ Ⓑ Ⓒ Ⓓ Ⓔ	38. Ⓐ Ⓑ Ⓒ Ⓓ Ⓔ	70. Ⓐ Ⓑ Ⓒ Ⓓ Ⓔ	102. Ⓐ Ⓑ Ⓒ Ⓓ Ⓔ
7. Ⓐ Ⓑ Ⓒ Ⓓ Ⓔ	39. Ⓐ Ⓑ Ⓒ Ⓓ Ⓔ	71. Ⓐ Ⓑ Ⓒ Ⓓ Ⓔ	103. Ⓐ Ⓑ Ⓒ Ⓓ Ⓔ
8. Ⓐ Ⓑ Ⓒ Ⓓ Ⓔ	40. Ⓐ Ⓑ Ⓒ Ⓓ Ⓔ	72. Ⓐ Ⓑ Ⓒ Ⓓ Ⓔ	104. Ⓐ Ⓑ Ⓒ Ⓓ Ⓔ
9. Ⓐ Ⓑ Ⓒ Ⓓ Ⓔ	41. Ⓐ Ⓑ Ⓒ Ⓓ Ⓔ	73. Ⓐ Ⓑ Ⓒ Ⓓ Ⓔ	105. Ⓐ Ⓑ Ⓒ Ⓓ Ⓔ
10. Ⓐ Ⓑ Ⓒ Ⓓ Ⓔ	42. Ⓐ Ⓑ Ⓒ Ⓓ Ⓔ	74. Ⓐ Ⓑ Ⓒ Ⓓ Ⓔ	106. Ⓐ Ⓑ Ⓒ Ⓓ Ⓔ
11. Ⓐ Ⓑ Ⓒ Ⓓ Ⓔ	43. Ⓐ Ⓑ Ⓒ Ⓓ Ⓔ	75. Ⓐ Ⓑ Ⓒ Ⓓ Ⓔ	107. Ⓐ Ⓑ Ⓒ Ⓓ Ⓔ
12. Ⓐ Ⓑ Ⓒ Ⓓ Ⓔ	44. Ⓐ Ⓑ Ⓒ Ⓓ Ⓔ	76. Ⓐ Ⓑ Ⓒ Ⓓ Ⓔ	108. Ⓐ Ⓑ Ⓒ Ⓓ Ⓔ
13. Ⓐ Ⓑ Ⓒ Ⓓ Ⓔ	45. Ⓐ Ⓑ Ⓒ Ⓓ Ⓔ	77. Ⓐ Ⓑ Ⓒ Ⓓ Ⓔ	109. Ⓐ Ⓑ Ⓒ Ⓓ Ⓔ
14. Ⓐ Ⓑ Ⓒ Ⓓ Ⓔ	46. Ⓐ Ⓑ Ⓒ Ⓓ Ⓔ	78. Ⓐ Ⓑ Ⓒ Ⓓ Ⓔ	110. Ⓐ Ⓑ Ⓒ Ⓓ Ⓔ
15. Ⓐ Ⓑ Ⓒ Ⓓ Ⓔ	47. Ⓐ Ⓑ Ⓒ Ⓓ Ⓔ	79. Ⓐ Ⓑ Ⓒ Ⓓ Ⓔ	111. Ⓐ Ⓑ Ⓒ Ⓓ Ⓔ
16. Ⓐ Ⓑ Ⓒ Ⓓ Ⓔ	48. Ⓐ Ⓑ Ⓒ Ⓓ Ⓔ	80. Ⓐ Ⓑ Ⓒ Ⓓ Ⓔ	112. Ⓐ Ⓑ Ⓒ Ⓓ Ⓔ
17. Ⓐ Ⓑ Ⓒ Ⓓ Ⓔ	49. Ⓐ Ⓑ Ⓒ Ⓓ Ⓔ	81. Ⓐ Ⓑ Ⓒ Ⓓ Ⓔ	113. Ⓐ Ⓑ Ⓒ Ⓓ Ⓔ
18. Ⓐ Ⓑ Ⓒ Ⓓ Ⓔ	50. Ⓐ Ⓑ Ⓒ Ⓓ Ⓔ	82. Ⓐ Ⓑ Ⓒ Ⓓ Ⓔ	114. Ⓐ Ⓑ Ⓒ Ⓓ Ⓔ
19. Ⓐ Ⓑ Ⓒ Ⓓ Ⓔ	51. Ⓐ Ⓑ Ⓒ Ⓓ Ⓔ	83. Ⓐ Ⓑ Ⓒ Ⓓ Ⓔ	115. Ⓐ Ⓑ Ⓒ Ⓓ Ⓔ
20. Ⓐ Ⓑ Ⓒ Ⓓ Ⓔ	52. Ⓐ Ⓑ Ⓒ Ⓓ Ⓔ	84. Ⓐ Ⓑ Ⓒ Ⓓ Ⓔ	116. Ⓐ Ⓑ Ⓒ Ⓓ Ⓔ
21. Ⓐ Ⓑ Ⓒ Ⓓ Ⓔ	53. Ⓐ Ⓑ Ⓒ Ⓓ Ⓔ	85. Ⓐ Ⓑ Ⓒ Ⓓ Ⓔ	117. Ⓐ Ⓑ Ⓒ Ⓓ Ⓔ
22. Ⓐ Ⓑ Ⓒ Ⓓ Ⓔ	54. Ⓐ Ⓑ Ⓒ Ⓓ Ⓔ	86. Ⓐ Ⓑ Ⓒ Ⓓ Ⓔ	118. Ⓐ Ⓑ Ⓒ Ⓓ Ⓔ
23. Ⓐ Ⓑ Ⓒ Ⓓ Ⓔ	55. Ⓐ Ⓑ Ⓒ Ⓓ Ⓔ	87. Ⓐ Ⓑ Ⓒ Ⓓ Ⓔ	119. Ⓐ Ⓑ Ⓒ Ⓓ Ⓔ
24. Ⓐ Ⓑ Ⓒ Ⓓ Ⓔ	56. Ⓐ Ⓑ Ⓒ Ⓓ Ⓔ	88. Ⓐ Ⓑ Ⓒ Ⓓ Ⓔ	120. Ⓐ Ⓑ Ⓒ Ⓓ Ⓔ
25. Ⓐ Ⓑ Ⓒ Ⓓ Ⓔ	57. Ⓐ Ⓑ Ⓒ Ⓓ Ⓔ	89. Ⓐ Ⓑ Ⓒ Ⓓ Ⓔ	121. Ⓐ Ⓑ Ⓒ Ⓓ Ⓔ
26. Ⓐ Ⓑ Ⓒ Ⓓ Ⓔ	58. Ⓐ Ⓑ Ⓒ Ⓓ Ⓔ	90. Ⓐ Ⓑ Ⓒ Ⓓ Ⓔ	122. Ⓐ Ⓑ Ⓒ Ⓓ Ⓔ
27. Ⓐ Ⓑ Ⓒ Ⓓ Ⓔ	59. Ⓐ Ⓑ Ⓒ Ⓓ Ⓔ	91. Ⓐ Ⓑ Ⓒ Ⓓ Ⓔ	123. Ⓐ Ⓑ Ⓒ Ⓓ Ⓔ
28. Ⓐ Ⓑ Ⓒ Ⓓ Ⓔ	60. Ⓐ Ⓑ Ⓒ Ⓓ Ⓔ	92. Ⓐ Ⓑ Ⓒ Ⓓ Ⓔ	124. Ⓐ Ⓑ Ⓒ Ⓓ Ⓔ
29. Ⓐ Ⓑ Ⓒ Ⓓ Ⓔ	61. Ⓐ Ⓑ Ⓒ Ⓓ Ⓔ	93. Ⓐ Ⓑ Ⓒ Ⓓ Ⓔ	125. Ⓐ Ⓑ Ⓒ Ⓓ Ⓔ
30. Ⓐ Ⓑ Ⓒ Ⓓ Ⓔ	62. Ⓐ Ⓑ Ⓒ Ⓓ Ⓔ	94. Ⓐ Ⓑ Ⓒ Ⓓ Ⓔ	
31. Ⓐ Ⓑ Ⓒ Ⓓ Ⓔ	63. Ⓐ Ⓑ Ⓒ Ⓓ Ⓔ	95. Ⓐ Ⓑ Ⓒ Ⓓ Ⓔ	
32. Ⓐ Ⓑ Ⓒ Ⓓ Ⓔ	64. Ⓐ Ⓑ Ⓒ Ⓓ Ⓔ	96. Ⓐ Ⓑ Ⓒ Ⓓ Ⓔ	

PART C

1. Ⓐ Ⓑ Ⓒ Ⓓ Ⓔ	15. Ⓐ Ⓑ Ⓒ Ⓓ Ⓔ	29. Ⓐ Ⓑ Ⓒ Ⓓ Ⓔ	43. Ⓐ Ⓑ Ⓒ Ⓓ Ⓔ
2. Ⓐ Ⓑ Ⓒ Ⓓ Ⓔ	16. Ⓐ Ⓑ Ⓒ Ⓓ Ⓔ	30. Ⓐ Ⓑ Ⓒ Ⓓ Ⓔ	44. Ⓐ Ⓑ Ⓒ Ⓓ Ⓔ
3. Ⓐ Ⓑ Ⓒ Ⓓ Ⓔ	17. Ⓐ Ⓑ Ⓒ Ⓓ Ⓔ	31. Ⓐ Ⓑ Ⓒ Ⓓ Ⓔ	45. Ⓐ Ⓑ Ⓒ Ⓓ Ⓔ
4. Ⓐ Ⓑ Ⓒ Ⓓ Ⓔ	18. Ⓐ Ⓑ Ⓒ Ⓓ Ⓔ	32. Ⓐ Ⓑ Ⓒ Ⓓ Ⓔ	46. Ⓐ Ⓑ Ⓒ Ⓓ Ⓔ
5. Ⓐ Ⓑ Ⓒ Ⓓ Ⓔ	19. Ⓐ Ⓑ Ⓒ Ⓓ Ⓔ	33. Ⓐ Ⓑ Ⓒ Ⓓ Ⓔ	47. Ⓐ Ⓑ Ⓒ Ⓓ Ⓔ
6. Ⓐ Ⓑ Ⓒ Ⓓ Ⓔ	20. Ⓐ Ⓑ Ⓒ Ⓓ Ⓔ	34. Ⓐ Ⓑ Ⓒ Ⓓ Ⓔ	48. Ⓐ Ⓑ Ⓒ Ⓓ Ⓔ
7. Ⓐ Ⓑ Ⓒ Ⓓ Ⓔ	21. Ⓐ Ⓑ Ⓒ Ⓓ Ⓔ	35. Ⓐ Ⓑ Ⓒ Ⓓ Ⓔ	49. Ⓐ Ⓑ Ⓒ Ⓓ Ⓔ
8. Ⓐ Ⓑ Ⓒ Ⓓ Ⓔ	22. Ⓐ Ⓑ Ⓒ Ⓓ Ⓔ	36. Ⓐ Ⓑ Ⓒ Ⓓ Ⓔ	50. Ⓐ Ⓑ Ⓒ Ⓓ Ⓔ
9. Ⓐ Ⓑ Ⓒ Ⓓ Ⓔ	23. Ⓐ Ⓑ Ⓒ Ⓓ Ⓔ	37. Ⓐ Ⓑ Ⓒ Ⓓ Ⓔ	51. Ⓐ Ⓑ Ⓒ Ⓓ Ⓔ
10. Ⓐ Ⓑ Ⓒ Ⓓ Ⓔ	24. Ⓐ Ⓑ Ⓒ Ⓓ Ⓔ	38. Ⓐ Ⓑ Ⓒ Ⓓ Ⓔ	52. Ⓐ Ⓑ Ⓒ Ⓓ Ⓔ
11. Ⓐ Ⓑ Ⓒ Ⓓ Ⓔ	25. Ⓐ Ⓑ Ⓒ Ⓓ Ⓔ	39. Ⓐ Ⓑ Ⓒ Ⓓ Ⓔ	53. Ⓐ Ⓑ Ⓒ Ⓓ Ⓔ
12. Ⓐ Ⓑ Ⓒ Ⓓ Ⓔ	26. Ⓐ Ⓑ Ⓒ Ⓓ Ⓔ	40. Ⓐ Ⓑ Ⓒ Ⓓ Ⓔ	54. Ⓐ Ⓑ Ⓒ Ⓓ Ⓔ
13. Ⓐ Ⓑ Ⓒ Ⓓ Ⓔ	27. Ⓐ Ⓑ Ⓒ Ⓓ Ⓔ	41. Ⓐ Ⓑ Ⓒ Ⓓ Ⓔ	55. Ⓐ Ⓑ Ⓒ Ⓓ Ⓔ
14. Ⓐ Ⓑ Ⓒ Ⓓ Ⓔ	28. Ⓐ Ⓑ Ⓒ Ⓓ Ⓔ	42. Ⓐ Ⓑ Ⓒ Ⓓ Ⓔ	

PART A—CLERICAL ABILITY

Sample Questions

There are four kinds of questions in Part A. Each kind of question has its own set of directions, and each portion of the part is timed separately. The four kinds of questions are:

Sequencing	3 minutes,	20 questions
Comparisons	5 minutes,	30 questions
Spelling	3 minutes,	20 questions
Computations	8 minutes,	15 questions

Directions for sequencing questions: For each question there is a name, number, or code in a box at the left and four other names or codes in alphabetical or numerical order at the right. Find the correct space for the boxed name or number so that it will be in alphabetical and/or numerical order with the others and mark the letter of that space on your answer sheet.

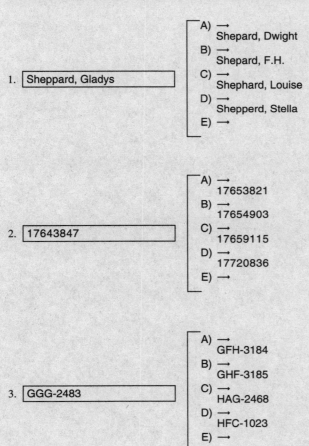

1. Sheppard, Gladys

A) →
Shepard, Dwight
B) →
Shepard, F.H.
C) →
Shephard, Louise
D) →
Shepperd, Stella
E) →

2. 17643847

A) →
17653821
B) →
17654903
C) →
17659115
D) →
17720836
E) →

3. GGG-2483

A) →
GFH-3184
B) →
GHF-3185
C) →
HAG-2468
D) →
HFC-1023
E) →

Directions for comparisons questions: In each line across the page there are three names, addresses, or codes that are very much alike. Compare the three and decide which ones are EXACTLY alike. On your answer sheet, mark:

A   if **ALL THREE** names, addresses, or codes are exactly **ALIKE**
B   if only the **FIRST** and **SECOND** names, addresses, or codes are exactly **ALIKE**
C   if only the **FIRST** and **THIRD** names, addresses, or codes are exactly **ALIKE**
D   if only the **SECOND** and **THIRD** names, addresses, or codes are exactly **ALIKE**
E   if **ALL THREE** names, addresses, or codes are **DIFFERENT**

4. H. Merritt Audubon	H. Merriott Audubon	H. Merritt Audubon
5. 2395890	2395890	2395890
6. 3418 W. 42nd St.	3418 W. 42nd Ave.	3148 W. 42nd Ave.

Directions for spelling questions: Find the correct spelling of the word and darken the appropriate space on the answer sheet. If none of the spellings is correct, darken space D.

7.   (A) exceed
     (B) excede
     (C) exseed
     (D) none of these

8.   (A) maneuver
     (B) manuver
     (C) manuever
     (D) none of these

9.   (A) corellation
     (B) corrolation
     (C) corralation
     (D) none of these

Directions for computations questions: Perform the computation as indicated in the question and find the answer among the list of alternative responses. If the correct answer is not given among the choices, mark E.

10. $2\overline{)142}$ (A) 70
                (B) 72
                (C) 74
                (D) 76
                (E) none of these

11. 25   (A) 5
    -10 (B) 10
                (C) 15
                (D) 20
                (E) none of these

12. 18   (A) 108
    $\times\ 6$ (B) 116
                (C) 118
                (D) 124
                (E) none of these

Sample Answer Sheet

1 Ⓐ Ⓑ Ⓒ Ⓓ Ⓔ   4 Ⓐ Ⓑ Ⓒ Ⓓ Ⓔ   7 Ⓐ Ⓑ Ⓒ Ⓓ Ⓔ   10 Ⓐ Ⓑ Ⓒ Ⓓ Ⓔ
2 Ⓐ Ⓑ Ⓒ Ⓓ Ⓔ   5 Ⓐ Ⓑ Ⓒ Ⓓ Ⓔ   8 Ⓐ Ⓑ Ⓒ Ⓓ Ⓔ   11 Ⓐ Ⓑ Ⓒ Ⓓ Ⓔ
3 Ⓐ Ⓑ Ⓒ Ⓓ Ⓔ   6 Ⓐ Ⓑ Ⓒ Ⓓ Ⓔ   9 Ⓐ Ⓑ Ⓒ Ⓓ Ⓔ   12 Ⓐ Ⓑ Ⓒ Ⓓ Ⓔ

Correct Answers to Sample Questions

1 Ⓐ Ⓑ Ⓒ ● Ⓔ   4 Ⓐ Ⓑ ● Ⓓ Ⓔ   7 ● Ⓑ Ⓒ Ⓓ Ⓔ   10 Ⓐ Ⓑ Ⓒ Ⓓ ●
2 ● Ⓑ Ⓒ Ⓓ Ⓔ   5 ● Ⓑ Ⓒ Ⓓ Ⓔ   8 ● Ⓑ Ⓒ Ⓓ Ⓔ   11 Ⓐ Ⓑ ● Ⓓ Ⓔ
3 Ⓐ ● Ⓒ Ⓓ Ⓔ   6 Ⓐ Ⓑ Ⓒ Ⓓ ●   9 Ⓐ Ⓑ Ⓒ ● Ⓔ   12 ● Ⓑ Ⓒ Ⓓ Ⓔ

Sequencing

Time: 3 Minutes. 20 Questions.

Directions: *For each question there is a name, number, or code in a box at the left and four other names, numbers, or codes in alphabetical or numerical order at the right. Find the correct space for the boxed name or number so that it will be in alphabetical and/or numerical order with the others and mark the letter of that space on your answer sheet.*

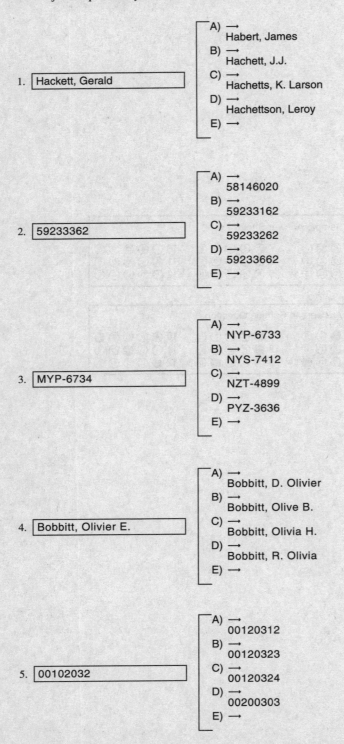

1. | Hackett, Gerald |

A) →
  Habert, James
B) →
  Hachett, J.J.
C) →
  Hachetts, K. Larson
D) →
  Hachettson, Leroy
E) →

2. | 59233362 |

A) →
  58146020
B) →
  59233162
C) →
  59233262
D) →
  59233662
E) →

3. | MYP-6734 |

A) →
  NYP-6733
B) →
  NYS-7412
C) →
  NZT-4899
D) →
  PYZ-3636
E) →

4. | Bobbitt, Olivier E. |

A) →
  Bobbitt, D. Olivier
B) →
  Bobbitt, Olive B.
C) →
  Bobbitt, Olivia H.
D) →
  Bobbitt, R. Olivia
E) →

5. | 00102032 |

A) →
  00120312
B) →
  00120323
C) →
  00120324
D) →
  00200303
E) →

6. | LPD-6100 |

A) →
LPD-5865
B) →
LPD-6001
C) →
LPD-6101
D) →
LPD-6106
E) →

7. | Vanstory, George |

A) →
Vanover, Eva
B) →
VanSwinderen, Floyd
C) →
VanSyckle, Harry
D) →
Vanture, Laurence
E) →

8. | Fitzsimmons, Hugh |

A) →
Fitts, Harold
B) →
Fitzgerald, June
C) →
FitzGibbon, Junius
D) →
FitzSimons, Martin
E) →

9. | 01066010 |

A) →
01006040
B) →
01006051
C) →
01016053
D) →
01016060
E) →

10. | AAZ-2687 |

A) →
AAA-2132
B) →
AAS-4623
C) →
ASA-3216
D) →
ASZ-5490
E) →

11. | Pawlowicz, Ruth M. |

A) →
Pawalek, Edward
B) →
Pawelek, Flora G.
C) →
Pawlowski, Joan M.
D) →
Pawtowski, Wanda
E) →

12. NCD-7834

A) →
NBJ-4682
B) →
NBT-5066
C) →
NCD-7710
D) →
NCD-7868
E) →

13. 36270013

A) →
36260006
B) →
36270000
C) →
36270030
D) →
36670012
E) →

14. Freedenburg, C. Erma

A) →
Freedenberg, Emerson
B) →
Freedenberg, Erma
C) →
Freedenberg, Erma E.
D) →
Freedinberg, Erma F.
E) →

15. Prouty, Martha

A) →
Proutey, Margaret
B) →
Proutey, Maude
C) →
Prouty, Myra
D) →
Prouty, Naomi
E) →

16. 58006021

A) →
58006130
B) →
58097222
C) →
59000599
D) →
59909000
E) →

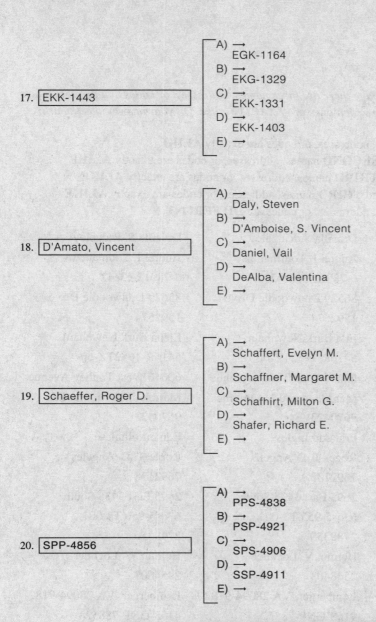

17. EKK-1443

   A) →
      EGK-1164
   B) →
      EKG-1329
   C) →
      EKK-1331
   D) →
      EKK-1403
   E) →

18. D'Amato, Vincent

   A) →
      Daly, Steven
   B) →
      D'Amboise, S. Vincent
   C) →
      Daniel, Vail
   D) →
      DeAlba, Valentina
   E) →

19. Schaeffer, Roger D.

   A) →
      Schaffert, Evelyn M.
   B) →
      Schaffner, Margaret M.
   C) →
      Schafhirt, Milton G.
   D) →
      Shafer, Richard E.
   E) →

20. SPP-4856

   A) →
      PPS-4838
   B) →
      PSP-4921
   C) →
      SPS-4906
   D) →
      SSP-4911
   E) →

END OF SEQUENCING QUESTIONS

Comparisons

Time: 5 Minutes. 30 Questions.

Directions: *In each line across the page there are three names, addresses, or codes that are very much alike. Compare the three and decide which ones are EXACTLY alike. On your answer sheet, mark:*

A   if **ALL THREE** names, addresses, or codes are exactly **ALIKE**
B   if only the **FIRST** and **SECOND** names, addresses, or codes are exactly **ALIKE**
C   if only the **FIRST** and **THIRD** names, addresses, or codes are exactly **ALIKE**
D   if only the **SECOND** and **THIRD** names, addresses, or codes are exactly **ALIKE**
E   if **ALL THREE** names, addresses, or codes are **DIFFERENT**

21.	Drusilla S. Ridgeley	Drusilla S. Ridgeley	Drusilla S. Ridgeley
22.	Andrei I. Toumantzev	Andrei I. Tourmantzev	Andrei I. Toumantzov
23.	6-78912-e3e42	6-78912-3e3e42	6-78912-e3e42
24.	86529 Dunwoodie Drive	86529 Dunwoodie Drive	85629 Dunwoodie Drive
25.	1592514	1592574	1592574
26.	Ella Burk Newham	Ella Burk Newnham	Elena Burk Newnham
27.	5416R-1952TZ-op	5416R-1952TZ-op	5416R-1952TZ-op
28.	60646 West Touhy Avenue	60646 West Touhy Avenue	60646 West Touhey Avenue
29.	Mardikian & Moore, Inc.	Mardikian and Moore, Inc.	Mardikian & Moore, Inc.
30.	9670243	9670423	9670423
31.	Eduardo Ingles	Eduardo Inglese	Eduardo Inglese
32.	Roger T. DeAngelis	Roger T. D'Angelis	Roger T. DeAngeles
33.	7692138	7692138	7692138
34.	2695 East 3435 South	2695 East 3435 South	2695 East 3435 South
35.	63qs5-95YT3-001	63qs5-95YT3-001	63qs5-95YT3-001
36.	2789350	2789350	2798350
37.	Helmut V. Lochner	Helmut V. Lockner	Helmut W. Lochner
38.	2454803	2548403	2454803
39.	Lemberger, WA 28094-9182	Lemberger, VA 28094-9182	Lemberger, VA 28094-9182
40.	4168-GNP-78852	4168-GNP-78852	4168-GNP-78852
41.	Yoshihito Saito	Yoshihito Saito	Yoshihito Saito
42.	5927681	5927861	5927681
43.	O'Reilly Bay, LA 56212	O'Reillys Bay, LA 56212	O'Reilly Bay, LA 56212
44.	Francis Ransdell	Frances Ramsdell	Francis Ramsdell
45.	5634-OotV5a-16867	5634-Ootv5a-16867	5634-Ootv5a-16867
46.	Dolores Mollicone	Dolores Mollicone	Doloras Mollicone
47.	David C. Routzon	David E. Routzon	David C. Routzron
48.	8932 Shimabui Hwy.	8932 Shimabui Hwy.	8932 Shimabui Hwy.
49.	6177396	6177936	6177396
50.	A8987-B73245	A8987-B73245	A8987-B73245

END OF COMPARISONS QUESTIONS

Spelling

Time: 3 Minutes. 20 Questions.

Directions: *Find the correct spelling of the word and darken the appropriate space on your answer sheet. If none of the spellings is correct, darken space D.*

51. (A) anticipate
     (B) antisipate
     (C) anticapate
     (D) none of these

52. (A) similiar
     (B) simmilar
     (C) similar
     (D) none of these

53. (A) sufficiantly
     (B) suficeintly
     (C) sufficiently
     (D) none of these

54. (A) intelligence
     (B) inteligence
     (C) intellegence
     (D) none of these

55. (A) referance
     (B) referrence
     (C) referense
     (D) none of these

56. (A) conscious
     (B) consious
     (C) conscius
     (D) none of these

57. (A) paralell
     (B) parellel
     (C) parellell
     (D) none of these

58. (A) abundence
     (B) abundance
     (C) abundants
     (D) none of these

59. (A) corregated
     (B) corrigated
     (C) corrugated
     (D) none of these

60. (A) accumalation
    (B) accumulation
    (C) accumullation
    (D) none of these

61. (A) resonance
    (B) resonence
    (C) resonnance
    (D) none of these

62. (A) benaficial
    (B) benefitial
    (C) beneficial
    (D) none of these

63. (A) spesifically
    (B) specificially
    (C) specifically
    (D) none of these

64. (A) elemanate
    (B) elimenate
    (C) elliminate
    (D) none of these

65. (A) collosal
    (B) colosal
    (C) collossal
    (D) none of these

66. (A) auxillary
    (B) auxilliary
    (C) auxiliary
    (D) none of these

67. (A) inimitable
    (B) inimitible
    (C) inimatable
    (D) none of these

68. (A) disapearance
    (B) dissapearance
    (C) disappearence
    (D) none of these

69. (A) appelate
    (B) appellate
    (C) apellate
    (D) none of these

70. (A) esential
    (B) essential
    (C) essencial
    (D) none of these

END OF SPELLING QUESTIONS

Computations

Time: 8 Minutes. 15 Questions.

Directions: *Perform the computation as indicated in the question and find the answer among the list of alternative responses. If the correct answer is not given among the choices, mark E.*

71. 83
   −56
- (A) 23
- (B) 29
- (C) 33
- (D) 37
- (E) none of these

72. 15
  +17
- (A) 22
- (B) 32
- (C) 39
- (D) 42
- (E) none of these

73. 32
  ×7
- (A) 224
- (B) 234
- (C) 324
- (D) 334
- (E) none of these

74. 39
  ×2
- (A) 77
- (B) 78
- (C) 79
- (D) 81
- (E) none of these

75. 43
  −15
- (A) 23
- (B) 32
- (C) 33
- (D) 35
- (E) none of these

76. 50
  +49
- (A) 89
- (B) 90
- (C) 99
- (D) 109
- (E) none of these

77. $6\overline{)366}$
- (A) 11
- (B) 31
- (C) 36
- (D) 66
- (E) none of these

78. 38
  ×3
- (A) 111
- (B) 113
- (C) 115
- (D) 117
- (E) none of these

79. 19   (A) 20
     +21   (B) 30
               (C) 40
               (D) 50
               (E) none of these

80. 13   (A) 5
     − 6   (B) 7
               (C) 9
               (D) 11
               (E) none of these

81. 6√180   (A) 29
               (B) 31
               (C) 33
               (D) 39
               (E) none of these

82. 10   (A) 0
     × 1   (B) 1
               (C) 10
               (D) 100
               (E) none of these

83. 7√287   (A) 21
               (B) 27
               (C) 31
               (D) 37
               (E) none of these

84. 12   (A) 21
     +11   (B) 22
               (C) 23
               (D) 24
               (E) none of these

85. 85   (A) 19
     −64   (B) 21
               (C) 29
               (D) 31
               (E) none of these

END OF COMPUTATIONS QUESTIONS

END OF PART A

PART B—VERBAL ABILITY

Sample Questions

There are four kinds of questions in Part B. Each kind of question has its own set of directions, but the portions containing the different kinds of questions are not separately timed. There are 55 questions in Part B, and candidates are allowed 50 minutes to complete the entire part. The four kinds of questions are:

Following Written Instructions	20 questions
Grammar/Punctuation	20 questions
Vocabulary	15 questions altogether
Reading Comprehension	

Directions for following written instructions: These questions test your ability to follow instructions. Each question directs you to mark a specific number and letter combination on your answer sheet. The questions require your total concentration because the answers that you are instructed to mark are, for the most part, NOT in numerical sequence (i.e., you would not use Number 1 on your answer sheet to answer Question 1; Number 2 for Question 2; etc.). Instead, you must mark the number and space specifically designated in each test question.

1. Look at the numbers below. Draw one line under the lowest number. Now, on your answer sheet, find that number and darken letter C for that number.

    4   2   3   6

2. Circle the middle letter in the line below. Now, on your answer sheet, find the number 3 and darken the space for the letter you just circled.

    F   A   D   B   E

3. Subtract 8 from 9 and write your answer on the line below. Now, on your answer sheet, darken space D for the space of the number you wrote.

    _____

The remaining questions are to be answered on the answer sheet in numerical sequence: Question 4 is to be answered in Space 4, Question 5 in Space 5, and so forth.

Directions for Grammar/Punctuation Questions: Each question consists of a sentence written in four different ways. Choose the sentence that is most appropriate with respect to grammar, usage, and punctuation, so as to be suitable for a business letter or report, and darken its letter on your answer sheet.

4. (A) Your pen is different from mine.
    (B) Your pen is different to mine.
    (C) Your pen is different than mine.
    (D) Your pen is different with mine.

Directions for Vocabulary Questions: Each question consists of a sentence containing a word in boldface type. Choose the best meaning for the word in boldface type and darken its letter on your answer sheet.

5. A passing grade on the special exam may **exempt** the applicant from the experience requirements for that job. **Exempt** most nearly means

(A) prohibit
(B) excuse
(C) subject
(D) specify

Directions for Reading Comprehension Questions: Read each paragraph and answer the question that follows it by darkening the letter of the correct answer on your answer sheet.

6. The work goals of an agency can best be reached if the employees understand and agree with these goals. One way to gain such understanding and agreement is for management to encourage and seriously consider suggestions from employees in the setting of agency goals.

The paragraph best supports the statement that understanding and agreement with agency goals can be gained by

(A) allowing the employees to set agency goals
(B) reaching agency goals quickly
(C) legislative review of agency operations
(D) employee participation in setting agency goals

Sample Answer Sheet

1. Ⓐ Ⓑ Ⓒ Ⓓ Ⓔ   3. Ⓐ Ⓑ Ⓒ Ⓓ Ⓔ   5. Ⓐ Ⓑ Ⓒ Ⓓ Ⓔ
2. Ⓐ Ⓑ Ⓒ Ⓓ Ⓔ   4. Ⓐ Ⓑ Ⓒ Ⓓ Ⓔ   6. Ⓐ Ⓑ Ⓒ Ⓓ Ⓔ

Correct Answers to Sample Questions

1. Ⓐ Ⓑ Ⓒ ● Ⓔ   3. Ⓐ Ⓑ Ⓒ ● Ⓔ   5. Ⓐ ● Ⓒ Ⓓ Ⓔ
2. Ⓐ Ⓑ ● Ⓓ Ⓔ   4. ● Ⓑ Ⓒ Ⓓ Ⓔ   6. Ⓐ Ⓑ Ⓒ ● Ⓔ

Part B

Time: 50 Minutes. 55 Questions.

Directions: *Questions 1–20 test your ability to follow instructions. Each question directs you to mark a specific number and letter combination on your answer sheet. The questions require your total concentration because the answers that you are instructed to mark are, for the most part, NOT in numerical sequence (i.e., you would not use Number 1 on your answer sheet to answer Question 1; Number 2 for Question 2; etc.). Instead, you must mark the number and space specifically designated in each test question.*

1. Look at the letters below. Draw a circle around the letter that comes first in the alphabet. Now, on your answer sheet, find Number 12 and darken the space for the letter you just circled.

    E   G   D   Z   B   F

2. Draw a line under the odd number below that is more than 5 but less than 10. Find this number on your answer sheet and darken space E.

    8   10   5   6   11   9

3. Divide the number 16 by 4 and write your answer on the line below. Now find this number on your answer sheet and darken space A.

    _____

4. Write the letter C on the line next to the left hand number below. Now, on your answer sheet, darken the space for the number-letter combination you see.

    5 _____   19 _____   7 _____

5. If in any week Wednesday comes before Tuesday, write the number 15 on the line below. If not, write the number 18. Now, on your answer sheet, darken the letter A for the number you just wrote.

    _____

6. Count the number of Bs in the line below and write that number at the end of the line. Now, on your answer sheet, darken the letter D for the number you wrote.

    A   D   A   E   B   D   C   A _____

7. Write the letter B on the line with the highest number. Now, on your answer sheet, darken the number-letter combination that appears on that line.

    16 _____   9 _____   20 _____   11 _____

8. If the product of 6×4 is greater than the product of 8×3, write the letter E on the line below. If not, write the letter C. Now, on your answer sheet find number 8 and darken the space for the letter you just wrote.

    _____

9. Write the number 2 in the largest circle below. Now, on your answer sheet, darken the space for the number-letter combination in that circle.

_____A   _____D   _____C   _____B

10. Write the letter D on the line next to the number that is the sum of 7 + 4 + 4. Now, on your answer sheet, darken the space for that number-letter combination.

13 _____   14 _____   15 _____   16 _____   17 _____

11. If 5 × 5 equals 25 and 5 + 5 equals 10, write the number 17 on the line below. If not, write the number 10. Now, on your answer sheet, darken space E for the number you just wrote.

_____

12. Circle the second letter below. On the line beside that letter write the number that represents the number of days in a week. Now, on your answer sheet, darken the space for that number-letter combination.

_____ C   _____ D   _____ B   _____ E

13. If a triangle has more angles than a rectangle, write the number 13 in the circle below. If not, write the number 14 in the square. Now, on your answer sheet, darken the space for the number-letter combination in the figure that you just wrote in.

_____A   _____C   _____E

14. Count the number of Bs below and write that number at the end of the line. Subtract 2 from that number. Now, on your answer sheet, darken space E for the number that represents 2 less than the number of Bs in the line.

B E A D E C C B B B A E B D_____

15. The numbers below represent morning pick-up times from neighborhood letter boxes. Draw a line under the number that represents the latest pick-up time. Now, on your answer sheet, darken space D for the number that is the same as the "minutes" of the time that you underlined.

9:19   10:16   10:10

16. If a person who is 6 feet tall is taller than a person who is 5 feet tall and if a pillow is softer than a rock, darken space 11A on your answer sheet. If not, darken space 6B.

17. Write the fourth letter of the alphabet on the line next to the third number below. Now, on your answer sheet, darken that number-letter combination.

10 _____   19 _____   13 _____   4 _____

18. Write the letter B in the box containing the next to smallest number. On your answer sheet, darken the space for that number-letter combination.

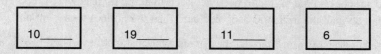

| 10_____ | 19_____ | 11_____ | 6_____ |

19. Directly below you will see three boxes and three words. Write the third letter of the first word on the line in the second box. Now, on your answer sheet, darken the space for that number-letter combination.

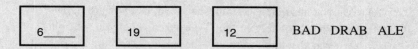

| 6_____ | 19_____ | 12_____ | BAD   DRAB   ALE |

20. Count the number of points on the figure below. If there are five or more points, darken the space for 6E on your answer sheet. If there are fewer than five points, darken 6A.

Directions: Each question from 21 through 40 consists of a sentence written in four different ways. Choose the sentence that is most appropriate with respect to grammar, usage, and punctuation, so as to be suitable for a business letter or report and darken its letter on your answer sheet. Answer each question in the answer space with the corresponding number.

21. (A) Double parking is when you park your car alongside one that is already having been parked.
    (B) When one double parks, you park your car alongside one that is already parked.
    (C) Double parking is parking alongside a car already parked.
    (D) To double park is alongside a car already parked.

22. (A) This is entirely among you and he.
    (B) This is completely among him and you.
    (C) This is between you and him.
    (D) This is between he and you.

23. (A) As I said, "neither of them are guilty."
    (B) As I said, "neither of them are guilty".
    (C) As I said, "neither of them is guilty."
    (D) As I said, neither of them is guilty.

24. (A) I think that they will promote whoever has the best record.
    (B) The firm would have liked to have promoted all employees with good records.
    (C) Such of them that have the best records have excellent prospects of promotion.
    (D) I feel sure they will give the promotion to whomever has the best record.

25. (A) The receptionist must answer courteously the questions of all them callers.
    (B) The receptionist must answer courteously the questions what are asked by the callers.
    (C) There would have been no trouble if the receptionist had have always answered courteously.
    (D) The receptionist should answer courteously the questions of all callers.

26. (A) Since the report lacked the needed information, it was of no use to them.
    (B) This report was useless to them because there were no needed information in it.
    (C) Since the report did not contain the needed information, it was not real useful to them.
    (D) Being that the report lacked the needed information, they could not use it.

27. (A) The company had hardly declared the dividend till the notices were prepared for mailing.
    (B) They had no sooner declared the dividend when they sent the notices to the stockholders.
    (C) No sooner had the dividend been declared than the notices were prepared for mailing.
    (D) Scarcely had the dividend been declared than the notices were sent out.

28. (A) The supervisors reprimanded the typists, whom she believed had made careless errors.
    (B) The typists would have corrected the errors had they of known that the supervisor would see the report.
    (C) The errors in the typed reports were so numerous that they could hardly be overlooked.
    (D) Many errors were found in the reports which they typed and could not disregard them.

29. (A) "Are you absolutely certain, she asked, that you are right?"
    (B) "Are you absolutely certain," she asked, "that you are right?"
    (C) "Are you absolutely certain," she asked, "That you are right"?
    (D) "Are you absolutely certain", she asked, "That you are right?"

30. (A) He goes only to church on Christmas and Easter.
    (B) He only goes to church on Christmas and Easter.
    (C) He goes to only church on Christmas and Easter.
    (D) He goes to church only on Christmas and Easter.

31. (A) Most all these statements have been supported by persons who are reliable and can be depended upon.
    (B) The persons which have guaranteed these statements are reliable.
    (C) Reliable persons guarantee the facts with regards to the truth of these statements.
    (D) These statements can be depended on, for their truth has been guaranteed by reliable persons.

32. (A) The success of the book pleased both the publisher and authors.
    (B) Both the publisher and they was pleased with the success of the book.
    (C) Neither they or their publisher was disappointed with the success of the book.
    (D) Their publisher was as pleased as they with the success of the book.

33. (A) In reviewing the typists' work reports, the job analyst found records of unusual typing speeds.
    (B) It says in the job analyst's report that some employees type with great speed.
    (C) The job analyst found that, in reviewing the typists' work reports, that some unusual typing speeds had been made.
    (D) In the reports of typists' speeds, the job analyst found some records that are kind of unusual.

34. (A) Every carrier should always have something to throw; not something to throw at the dog but something what will divert its attention.
    (B) Every carrier should have something to throw—not something to throw at the dog but something to divert its attention.
    (C) Every carrier should always carry something to throw not something to throw at the dog but something that will divert it's attention.
    (D) Every carrier should always carry something to throw, not something to throw at the dog, but, something that will divert its' attention.

35. (A) Brown's & Company employees have recently received increases in salary.
    (B) Brown & Company recently increased the salaries of all its employees.
    (C) Recently Brown & Company has increased their employees' salaries.
    (D) Brown & Company have recently increased the salaries of all its employees.

36. (A) If properly addressed, the letter will reach my mother and I.
     (B) The letter had been addressed to myself and my mother.
     (C) I believe the letter was addressed to either my mother or I.
     (D) My mother's name, as well as mine, was on the letter.

37. (A) One of us have to make the reply before tomorrow.
     (B) Making the reply before tomorrow will have to be done by one of us.
     (C) One of us has to reply before tomorrow.
     (D) Anyone has to reply before tomorrow.

38. (A) You have got to get rid of some of these people if you expect to have the quality of the work improve.
     (B) The quality of the work would improve if they would leave fewer people do it.
     (C) I believe it would be desirable to have fewer persons doing this work.
     (D) If you had planned on employing fewer people than this to do the work, this situation would not have arose.

39. (A) The paper we use for this purpose must be light, glossy, and stand hard usage as well.
     (B) Only a light and a glossy, but durable, paper must be used for this purpose.
     (C) For this purpose, we want a paper that is light, glossy, but that will stand hard wear.
     (D) For this purpose, paper that is light, glossy, and durable is essential.

40. (A) This letter, together with the reports, are to be sent to the postmaster.
     (B) The reports, together with this letter, is to be sent to the postmaster.
     (C) The reports and this letter is to be sent to the postmaster.
     (D) This letter, together with the reports, is to be sent to the postmaster.

*Directions: Each question from 41 through 48 consists of a sentence containing a word in **boldface** type. Choose the best meaning for the word in **boldface** type and darken its letter on your answer sheet. Answer each question in the answer space with the corresponding number.*

41. Please consult your office **manual** to learn the proper operation of our copying machine. **Manual** means most nearly

     (A) labor
     (B) handbook
     (C) typewriter
     (D) handle

42. There is a specified punishment for each **infraction** of the rules. **Infraction** means most nearly

     (A) violation
     (B) use
     (C) interpretation
     (D) part

43. The order was **rescinded** within the week. **Rescinded** means most nearly

     (A) revised
     (B) canceled
     (C) misinterpreted
     (D) confirmed

44. If you have a question, please raise your hand to **summon** the test proctor. **Summon** means most nearly

    (A) ticket
    (B) fine
    (C) give
    (D) call

45. We dared not prosecute the terrorist for fear of **reprisal. Reprisal** means most nearly

    (A) retaliation
    (B) advantage
    (C) warning
    (D) denial

46. The increased use of dictation machines has severely **reduced** the need for office stenographers. **Reduced** means most nearly

    (A) enlarged
    (B) cut out
    (C) lessened
    (D) expanded

47. Frequent use of marijuana may **impair** your judgment. **Impair** means most nearly

    (A) weaken
    (B) conceal
    (C) improve
    (D) expose

48. It is altogether **fitting** that the parent discipline the child. **Fitting** means most nearly

    (A) illegal
    (B) bad practice
    (C) appropriate
    (D) required

Directions: *For questions 49 through 55, read each paragraph and answer the question that follows it by darkening the letter of the correct answer on your answer sheet. Answer each question in the answer space with the corresponding number.*

49. A survey to determine the subjects that have helped students most in their jobs shows that typewriting leads all other subjects in the business group. It also leads among the subjects college students consider most valuable and would take again if they were to return to high school.

    The paragraph best supports the statement that

    (A) the ability to type is an asset in business and in school
    (B) students who return to night school take typing
    (C) students with a knowledge of typing do superior work in college
    (D) success in business is assured those who can type

50. Telegrams should be clear, concise, and brief. Omit all unnecessary words. The parts of speech most often used in telegrams are nouns, verbs, adjectives, and adverbs. If possible, do without pronouns, prepositions, articles, and copulative verbs. Use simple sentences, rather than complex and compound.

The paragraph best supports the statement that in writing telegrams one should always use

(A) common and simple words
(B) only nouns, verbs, adjectives, and adverbs
(C) incomplete sentences
(D) only words essential to the meaning

51. Since the government can spend only what it obtains from the people, and this amount is ultimately limited by their capacity and willingness to pay taxes, it is very important that the people be given full information about the work of the government.

The paragraph best supports the statement that

(A) governmental employees should be trained not only in their own work, but also in how to perform the duties of other employees in their agency
(B) taxation by the government rests upon the consent of the people
(C) the release of full information on the work of the government will increase the efficiency of governmental operations
(D) the work of the government, in recent years, has been restricted because of reduced tax collections.

52. Both the high school and the college should take the responsibility for preparing the student to get a job. Since the ability to write a good application letter is one of the first steps toward this goal, every teacher should be willing to do what he can to help the student learn to write such letters.

The paragraph best supports the statement that

(A) inability to write a good letter often reduces one's job prospects
(B) the major responsibility of the school is to obtain jobs for its students
(C) success is largely a matter of the kind of work the student applies for first
(D) every teacher should teach a course in the writing of application letters

53. Direct lighting is the least satisfactory lighting arrangement. The desk or ceiling light with a reflector that diffuses all the rays downward is sure to cause a glare on the working surface.

The paragraph best supports the statement that direct lighting is least satisfactory as a method of lighting chiefly because

(A) the light is diffused causing eye strain
(B) the shade on the individual desk lamp is not constructed along scientific lines
(C) the working surface is usually obscured by the glare
(D) direct lighting is injurious to the eyes

54. "White collar" is a term used to describe one of the largest groups of workers in American industry and trade. It distinguishes those who work with the pencil and the mind from those who depend on their hands and the machine. It suggests occupations in which physical exertion and handling of materials are not primary features of the job.

The paragraph best supports the statement that "white collar" workers are

(A) not so strong physically as those who work with their hands
(B) those who supervise workers handling materials
(C) all whose work is entirely indoors
(D) not likely to use machines as much as are other groups of workers

55.   In large organizations some standardized, simple, inexpensive method of giving employees information about company policies and rules, as well as specific instructions regarding their duties, is practically essential. This is the purpose of all office manuals of whatever type.

The paragraph best supports the statement that office manuals

(A) are all about the same
(B) should be simple enough for the average employee to understand
(C) are necessary to large organizations
(D) act as constant reminders to the employee of his duties

END OF PART B

PART C—STENOGRAPHY

Sample Dictation

Have someone dictate the sample passage below to you. It should take 3 minutes. Take notes on your own paper.

Directions to person dictating: This practice dictation should be dictated at the rate of 80 words a minute. Do not dictate the punctuation except for periods, but dictate with the expression the punctuation indicates. Use a watch with a second hand to enable you to read the exercises at the proper speed.

Exactly on a minute start dictating.	Finish reading each two lines at the number of seconds indicated below.
I realize that this practice dictation is not a part of the examination	10
proper and is not to be scored. (Period) The work of preventing and correcting	20
physical defects in children is becoming more effective as a result of change	30
in the attitude of many parents. (Period) In order to bring about this change,	40
parents have been invited to visit the schools when their children are being examined	50
and to discuss the treatment necessary for the correction of defects. (Period)	1 min.
There is a distinct value in having a parent see that his or her child is not the	10
only one who needs attention. (Period) Otherwise a few parents might feel that they	20
were being criticized by having the defects of their children singled out for medical	30
treatment. (Period) The special classes that have been set up have shown the value of	40
the scientific knowledge that has been applied in the treatment of children. (Period)	50
In these classes the children have been taught to exercise by a trained teacher	2 min.
under medical supervision. (Period) The hours of the school day have been divided	10
between school work and physical activity that helps not only to correct their defects	20

but also to improve their general physical
condition. (Period) This method of treatment   30

has been found to be very effective
except for those who have severe medical   40

defects. (Period) Most parents now see
how desirable it is to have these classes   50

that have been set up in the regular
school system to meet special needs. (Period)   3 min.

After dictating the practice, pause for 15 seconds to permit the competitor to complete notetaking. Then continue in accordance with the directions. After the sample dictation transcript has been completed, dictate the test on page 161.

Sample Dictation Transcript Sheet

The transcript below is part of the material that was dictated to you for practice, except that many of the words have been left out. From your notes, you are to tell what the missing words are. Proceed as follows:

Compare your notes with the transcript and, when you come to a blank in the transcript, decide what word (or words) belongs there. For example, you will find that the word "practice" belongs in blank number 1. Look at the word list to see whether you can find the same word there. Notice what letter (A, B, C, or D) is printed beside it, and write that letter in the blank. For example, the word "practice" is listed, followed by the letter B. We have already written B in blank number 1 to show you how you are to record your choice. Now decide what belongs in each of the other blanks. (You may also write the word or words, or the shorthand for them, if you wish.) The same word may belong in more than one blank. If the exact answer is not listed, write E in the blank.

ALPHABETIC WORD LIST
Write E if the answer is **not** listed.

about—B	paper—B
against—C	parents—B
attitude—A	part—C
being—D	physical—D
childhood—B	portion—D
children—A	practical—A
correcting—C	practice—B
doctors—B	preliminary—D
effective—D	preventing—B
efficient—A	procedure—A
examination—A	proper—C
examining—C	reason for—A
for—B	result—B
health—B	result of—C
mothers—C	schools—C
never—C	to be—C
not—D	to prevent—A

TRANSCRIPT

I realize that this <u>B</u> dictation is ___
                                   1   2
a ___ of the ____ ____ and is ___ ___
3   4   5   6   7
scored.

The work ___ and ___ ___ defects
          8   9   10
in ___ is becoming more ___ as a ___
11   12   13
a change in the ___ of many ___.
              14   15

ALPHABETIC WORD LIST		TRANSCRIPT (Continued)

ALPHABETIC WORD LIST

Write E if the answer is **not** listed.

all—A	reducing—A
at—C	satisfied—D
bring—A	say—C
collection—B	see—B
correction—C	soon—C
discuss—C	their—D
during—D	to discover—A
friend—A	to discuss—D
indicated—C	to endorse—C
insisted—D	to visit—B
is—B	treatments—A
is not—A	understand—D
know—A	undertake—B
knows—D	virtue—D
needed—B	visit—A
promote—B	volume—B
recognizing—D	young—C

TRANSCRIPT (Continued)

In order to ___ ___ this change,
    16   17
parents have been invited ____ the
                            18
schools when ___ children are being
                19
examined and ___ the ___ necessary for
            20   21
the ___ of defects. There is a distinct
    22
___ in having a parent ___ that his or her
23   24
child ___ the only one who needs
        25
attention....(The rest of the sample

dictation is not transcribed here.)

Answer Sheet for Sample Dictation

1. Ⓐ Ⓑ Ⓒ Ⓓ Ⓔ   8. Ⓐ Ⓑ Ⓒ Ⓓ Ⓔ   14. Ⓐ Ⓑ Ⓒ Ⓓ Ⓔ   20. Ⓐ Ⓑ Ⓒ Ⓓ Ⓔ
2. Ⓐ Ⓑ Ⓒ Ⓓ Ⓔ   9. Ⓐ Ⓑ Ⓒ Ⓓ Ⓔ   15. Ⓐ Ⓑ Ⓒ Ⓓ Ⓔ   21. Ⓐ Ⓑ Ⓒ Ⓓ Ⓔ
3. Ⓐ Ⓑ Ⓒ Ⓓ Ⓔ   10. Ⓐ Ⓑ Ⓒ Ⓓ Ⓔ   16. Ⓐ Ⓑ Ⓒ Ⓓ Ⓔ   22. Ⓐ Ⓑ Ⓒ Ⓓ Ⓔ
4. Ⓐ Ⓑ Ⓒ Ⓓ Ⓔ   11. Ⓐ Ⓑ Ⓒ Ⓓ Ⓔ   17. Ⓐ Ⓑ Ⓒ Ⓓ Ⓔ   23. Ⓐ Ⓑ Ⓒ Ⓓ Ⓔ
5. Ⓐ Ⓑ Ⓒ Ⓓ Ⓔ   12. Ⓐ Ⓑ Ⓒ Ⓓ Ⓔ   18. Ⓐ Ⓑ Ⓒ Ⓓ Ⓔ   24. Ⓐ Ⓑ Ⓒ Ⓓ Ⓔ
6. Ⓐ Ⓑ Ⓒ Ⓓ Ⓔ   13. Ⓐ Ⓑ Ⓒ Ⓓ Ⓔ   19. Ⓐ Ⓑ Ⓒ Ⓓ Ⓔ   25. Ⓐ Ⓑ Ⓒ Ⓓ Ⓔ
7. Ⓐ Ⓑ Ⓒ Ⓓ Ⓔ

The correct answers for the sample dictation are:

1. B	8. B	14. A	20. D
2. D	9. C	15. B	21. E
3. C	10. D	16. A	22. C
4. A	11. A	17. E	23. E
5. C	12. D	18. B	24. B
6. D	13. C	19. D	25. A
7. C			

Compare your answers with the correct ones. If one of your answers does not agree with the correct answer, again compare your notes with the samples and make certain you understand the instructions.

Your notes should show that the word "bring" goes in blank 16, and "about" in blank 17. But "about" is *not in the list;* so E should be your answer for question 17.

The two words, "to visit—B," are needed for 18, and the one word "visit—A," would be an incorrect answer.

For the actual test you will use a separate answer sheet. As scoring will be done by an electronic machine, it is important that you follow directions carefully. Use the special pencil if one is furnished by the examiner. If no pencil is furnished, use only a number 2 pencil, as directed. Make a heavy mark for each answer. If you have to change your mark for any question, be sure to erase the first mark completely (do not merely cross it out) before making another.

Correctly Filled Transcripts for Sample Dictation

Check your notes against the dictation; check your notes against the alphabetic list of words and the transcript sheet; check the transcript against your answer grid. Identify your errors.

I realize that this __B__ dictation is __D__
          1   2

a __C__ of the __A__ __C__ and is __D__ __C__
 3   4   5   6   7

scored.

    The work __B__ the __C__ __D__ defects
            8   9 10

in __A__ is becoming more __D__ as a __C__
  11   12   13

a change in the __A__ of many __B__ .
            14   15

In order to __A__ __E__ this change,
       16 17

parents have been invited __B__ the
                    18

schools when __D__ children are being
            19

examined and __D__ the __E__ necessary for
            20   21

the __C__ of defects. There is a distinct
    22

__E__ in having a parent __B__ that his or her
23   24

child __A__ the only one who needs
     25

attention....(The rest of the sample

dictation is not transcribed here.)

Part C

Dictation Time: 3 Minutes.

Exactly on a minute start dictating.	Finish reading each two lines at the number of seconds indicated below.
In recent years there has been a great increase in the need for capable stenographers,	10
not only in business offices but also in public service agencies, both	20
governmental and private. (Period) The high schools and business schools in many parts of	30
the country have tried to meet this need by offering complete commercial courses. (Period)	40
The increase in the number of persons who are enrolled in these courses shows that	50
students have become aware of the great demand for stenographers. (Period) A person	1 min.
who wishes to secure employment in this field must be able to take dictation	10
and to transcribe the notes with both speed and accuracy. (Period) The rate of	20
speed at which dictation is given in most offices is somewhat less than that of	30
ordinary speech. (Period) Thus, one who has had a thorough training in shorthand	40
should have little trouble in taking complete notes. (Period) Skill in taking dictation	50
at a rapid rate is of slight value if the stenographer cannot also type the notes	2 min.
in proper form. (Period) A manager sometimes dictates a rough draft of the ideas	10
he/she wishes to have included in a letter, and leaves to the stenographer the task	20
of putting them in good form. (Period) For this reason, knowledge of the essentials	30
of grammar and of composition is as important as the ability to take	40
dictation. (Period) In addition, a stenographer should be familiar with the sources of	50
general information that are most likely to be used in office work. (Period)	3 min.

Dictation Transcript

Time: 30 Minutes. 125 Questions.

ALPHABETIC WORD LIST
Write E if the answer is **not** listed.

also—A	offering—C
also in—C	officials—D
business—C	one—C
busy—D	only—B
capable—A	parts—A
commerce—C	private—C
commercial—D	public—D
county—B	recent—B
culpable—D	recurrent—A
decrease—A	school—C
governing—D	schools—B
governmental—C	servant—D
had been—B	stenographers—D
has been—D	stenos—A
many—A	their—D
most—D	there—B
need—C	tied—A
needy—D	to beat—C
offending—A	tried—B

TRANSCRIPT

In ___ years ___ ___ a great ___ in the
  1   2 3   4

___ for ___ ___, not ___ in ___ ___
5   6 7   8   9 10

but ___ in ___ ___ agencies, both ___
  11   12 13   14

and ___. The high ___ and ___ schools
   15   16   17

in ___ ___ of the ___ have ___ ___
  18 19   20   21 22

this ___ by ___ complete ___ courses.
   23   24   25

Continue on the next page without waiting for a signal.

ALPHABETIC WORD LIST

Write E if the answer is **not** listed.

awake—C	in a—B
aware—B	in the —A
be able—A	increase—C
be able to—C	increment—A
became—B	notations—B
better—A	notes—C
both—D	number—C
courses—D	numbers—D
curses—C	people—A
demand—C	person—C
demean—A	seclude—C
dictation—B	secure—B
dictation notes—C	speech—C
employing—A	speed—B
employment—D	students—C
enrolled—B	studies—D
enroute—D	the—C
feel—A	this—A
felt—D	transcribe—C
grate—D	transcript—D
great—A	who desires—C

TRANSCRIPT (continued)

The ___ ___ ___ of ___ who are ___ in
    26 27 28   29   30
these ___ shows ___ ___ have ___ ___
    31   32 33   34 35
of the ___ ___ for stenographers. A ___
      36 37   38
___ to ___ ___ in ___ ___ must ___
39   40 41   42 43   44
to take ___ and to ___ the ___ with ___
      45   46   47   48
___ and ___.
49   50

Continue on the next page without waiting for a signal.

ALPHABETIC WORD LIST

Write E if the answer is **not** listed.

also—D	rampant—B
also can—B	rate—C
at a—A	ratio—D
at the—C	should—D
compete—B	should not—A
complete—D	sight—C
dictates—B	slight—B
dictation—D	somehow—D
firm—C	speech—A
form—D	speed—A
gained—A	stenographer—C
give—D	taking—C
has—C	that—D
have—B	thorough—C
less—B	through—B
less than—A	treble—D
many—A	trial—A
most—D	typed—D
note—C	typewriter—A
notes—B	valuate—A
offices—C	value—C
orderly—C	what—C
ordinary—D	which—B
proffer—C	who gets—A
proper—A	who had—C

TRANSCRIPT (continued)

The ___ of ___ at ___ dictation is ___
    51   52   53   54

in ___ ___ is ___ ___ than ___ of ___
  55 56   57 58   59   60

___. Thus, one ___ had a ___ ___ in
 61   62   63 64

shorthand ___ ___ little ___ in ___ ___
         65 66   67   68 69

___. Skill in ___ ___ ___ ___ ___ is
 70   71 72 73 74 75

of ___ ___ if the ___ cannot ___ ___
    76 77   78   79 80

the ___ in ___ ___.
   81   82 83

Continue on the next page without waiting for a signal.

ALPHABETIC WORD LIST		**TRANSCRIPT (continued)**

Write E if the answer is **not** listed.

ability—B	letter—D	A ___ ___ ___ a ___ ___ ___ ___
adding—C	like—A	84 85 86 87 88 89 90
addition—A	likely—C	s/he ___ to ___ ___ in a ___, and ___
are—D	manager—A	91 92 93 94 95
as—A	management—B	to the ___ the ___ of ___ them in ___
composing—A	of the —D	96 97 98 99
composition—C	of these—A	___. For ___ ___ ___ ___ ___ of ___
dictates—B	office—A	100 101 102 103 104 105 106
essence—B	official—B	and of ___ is ___ ___ ___ ___ to ___
essentials—C	put in—D	107 108 109 110 111 112
form—A	putting—C	dictation. In ___ ___ stenographer ___
familial—C	reasoning—B	113 114 115
familiar—A	rough—A	be ___ ___ ___ of ___ ___ that ___
general—C	roughly—D	116 117 118 119 120 121
generous—A	sauces—A	most ___ ___ ___ in ___ work.
good—C	shall—D	122 123 124 125
grammatical—D	should—B	
great—A	some times—A	
had—A	somethings—D	
have—B	source—D	
ideals—C	stenographic—A	
ideas—A	take—D	
included—C	task—D	
inclusive—A	this—A	
information—D	to—A	
important—B	to be—B	
impotent—A	used—C	
knowledge—B	useful—A	
knowledgeable—C	wished—D	
leaves—B	wishes—A	
lets—C	with the—D	

You will now have ten minutes to transfer your answers to the Part C answer sheet.

END OF EXAM

CORRECT ANSWERS FOR MODEL EXAMINATION 2

PART A—CLERICAL ABILITY

1. E	16. A	31. D	46. B	61. A	76. C
2. D	17. E	32. E	47. E	62. C	77. E
3. A	18. B	33. A	48. A	63. C	78. E
4. D	19. A	34. A	49. C	64. D	79. C
5. A	20. C	35. A	50. A	65. D	80. B
6. C	21. A	36. B	51. A	66. C	81. E
7. B	22. E	37. E	52. C	67. A	82. C
8. D	23. C	38. C	53. C	68. D	83. E
9. E	24. B	39. D	54. A	69. B	84. C
10. C	25. D	40. A	55. D	70. B	85. B
11. C	26. E	41. A	56. A	71. E	
12. D	27. A	42. C	57. D	72. B	
13. C	28. B	43. C	58. B	73. A	
14. D	29. C	44. E	59. C	74. B	
15. C	30. D	45. D	60. B	75. E	

Explanations

1. **(E)** Ha<u>c</u>hettson; Ha<u>c</u>kett

2. **(D)** 59233<u>2</u>62; 59233<u>3</u>62

3. **(A)** <u>M</u>YP; <u>N</u>YP

4. **(D)** Oliv<u>ia</u> H.; Oliv<u>ier</u> E.; <u>R</u>. Olivia

5. **(A)** 00<u>10</u>; 00<u>12</u>

6. **(C)** 6<u>001</u>; 6<u>100</u>; 6<u>101</u>

7. **(B)** Va<u>no</u>ver; Va<u>ns</u>tory; Van<u>Sw</u>inderen

8. **(D)** Fitz<u>G</u>ibbon; Fitz<u>s</u>immons; Fitz<u>Sim</u>ons

9. **(E)** 01<u>016</u>060; 01<u>066</u>010

10. **(C)** A<u>AS</u>; A<u>AZ</u>; A<u>SA</u>

11. **(C)** Pa<u>wel</u>ek; Pa<u>wlowi</u>cz; Pa<u>wlows</u>ki

12. **(D)** 77<u>10</u>; 78<u>34</u>; 78<u>68</u>

13. **(C)** 36270<u>000</u>; 36270<u>013</u>; 36270<u>030</u>

14. **(D)** Freed<u>enb</u>erg; Freed<u>enb</u>urg; Freed<u>inb</u>erg

15. **(C)** Prou<u>tey</u>; Prouty, <u>Ma</u>rtha; Prouty, <u>My</u>ra

16. **(A)** 58006<u>021</u>; 58006<u>130</u>

17. **(E)** EKK-14<u>03</u>; EKK-14<u>43</u>

18. **(B)** <u>Daly</u>; <u>D'Amato</u>; <u>D'Amb</u>oise

19. **(A)** Sch<u>ae</u>ffer; Sch<u>a</u>ffert

20. **(C)** <u>PSP</u>; <u>SPP</u>; SPS

21. **(A)** Drusilla S. Ridgeley   Drusilla S. Ridgeley   Drusilla S. Ridgeley

22. **(E)** Andrei I. Toumantzev   Andrei I. Tou<u>rm</u>antzev   Andrei I. Touman<u>tzov</u>

23. **(C)** 6-78912-e3e42   6-78912-<u>3e</u>3e42   6-78912-e3e42

24. **(B)** 86529 Dunwoodie Drive   86529 Dunwoodie Drive   8<u>5</u>629 Dunwoodie Drive

25. **(D)** 1592<u>514</u>   1592574   1592574

26. **(E)** Ella Burk N<u>ew</u>ham   Ella Burk Newnham   <u>Elena</u> Burk Newnham

27. **(A)** 5416R-1952TZ-op   5416R-1952TZ-op   5416R-1952TZ-op

28. **(B)** 60646 West Touhy Avenue   60646 West Touhy Avenue   60646 West Tou<u>hey</u> Avenue

29. **(C)** Mardikian & Moore, Inc.   Mardikian <u>and</u> Moore, Inc.   Mardikian & Moore, Inc.

30. **(D)** 9670<u>243</u>   9670423   9670423

31. **(D)** Eduardo Ingles_   Eduardo Inglese   Eduardo Inglese

32. **(E)** Roger T. DeAngelis   Roger T. <u>D'</u>Angelis   Roger T. DeAnge<u>les</u>

33. **(A)** 7692138   7692138   7692138

34. **(A)** 2695 East 3435 South   2695 East 3435 South   2695 East 3435 South

35. **(A)** 63qs5-95YT3-001   63qs5-95YT3-001   63qs5-95YT3-001

36. **(B)** 2789350   2789350   27<u>9</u>8350

37. **(E)** Helmut V. Lochner   Helmut V. Lo<u>ck</u>ner   Helmut <u>W.</u> Lochner

38. **(C)** 2454803   2<u>548</u>403   2454803

39. **(D)** Lemberger, <u>WA</u> 28094-9182   Lemberger, VA 28094-9182   Lemberger, VA 28094-9182

40. **(A)** 4168-GNP-78852	4168-GNP-78852	4168-GNP-78852
41. **(A)** Yoshihito Saito	Yoshihito Saito	Yoshihito Saito
42. **(C)** 5927681	592<u>786</u>1	5927681
43. **(C)** O'Reilly Bay, LA 56212	O'Reilly<u>s</u> Bay, LA 56212	O'Reilly Bay, LA 56212
44. **(E)** Francis Ra<u>ns</u>dell	Fran<u>ces</u> Ramsdell	Francis Ramsdell
45. **(D)** 5634-Oot<u>V5</u>a-16867	5634-Ootv5a-16867	5634-Ootv5a-16867
46. **(B)** Dolores Mollicone	Dolores Mollicone	Dolo<u>ras</u> Mollicone
47. **(E)** David C. Routzon	David <u>E</u>. Routzon	David C. Rout<u>zron</u>
48. **(A)** 8932 Shimabui Hwy.	8932 Shimabui Hwy.	8932 Shimabui Hwy.
49. **(C)** 6177396	6177<u>93</u>6	6177396
50. **(A)** A8987-B73245	A8987-B73245	A8987-B73245

51. **(A)** anticipate

52. **(C)** similar

53. **(C)** sufficiently

54. **(A)** intelligence

55. **(D)** reference

56. **(A)** conscious

57. **(D)** parallel

58. **(B)** abundance

59. **(C)** corrugated

60. **(B)** accumulation

61. **(A)** resonance

62. **(C)** beneficial

63. **(C)** specifically

64. **(D)** eliminate

65. **(D)** colossal

66. **(C)** auxiliary

67. **(A)** inimitable

68. **(D)** disappearance

69. **(B)** appellate

70. **(B)** essential

71. **(E)**   83
              −56
              27

72. **(B)**   15
             +17
              32

73. **(A)**   32
             × 7
             224

74. **(B)**   39
             ×2
             78

75. **(E)**   43
             −15
              28

76. **(C)**   50
             +49
              99

77. **(E)**   61
              6/366

78. **(E)**   38
             × 3
             114

79. **(C)**   19
             +21
              40

80. **(B)**   13
             − 6
              7

81. **(E)**   30
              6/180

82. **(C)**   10
             ×1
             10

83. **(E)**   41
              7/287

84. **(C)**   12
             +11
              23

85. **(B)**   85
             −64
              21

PART B—VERBAL ABILITY

1. D	12. B	23. D	34. B	45. A
2. C	13. D	24. A	35. B	46. C
3. E	14. A	25. D	36. D	47. A
4. A	15. D	26. A	37. C	48. C
5. C	16. D	27. C	38. C	49. A
6. E	17. E	28. C	39. D	50. D
7. D	18. A	29. B	40. D	51. B
8. C	19. D	30. D	41. B	52. A
9. E	20. B	31. D	42. A	53. C
10. B	21. C	32. D	43. B	54. D
11. A	22. C	33. A	44. D	55. C

Explanations

Questions 1–20. If you made any errors in the Following Written Instructions portion, go back and reread those questions more carefully.

21. **(C)** Sentence (C) is the best expression of the idea. Sentence (A) has two grammatical errors: the use of *when* to introduce a definition and the unacceptable verb form *is already having been parked.* Sentence (B) incorrectly shifts subjects from *one* to *you.* Sentence (D) does not make sense.

22. **(C)** Choice (B) is incorrect because only two persons are involved in this statement. *Between* is used when there are only two, *among* is reserved for three or more. (A) makes a similar error. In addition, both (A) and (D) use the pronoun *he.* The object of a preposition, in this case *between,* must be in the objective case, hence *him.*

23. **(D)** Punctuation aside, both (A) and (B) incorrectly place the verb in the plural, *are. Neither* is a singular indefinite pronoun. It means *not one and not the other* and requires a singular verb. The choice between (C) and (D) is more difficult, but basically this is a simple statement and not a direct quote.

24. **(A)** *Whoever* is the subject of the phrase *whoever has the best record.* Hence (A) is the correct answer and (D) is wrong. Both (B) and (C) are wordy and awkward.

25. **(D)** All the other choices contain obvious errors.

26. **(A)** Choice (B) uses the plural verb *were* with the singular subject *report.* (C) and (D) are colloquial and incorrect even for informal speech. They have no place in business writing.

27. **(C)** Choices (A) and (B) use adverbs incorrectly; choice (D) is awkward and unidiomatic.

28. **(C)** Choices (B) and (D) are obviously incorrect. In (A), the pronoun *who* should be the subject of the phrase, *who had made careless errors.*

29. **(B)** Only the quoted material should appear enclosed by quotation marks, so (A) is incorrect. Only the first word of a sentence should begin with a capital letter, so both (C) and (D) are wrong.

In addition, only the quoted material itself is a question; the entire sentence is a statement. Therefore, the question mark must be placed inside the quotes.

30. **(D)** Choices (A) and (B) imply that he stays in church all day on Christmas and Easter and goes nowhere else. Choice (C) makes the same implication and in addition splits the infinitive awkwardly. In (D) the modifier *only* is correctly placed to tell us that the only times he goes to church are on Christmas and Easter.

31. **(D)** Choice (A) might state either *most* or *all* but not both; choice (B) should read *persons who;* choice (C) should read *with regard to. . . .*

32. **(D)** Choice (A) is incorrect because *both* can refer to only two, but the publisher and authors implies at least three; choice (B) requires the plural verb *were;* choice (C) requires the correlative construction *neither . . . nor.*

33. **(A)** Choices (C) and (D) are glaringly poor. Choice (B) is not incorrect, but choice (A) is far better.

34. **(B)** Choice (A) incorrectly uses a semicolon to separate a complete clause from a sentence fragment. Additionally, (A) incorrectly uses *what* in place of *that.* Choice (C) is a run-on sentence that also misuses an apostrophe: *It's* is the contraction for *it is,* not the possessive of *it.* Choice (D) uses commas indiscriminately; it also misuses the apostrophe.

35. **(B)** In choice (A) the placement of the apostrophe is inappropriate; choices (C) and (D) use the plural, but there is only one company.

36. **(D)** Choices (A) and (C) are incorrect in use of the subject form *I* instead of the object of the preposition *me.* Choice (B) incorrectly uses the reflexive *myself.* Only I can address a letter to myself.

37. **(C)** Choice (A) incorrectly uses the plural verb form *have* with the singular subject *one.* (B) is awkward and wordy. (D) incorrectly changes the subject from *one of us* to *anyone.*

38. **(C)** (A) is wordy. In (B), the correct verb should be *have* in place of *leave.* In (D), the word *arose* should be *arisen.*

39. **(D)** The first three sentences lack parallel construction. All the words that modify *paper* must appear in the same form.

40. **(D)** The phrase, *together with … ,* is extra information and not a part of the subject; therefore, both (A) and (B) represent similar errors of agreement. Choice (C) also presents disagreement in number between subject and verb, but in this case the compound subject, indicated by the use of the conjunction, *and,* requires a plural verb.

41. **(B)** Even if you do not recognize the root *manu* meaning *hand* and relating directly to *handbook,* you should have no trouble getting this question right. If you substitute each of the choices in the sentence, you will readily see that only one makes sense.

42. **(A)** Within the context of the sentence, the thought of a specified punishment for use, interpretation, or an edition of the rules does not make too much sense. *Fraction* gives a hint of *part,* but you must also contend with the negative prefix *in.* Since it is reasonable to expect punishment for negative behavior with relation to the rules, *violation,* which is the meaning of INFRACTION, is the proper answer.

43. **(B)** The prefix should help you narrow your choices. The prefix *re* meaning *back* or *again* narrows the choices to (A) or (B). To RESCIND is to *take back* or to *cancel.*

44. **(D)** First eliminate (C) since it does not make sense in the sentence. Your experience with the word *summons* may be with relation to *tickets* and *fines,* but tickets and fines have nothing to do with asking questions while taking a test. Even if you are unfamiliar with the word SUMMON, you should be able to choose *call* as the best synonym in this context.

45. **(A)** REPRISAL means injury done for injury received or *retaliation.*

46. **(C)** To REDUCE is to *make smaller* or to *lessen.*

47. **(A)** To IMPAIR is to *make worse,* to *injure,* or to *weaken.*

48. **(C)** FITTING in this context means *suitable* or *appropriate.*

49. **(A)** The survey showed that of all subjects typing has helped most in business. It was also considered valuable by college students in their schoolwork.

50. **(D)** See the second sentence.

51. **(B)** According to the paragraph, the government can spend only what it obtains from the people. The government obtains money from the people by taxation. If the people are unwilling to pay taxes, the government has no source of funds.

52. **(A)** Step one in the job application process is often the application letter. If the letter is not effective, the applicant will not move on to the next step and job prospects will be greatly lessened.

53. **(C)** The second sentence states that direct lighting causes glare on the working surface.

54. **(D)** While all the answer choices are likely to be true, the answer suggested by the paragraph is that "white collar" workers work with their pencils and their minds rather than with their hands and machines.

55. **(C)** All the paragraph says is that office manuals are a necessity in large organizations.

PART C—STENOGRAPHY

1. B	26. C	51. C	76. B	101. A
2. B	27. A	52. A	77. C	102. E
3. D	28. C	53. B	78. C	103. B
4. E	29. E	54. E	79. D	104. D
5. C	30. B	55. D	80. E	105. C
6. A	31. D	56. C	81. B	106. E
7. D	32. E	57. E	82. A	107. C
8. B	33. C	58. B	83. D	108. A
9. C	34. E	59. D	84. A	109. B
10. E	35. B	60. D	85. E	110. E
11. A	36. A	61. A	86. B	111. B
12. D	37. C	62. E	87. A	112. D
13. E	38. C	63. C	88. E	113. A
14. C	39. E	64. E	89. D	114. E
15. C	40. B	65. D	90. A	115. B
16. B	41. D	66. B	91. A	116. A
17. C	42. A	67. E	92. B	117. D
18. A	43. E	68. C	93. C	118. E
19. A	44. A	69. D	94. D	119. C
20. E	45. B	70. B	95. B	120. D
21. E	46. C	71. C	96. E	121. D
22. E	47. C	72. D	97. D	122. C
23. C	48. D	73. A	98. C	123. B
24. C	49. B	74. E	99. C	124. C
25. D	50. E	75. C	100. A	125. A

Correctly Filled Transcript

In _B_ years _B_ _D_ a great _E_ in the
  1   2 3   4

_C_ for _A_ _D_ , not _B_ in _C_ _E_
 5   6 7   8   9 10

but _A_ in _D_ _E_ agencies, both _C_
   11   12 13   14

and _C_ . The high _B_ and _C_ schools
   15   16   17

in _A_ _A_ of the _E_ have _E_ _E_
  18 19   20   21 22

this _C_ by _C_ complete _D_ courses.
    23   24   25

The _C_ _A_ _C_ of _E_ who are _B_ in
   26 27 28 29   30

these _D_ shows _E_ _C_ have _E_ _B_
    31   32 33   34 35

of the _A_ _C_ for stenographers. A _C_
     36 37   38

_E_ to _B_ _D_ in _A_ _E_ must _A_
 39   40 41   42 43   44

to take _B_ and to _C_ the _C_ with _D_
     45   46   47   48

_B_ and _E_ .
49   50

The _C_ of _A_ at _B_ dictation is _E_
   51   52   53   54

in _D_ _C_ is _E_ _B_ than _D_ of _D_
  55 56   57 58   59   60

_A_ . Thus, one _E_ had a _C_ _E_ in
61   62   63 64

shorthand _D_ _B_ little _E_ in _C_ _D_
        65 66   67   68 69

_B_ . Skill in _C_ _D_ _A_ _E_ _C_ is
70   71 72 73 74 75

of _B_ _C_ if the _C_ cannot _D_ _E_
  76 77   78   79 80

the _B_ in _A_ _D_ .
   81 82 83

A <u>A</u> <u>E</u> <u>B</u> a <u>A</u> <u>E</u> <u>D</u> <u>A</u>
  84 85 86   87 88 89 90

s/he <u>A</u> to <u>B</u> <u>C</u> in a <u>D</u> , and <u>B</u>
   91   92 93   94   95

to the <u>E</u> the <u>D</u> of <u>C</u> them in <u>C</u>
    96   97   98   99

<u>A</u> . For <u>A</u> <u>E</u> <u>B</u> <u>D</u> <u>C</u> of <u>E</u>
100   101 102 103 104 105   106

and of <u>C</u> is <u>A</u> <u>B</u> <u>E</u> <u>B</u> to <u>D</u>
    107   108 109 110 111   112

dictation. In <u>A</u> , <u>E</u> stenographer <u>B</u>
          113 114   115

be <u>A</u> <u>D</u> <u>E</u> of <u>C</u> <u>D</u> that <u>D</u>
  116 117 118   119 120   121

most <u>C</u> <u>B</u> <u>C</u> in <u>A</u> work.
   122 123 124   125

Arco's *Practice for Clerical, Typing, and Stenographic Tests* offers techniques, strategies, and tips for taking dictation and answering stenography questions, along with lots of practice.

SCORE SHEET

Your score on Part A and Part B of the examination for Clerk-Typist, Clerk-Stenographer, and Data Conversion Operator is based only on the number of correct answers. Wrong answers have no effect on the score. Part A and Part B are timed and administered as two separate units, but they are not scored separately. There is no Clerical Ability score and no Verbal Ability score; there is only a single Exam 710 score.

To determine your raw score on this exam, count up all of your correct answers on the full exam.

Number Right equals Raw Score

_____ = _____

Since there is only a single Exam 710 score, your performance on any single question type does not matter. In order to earn a high score, however, you must do well on all parts of the exam. Enter your scores below to chart your performance on each question type. Then concentrate your efforts toward improvement in the areas with which you had the most difficulty.

Part A

Sequencing, Questions 1–20. Number right _____ out of 20.
Comparisons, Questions 21–50. Number right _____ out of 30.
Spelling, Questions 51–70. Number right _____ out of 20.
Computations, Questions 71–85. Number right _____ out of 15.

Part B

Following Written Instructions, Questions 1–20. Number right _____ out of 20.
Grammar/Punctuation, Questions 21–40. Number right _____ out of 20.
Vocabulary/Reading Comprehension, Questions 41–55. Number right _____ out of 15.

Now use the self evaluation chart below to see where your total score falls on a scale from Poor to Excellent.

Self Evaluation Chart

	Excellent	Good	Average	Fair	Poor
Exam 710	125–140	109–124	91–108	61–90	0–60

Part C

Your score on Part C, the stenography test, is based on your number of correct answers minus one fourth of your wrong answers. To determine your score, divide the number of answers you got wrong by 4 and subtract that number from the number of answers you got right.

Number Right	minus	Number Wrong (÷ 4)	equals	Raw Score
_____	–	_____	=	_____

Evaluate your performance on the stenography test by darkening the space in which your raw score falls in the chart below.

Self Evaluation Chart

Part C	Excellent	Good	Average	Fair	Poor
Stenography	111–125	96–110	81–95	51–80	0–50

Model Examination 3
Answer Sheet

Exam 911

Cleaner
Custodian
Custodial Laborer

1 Ⓐ Ⓑ Ⓒ Ⓓ Ⓔ	23 Ⓐ Ⓑ Ⓒ Ⓓ Ⓔ	45 Ⓐ Ⓑ Ⓒ Ⓓ Ⓔ	67 Ⓐ Ⓑ Ⓒ Ⓓ Ⓔ
2 Ⓐ Ⓑ Ⓒ Ⓓ Ⓔ	24 Ⓐ Ⓑ Ⓒ Ⓓ Ⓔ	46 Ⓐ Ⓑ Ⓒ Ⓓ Ⓔ	68 Ⓐ Ⓑ Ⓒ Ⓓ Ⓔ
3 Ⓐ Ⓑ Ⓒ Ⓓ Ⓔ	25 Ⓐ Ⓑ Ⓒ Ⓓ Ⓔ	47 Ⓐ Ⓑ Ⓒ Ⓓ Ⓔ	69 Ⓐ Ⓑ Ⓒ Ⓓ Ⓔ
4 Ⓐ Ⓑ Ⓒ Ⓓ Ⓔ	26 Ⓐ Ⓑ Ⓒ Ⓓ Ⓔ	48 Ⓐ Ⓑ Ⓒ Ⓓ Ⓔ	70 Ⓐ Ⓑ Ⓒ Ⓓ Ⓔ
5 Ⓐ Ⓑ Ⓒ Ⓓ Ⓔ	27 Ⓐ Ⓑ Ⓒ Ⓓ Ⓔ	49 Ⓐ Ⓑ Ⓒ Ⓓ Ⓔ	71 Ⓐ Ⓑ Ⓒ Ⓓ Ⓔ
6 Ⓐ Ⓑ Ⓒ Ⓓ Ⓔ	28 Ⓐ Ⓑ Ⓒ Ⓓ Ⓔ	50 Ⓐ Ⓑ Ⓒ Ⓓ Ⓔ	72 Ⓐ Ⓑ Ⓒ Ⓓ Ⓔ
7 Ⓐ Ⓑ Ⓒ Ⓓ Ⓔ	29 Ⓐ Ⓑ Ⓒ Ⓓ Ⓔ	51 Ⓐ Ⓑ Ⓒ Ⓓ Ⓔ	73 Ⓐ Ⓑ Ⓒ Ⓓ Ⓔ
8 Ⓐ Ⓑ Ⓒ Ⓓ Ⓔ	30 Ⓐ Ⓑ Ⓒ Ⓓ Ⓔ	52 Ⓐ Ⓑ Ⓒ Ⓓ Ⓔ	74 Ⓐ Ⓑ Ⓒ Ⓓ Ⓔ
9 Ⓐ Ⓑ Ⓒ Ⓓ Ⓔ	31 Ⓐ Ⓑ Ⓒ Ⓓ Ⓔ	53 Ⓐ Ⓑ Ⓒ Ⓓ Ⓔ	75 Ⓐ Ⓑ Ⓒ Ⓓ Ⓔ
10 Ⓐ Ⓑ Ⓒ Ⓓ Ⓔ	32 Ⓐ Ⓑ Ⓒ Ⓓ Ⓔ	54 Ⓐ Ⓑ Ⓒ Ⓓ Ⓔ	76 Ⓐ Ⓑ Ⓒ Ⓓ Ⓔ
11 Ⓐ Ⓑ Ⓒ Ⓓ Ⓔ	33 Ⓐ Ⓑ Ⓒ Ⓓ Ⓔ	55 Ⓐ Ⓑ Ⓒ Ⓓ Ⓔ	77 Ⓐ Ⓑ Ⓒ Ⓓ Ⓔ
12 Ⓐ Ⓑ Ⓒ Ⓓ Ⓔ	34 Ⓐ Ⓑ Ⓒ Ⓓ Ⓔ	56 Ⓐ Ⓑ Ⓒ Ⓓ Ⓔ	78 Ⓐ Ⓑ Ⓒ Ⓓ Ⓔ
13 Ⓐ Ⓑ Ⓒ Ⓓ Ⓔ	35 Ⓐ Ⓑ Ⓒ Ⓓ Ⓔ	57 Ⓐ Ⓑ Ⓒ Ⓓ Ⓔ	79 Ⓐ Ⓑ Ⓒ Ⓓ Ⓔ
14 Ⓐ Ⓑ Ⓒ Ⓓ Ⓔ	36 Ⓐ Ⓑ Ⓒ Ⓓ Ⓔ	58 Ⓐ Ⓑ Ⓒ Ⓓ Ⓔ	80 Ⓐ Ⓑ Ⓒ Ⓓ Ⓔ
15 Ⓐ Ⓑ Ⓒ Ⓓ Ⓔ	37 Ⓐ Ⓑ Ⓒ Ⓓ Ⓔ	59 Ⓐ Ⓑ Ⓒ Ⓓ Ⓔ	81 Ⓐ Ⓑ Ⓒ Ⓓ Ⓔ
16 Ⓐ Ⓑ Ⓒ Ⓓ Ⓔ	38 Ⓐ Ⓑ Ⓒ Ⓓ Ⓔ	60 Ⓐ Ⓑ Ⓒ Ⓓ Ⓔ	82 Ⓐ Ⓑ Ⓒ Ⓓ Ⓔ
17 Ⓐ Ⓑ Ⓒ Ⓓ Ⓔ	39 Ⓐ Ⓑ Ⓒ Ⓓ Ⓔ	61 Ⓐ Ⓑ Ⓒ Ⓓ Ⓔ	83 Ⓐ Ⓑ Ⓒ Ⓓ Ⓔ
18 Ⓐ Ⓑ Ⓒ Ⓓ Ⓔ	40 Ⓐ Ⓑ Ⓒ Ⓓ Ⓔ	62 Ⓐ Ⓑ Ⓒ Ⓓ Ⓔ	84 Ⓐ Ⓑ Ⓒ Ⓓ Ⓔ
19 Ⓐ Ⓑ Ⓒ Ⓓ Ⓔ	41 Ⓐ Ⓑ Ⓒ Ⓓ Ⓔ	63 Ⓐ Ⓑ Ⓒ Ⓓ Ⓔ	85 Ⓐ Ⓑ Ⓒ Ⓓ Ⓔ
20 Ⓐ Ⓑ Ⓒ Ⓓ Ⓔ	42 Ⓐ Ⓑ Ⓒ Ⓓ Ⓔ	64 Ⓐ Ⓑ Ⓒ Ⓓ Ⓔ	86 Ⓐ Ⓑ Ⓒ Ⓓ Ⓔ
21 Ⓐ Ⓑ Ⓒ Ⓓ Ⓔ	43 Ⓐ Ⓑ Ⓒ Ⓓ Ⓔ	65 Ⓐ Ⓑ Ⓒ Ⓓ Ⓔ	87 Ⓐ Ⓑ Ⓒ Ⓓ Ⓔ
22 Ⓐ Ⓑ Ⓒ Ⓓ Ⓔ	44 Ⓐ Ⓑ Ⓒ Ⓓ Ⓔ	66 Ⓐ Ⓑ Ⓒ Ⓓ Ⓔ	88 Ⓐ Ⓑ Ⓒ Ⓓ Ⓔ

TEAR HERE

SCORE SHEET

The worksheet is *not* scored. Raw score is based only upon the number of answers correctly gridded.

Number correctly gridded = Raw Score

_____ = _____

   The best possible score on this test is 28. If your score is lower than 24, you might find it helpful to purchase Arco's *Postal Clerk and Carrier*. There you will find useful instructions and lots of practice in answering Following Oral Instructions Questions.

FOLLOWING ORAL INSTRUCTIONS

Directions and Sample Instructions

LISTENING TO INSTRUCTIONS: When you are ready to try these sample questions, give the following instructions to a friend and have the friend read them aloud to you at the rate of 80 words per minute. Do not read them to yourself. Your friend will need a watch with a second hand. Listen carefully and do exactly what your friend tells you to do with the worksheet and answer sheet. Your friend will tell you some things to do with each item on the worksheet. After each set of instructions, your friend will give you time to mark your answer by darkening a circle on the sample answer sheet. Since B and D sound very much alike, your friend will say "B as in baker" when he or she means B and "D as in dog" when he or she means D.

> Before proceeding further, tear out the worksheet on page 183. Then hand this book to your friend.

TO THE PERSON WHO IS TO READ THE INSTRUCTIONS: The instructions are to be read at the rate of 80 words per minute. Do not read aloud the material that is in parentheses. Do not repeat any directions.

Read Aloud to the Candidate

Look at line 1 on the worksheet. (Pause slightly.)Write a D as in dog beside the middle number on line 1. (Pause 2 seconds.) Now, on your answer sheet, find the number beside which you just wrote the letter D and darken the space for that number-letter combination. (Pause 5 seconds.)

Look at line 2 on your worksheet. (Pause slightly.) Draw a circle around the largest number on the line. (Pause 2 seconds.) Now, on your answer sheet, find the number that you just circled and darken space A for that number. (Pause 5 seconds.)

Look at line 3 on your worksheet. (Pause slightly.) Draw two lines under the first letter in the word on line 3. (Pause 2 seconds.) Now, on your answer sheet, find the number 11 and darken the space for the letter under which you just drew two lines. (Pause 5 seconds.)

Look at line 4 on your worksheet. (Pause slightly.) Write the number 7 in the largest circle in line 4. (Pause 2 seconds.) Now, on your answer sheet, darken the space for the number-letter combination in the circle in which you just wrote. (Pause 5 seconds.)

Sample Worksheet

DIRECTIONS: Listening carefully to each set of instructions, mark each item on this worksheet as directed. Then complete each question by marking the sample answer sheet below as directed. For each answer you will darken the answer for a number-letter combination. Should you fall behind and miss an instruction, don't become excited. Let that one go and listen for the next one. If, when you start to darken a space for a number, you find that you have already darkened another space for that number, either erase the first mark and darken the space for the new combination or let the first mark stay and do not darken a space for the new combination. Write with a pencil that has a clean eraser. When you finish, you should have no more than one space darkened for each number.

1. 6 _____   1 _____   2 _____   11 _____   9 _____

2. 15   5   12   7

3. B   L   E   A   C   H

4.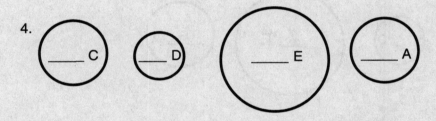

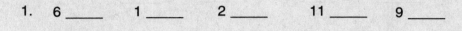

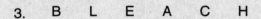

SAMPLE ANSWER SHEET

1. Ⓐ Ⓑ Ⓒ Ⓓ Ⓔ	6. Ⓐ Ⓑ Ⓒ Ⓓ Ⓔ	11. Ⓐ Ⓑ Ⓒ Ⓓ Ⓔ
2. Ⓐ Ⓑ Ⓒ Ⓓ Ⓔ	7. Ⓐ Ⓑ Ⓒ Ⓓ Ⓔ	12. Ⓐ Ⓑ Ⓒ Ⓓ Ⓔ
3. Ⓐ Ⓑ Ⓒ Ⓓ Ⓔ	8. Ⓐ Ⓑ Ⓒ Ⓓ Ⓔ	13. Ⓐ Ⓑ Ⓒ Ⓓ Ⓔ
4. Ⓐ Ⓑ Ⓒ Ⓓ Ⓔ	9. Ⓐ Ⓑ Ⓒ Ⓓ Ⓔ	14. Ⓐ Ⓑ Ⓒ Ⓓ Ⓔ
5. Ⓐ Ⓑ Ⓒ Ⓓ Ⓔ	10. Ⓐ Ⓑ Ⓒ Ⓓ Ⓔ	15. Ⓐ Ⓑ Ⓒ Ⓓ Ⓔ

TEAR HERE

CORRECT ANSWERS TO SAMPLE QUESTIONS

1. Ⓐ Ⓑ Ⓒ Ⓓ Ⓔ   6. Ⓐ Ⓑ Ⓒ Ⓓ Ⓔ   11. Ⓐ ● Ⓒ Ⓓ Ⓔ
2. Ⓐ Ⓑ Ⓒ ● Ⓔ   7. Ⓐ Ⓑ Ⓒ Ⓓ ●   12. Ⓐ Ⓑ Ⓒ Ⓓ Ⓔ
3. Ⓐ Ⓑ Ⓒ Ⓓ Ⓔ   8. Ⓐ Ⓑ Ⓒ Ⓓ Ⓔ   13. Ⓐ Ⓑ Ⓒ Ⓓ Ⓔ
4. Ⓐ Ⓑ Ⓒ Ⓓ Ⓔ   9. Ⓐ Ⓑ Ⓒ Ⓓ Ⓔ   14. Ⓐ Ⓑ Ⓒ Ⓓ Ⓔ
5. Ⓐ Ⓑ Ⓒ Ⓓ Ⓔ   10. Ⓐ Ⓑ Ⓒ Ⓓ Ⓔ   15. ● Ⓑ Ⓒ Ⓓ Ⓔ

Correctly Filled Worksheet

1. 6 ____   1 ____   2 **D**   11 ____   9 ____

2. (15)   5   12   7

3. B̲ L E A C H

4.

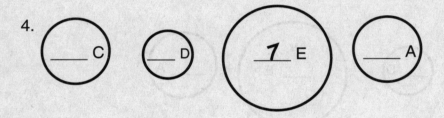

Following Oral Instructions

Time: 25 Minutes.

Listening to Instructions

DIRECTIONS: When you are ready to try this test, give the following instructions to a friend and have the friend read them aloud to you at the rate of 80 words per minute. Do NOT read them to yourself. Your friend will need a watch with a second hand. Listen carefully and do exactly what your friend tells you to do with the worksheet and with the answer sheet. Your friend will tell you some things to do with each item on the worksheet. After each set of instructions, your friend will give you time to mark your answer by darkening a circle on the answer sheet. Since B and D sound very much alike, your friend will say "B as in baker" when he or she means B and "D as in dog" when he or she means D.

> Before proceeding further, tear out the worksheet on page 187. Then hand this book to your friend.

TO THE PERSON WHO IS TO READ THE INSTRUCTIONS: The instructions are to be read at the rate of 80 words per minute. Do not read aloud the material that is in parentheses. Once you have begun the test itself, do not repeat any instructions. The next three paragraphs consist of approximately 120 words. Read these three paragraphs aloud to the candidate in about one and one-half minutes. You may reread these three paragraphs as often as necessary to establish an 80-words-per-minute reading speed.

Read Aloud to the Candidate

On the job you will have to listen to directions and then do what you have been told to do. In this test, I will read instructions to you. Try to understand them as I read them; I cannot repeat them. Once we begin, you may not ask any questions until the end of the test.

On the job you won't have to deal with pictures, numbers, and letters like those in the test, but you will have to listen to instructions and follow them. We are using this test to see how well you can follow instructions.

You are to mark your test booklet according to the instructions that I'll read to you. After each set of instructions, I'll give you time to record your answers on the separate answer sheet.

The actual test begins now.

Look at line 1 on your worksheet. Each number represents a length of rope. (Pause slightly.) Draw two lines under the number that represents the longest length of rope. (Pause 2 seconds.) Now, on your answer sheet, find the number under which you just drew two lines and darken B as in baker for that number. (Pause 5 seconds.)

Look at line 1 again. (Pause slightly.) Find the number that represents the shortest length of rope and draw one wavy line above that number. (Pause 2 seconds.) Now, on your answer sheet, darken space A for the number over which you just drew the wavy line. (Pause 5 seconds.)

Look at line 2 on your worksheet. The number in each carton represents the number of boxes of soap powder in the carton. (Pause slightly.) Write the letter D as in dog in the carton that is closest to empty. (Pause 2 seconds.) Now, on your answer sheet, darken the space for the number-letter combination in the carton you just wrote in. (Pause 5 seconds.)

Look at line 3 on your worksheet. (Pause slightly.) If Christmas is always on a Thursday, write the letter C next to the first number on line 3; if not, write the letter E next to the second number. (Pause 5 seconds.) Now, on your answer sheet, darken the space for the number next to which you just wrote a letter. (Pause 5 seconds.)

Look at line 3 again. (Pause slightly.) Write the second letter of the alphabet next to the lowest number on line 3. (Pause 2 seconds.) Now, on your answer sheet, darken the space for the number-letter combination you just wrote. (Pause 5 seconds.)

Look at line 4 on your worksheet. (Pause slightly.) Count the number of letters in the word and write the number of letters at the end of line 4. (Pause 2 seconds.) Now, on your answer sheet, darken letter C for the number you just wrote. (Pause 5 seconds.)

Look at line 4 again. (Pause slightly.) Draw a circle around the fifth letter in the word. (Pause 2 seconds.) Now, on your answer sheet, find number 64 and darken the space for the letter you just circled. (Pause 5 seconds.)

Look at line 5 on your worksheet. The numbers represent days of the month. Floors are to be washed on odd-numbered days. (Pause slightly.) Draw one line under the number of each day on which floors should be washed. (Pause 5 seconds.) Now, on your answer sheet, darken letter D as in dog for each number under which you drew a line. (Pause 10 seconds.)

Look at line 6 on your worksheet. (Pause slightly.) Write the letter C on the line in the bucket with the highest number. (Pause 2 seconds.) Now, on your answer sheet, darken the space for the number-letter combination in that bucket. (Pause 5 seconds.)

Look at line 6 again. (Pause slightly.) Write the letter B as in baker on the line in the middle bucket. (Pause 2 seconds.) Now, on your answer sheet, darken the space for the number-letter combination in that bucket. (Pause 5 seconds.)

Look at line 7 on your worksheet. (Pause slightly.) Count the number of times the letter A appears on line 7 and write that number at the end of the line. (Pause 2 seconds.) Add 10 to the number you just wrote. Now, on your answer sheet, find the number that represents the sum of the number you wrote plus 10 and darken space E for that number. (Pause 10 seconds.)

Look at line 8 on your worksheet. Each item on line 8 represents a key code. Only keys with odd-numbered codes open the restroom doors in the post office. (Pause slightly.) Draw two lines under the code for each key that will open a restroom door. (Pause 5 seconds.) Now, on your answer sheet, darken each space that represents a key that will open a restroom. (Pause 15 seconds.)

Look at line 9 on your worksheet. Each box contains a different kind of screw. (Pause slightly.) The box with the higher number holds wood screws, and the box with the lower number holds sheet-metal screws. (Pause 2 seconds.) Write the letter A in the box that holds sheet-metal screws. (Pause 2 seconds.) Write the letter E in the box that holds wood screws. (Pause 2 seconds.) Now, on your answer sheet, darken the spaces for the number-letter combinations in the boxes. (Pause 10 seconds.)

Look at line 10 on your worksheet. (Pause slightly.) If brooms are used for sweeping floors, write B as in baker in the triangle. If not, write D as in dog in the square. (Pause 2 seconds.) Now, on your answer sheet, darken the space for the number-letter combination in the figure you just wrote in. (Pause 5 seconds.)

Look at line 10 again. (Pause slightly.) Write the letter C in every figure that has no angles. (Pause 5 seconds.) Now, on your answer sheet, darken the number-letter combination in each figure that you just wrote in. (Pause 10 seconds.)

Look at line 11 on your worksheet. (Pause slightly.) The third mailbox on line 11 has a broken lock and must be reported for repair. Write the letter D as in dog on the line in the broken mailbox. (Pause 2 seconds.) Now, on your answer sheet, darken the space for the number-letter combination in the mailbox with the broken lock. (Pause 5 seconds.)

Look at line 11 again. (Pause slightly.) The first mailbox belongs to Mr. and Mrs. Dana. Write the second letter of the Danas's name in their mailbox. (Pause 2 seconds.) Now, on your answer sheet, darken the space for the number-letter combination in the Danas's mailbox. (Pause 5 seconds.)

Look at line 12 on your worksheet. (Pause slightly.) Write the number of minutes in an hour next to the fourth letter of the alphabet. (Pause 2 seconds.) Now, on your answer sheet, darken the space for the number-letter combination you just wrote. (Pause 5 seconds.)

Look at the brooms on line 13 on your worksheet. (Pause slightly.) Write the first letter of the word "broom" on the line under the first broom. (Pause 2 seconds.) Now, on your answer sheet, darken the space for the number-letter combination under the broom. (Pause 5 seconds.)

Look at the brooms on line 13 again. (Pause slightly.) Write the letter E on the line under the broom that is different from the other brooms. (Pause 2 seconds.) Now, on your answer sheet, darken the space for the number-letter combination under the broom. (Pause 5 seconds.)

Following Oral Instructions

Worksheet

DIRECTIONS: Listening carefully to each set of instructions, mark each item on this worksheet as directed. Then complete each question by marking the answer sheet as directed. For each answer you will darken the space for a number-letter combination. Should you fall behind and miss an instruction, don't get excited. Let that one go and listen for the next one. If, when you start to darken a space for a number, you find that you have already darkened another space for that number, either erase the first mark and darken the space for the new combination or let the first mark stay and do not darken a space for the new combination. Write with a pencil that has a clean eraser. When you finish, you should have no more than one space darkened for each number. Correct answers are on page 191.

1.   3ft.   5yds.   10 in.   7 yds.

2.   ☐ 6__   ☐ 2__   ☐ 12__   ☐ 3__

3.   51___   77___   46___

4.   I N F L A M M A B L E ___

5.   19   24   25   26   27   30

6.   55__   87__   42__   18__   63__

7.   G A D A G G A A D ___

8.   83A   50C   59E   37B   32C   69C

9.   50__   12__

10.   79__   73__   30__   19__   40__

11.   75__   69__   56__   28__

12.   ___D   ___B   ___A   ___E   ___C

13.

53__   21__   33__   85__   46__

END OF EXAM

Correctly Filled Worksheet

1.   3ft.   5yds.   10 in.   <u>7 yds.</u>

2.   [6__]   [2 *D*]   [12__]   [3__]

3.   51___   77 *E*   46 *B*

4.   I N F L Ⓐ M M A B L E   ⊥⊥

5.   <u>19</u>   24   <u>25</u>   26   <u>27</u>   30

6.   55__   87 *C*   42 *B*   18__   63__

7.   G A D A G G A A D   <u>4</u>

8. <u>83A</u>   50C   <u>59E</u>   <u>37B</u>   32C   <u>69C</u>

9. [50 _E_]   [22 _A_]

10. (79 _C_)   △73 _B_   (30 _C_)   [19 ___]   (40 _C_)

11. [75 _A_ •]   [69 ___ •]   [56 _D_ •]   [28 ___ •]

12. **_60_** D   ___ B   ___ A   ___ E   ___ C

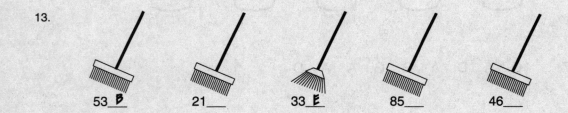

13.

53 _B_   21 ___   33 _E_   85 ___   46 ___

Correctly Filled Answer Grid

1 Ⓐ Ⓑ Ⓒ Ⓓ Ⓔ	23 Ⓐ Ⓑ Ⓒ Ⓓ Ⓔ	45 Ⓐ Ⓑ Ⓒ Ⓓ Ⓔ	67 Ⓐ Ⓑ Ⓒ Ⓓ Ⓔ
2 Ⓐ Ⓑ Ⓒ ● Ⓔ	24 Ⓐ Ⓑ Ⓒ Ⓓ Ⓔ	46 Ⓐ ● Ⓒ Ⓓ Ⓔ	68 Ⓐ Ⓑ Ⓒ Ⓓ Ⓔ
3 Ⓐ Ⓑ Ⓒ Ⓓ Ⓔ	25 Ⓐ Ⓑ Ⓒ ● Ⓔ	47 Ⓐ Ⓑ Ⓒ Ⓓ Ⓔ	69 Ⓐ Ⓑ ● Ⓓ Ⓔ
4 Ⓐ Ⓑ Ⓒ Ⓓ Ⓔ	26 Ⓐ Ⓑ Ⓒ Ⓓ Ⓔ	48 Ⓐ Ⓑ Ⓒ Ⓓ Ⓔ	70 Ⓐ Ⓑ Ⓒ Ⓓ Ⓔ
5 Ⓐ Ⓑ Ⓒ Ⓓ Ⓔ	27 Ⓐ Ⓑ Ⓒ ● Ⓔ	49 Ⓐ Ⓑ Ⓒ Ⓓ Ⓔ	71 Ⓐ Ⓑ Ⓒ Ⓓ Ⓔ
6 Ⓐ Ⓑ Ⓒ Ⓓ Ⓔ	28 Ⓐ Ⓑ Ⓒ Ⓓ Ⓔ	50 Ⓐ Ⓑ Ⓒ Ⓓ ●	72 Ⓐ Ⓑ Ⓒ Ⓓ Ⓔ
7 Ⓐ ● Ⓒ Ⓓ Ⓔ	29 Ⓐ Ⓑ Ⓒ Ⓓ Ⓔ	51 Ⓐ Ⓑ Ⓒ Ⓓ Ⓔ	73 Ⓐ ● Ⓒ Ⓓ Ⓔ
8 Ⓐ Ⓑ Ⓒ Ⓓ Ⓔ	30 Ⓐ Ⓑ ● Ⓓ Ⓔ	52 Ⓐ Ⓑ Ⓒ Ⓓ Ⓔ	74 Ⓐ Ⓑ Ⓒ Ⓓ Ⓔ
9 Ⓐ Ⓑ Ⓒ Ⓓ Ⓔ	31 Ⓐ Ⓑ Ⓒ Ⓓ Ⓔ	53 Ⓐ ● Ⓒ Ⓓ Ⓔ	75 ● Ⓑ Ⓒ Ⓓ Ⓔ
10 ● Ⓑ Ⓒ Ⓓ Ⓔ	32 Ⓐ Ⓑ Ⓒ Ⓓ Ⓔ	54 Ⓐ Ⓑ Ⓒ Ⓓ Ⓔ	76 Ⓐ Ⓑ Ⓒ Ⓓ Ⓔ
11 Ⓐ Ⓑ ● Ⓓ Ⓔ	33 Ⓐ Ⓑ Ⓒ Ⓓ ●	55 Ⓐ Ⓑ Ⓒ Ⓓ Ⓔ	77 Ⓐ Ⓑ Ⓒ Ⓓ ●
12 Ⓐ Ⓑ Ⓒ Ⓓ Ⓔ	34 Ⓐ Ⓑ Ⓒ Ⓓ Ⓔ	56 Ⓐ Ⓑ Ⓒ ● Ⓔ	78 Ⓐ Ⓑ Ⓒ Ⓓ Ⓔ
13 Ⓐ Ⓑ Ⓒ Ⓓ Ⓔ	35 Ⓐ Ⓑ Ⓒ Ⓓ Ⓔ	57 Ⓐ Ⓑ Ⓒ Ⓓ Ⓔ	79 Ⓐ Ⓑ ● Ⓓ Ⓔ
14 Ⓐ Ⓑ Ⓒ Ⓓ ●	36 Ⓐ Ⓑ Ⓒ Ⓓ Ⓔ	58 Ⓐ Ⓑ Ⓒ Ⓓ Ⓔ	80 Ⓐ Ⓑ Ⓒ Ⓓ Ⓔ
15 Ⓐ Ⓑ Ⓒ Ⓓ Ⓔ	37 Ⓐ ● Ⓒ Ⓓ Ⓔ	59 Ⓐ Ⓑ Ⓒ Ⓓ ●	81 Ⓐ Ⓑ Ⓒ Ⓓ Ⓔ
16 Ⓐ Ⓑ Ⓒ Ⓓ Ⓔ	38 Ⓐ Ⓑ Ⓒ Ⓓ Ⓔ	60 Ⓐ Ⓑ Ⓒ ● Ⓔ	82 Ⓐ Ⓑ Ⓒ Ⓓ Ⓔ
17 Ⓐ Ⓑ Ⓒ Ⓓ Ⓔ	39 Ⓐ Ⓑ Ⓒ Ⓓ Ⓔ	61 Ⓐ Ⓑ Ⓒ Ⓓ Ⓔ	83 ● Ⓑ Ⓒ Ⓓ Ⓔ
18 Ⓐ Ⓑ Ⓒ Ⓓ Ⓔ	40 Ⓐ Ⓑ ● Ⓓ Ⓔ	62 Ⓐ Ⓑ Ⓒ Ⓓ Ⓔ	84 Ⓐ Ⓑ Ⓒ Ⓓ Ⓔ
19 Ⓐ Ⓑ Ⓒ Ⓓ Ⓔ	41 Ⓐ Ⓑ Ⓒ Ⓓ Ⓔ	63 Ⓐ Ⓑ Ⓒ Ⓓ Ⓔ	85 Ⓐ Ⓑ Ⓒ Ⓓ Ⓔ
20 Ⓐ Ⓑ Ⓒ Ⓓ Ⓔ	42 Ⓐ ● Ⓒ Ⓓ Ⓔ	64 ● Ⓑ Ⓒ Ⓓ Ⓔ	86 Ⓐ Ⓑ Ⓒ Ⓓ Ⓔ
21 Ⓐ Ⓑ Ⓒ Ⓓ Ⓔ	43 Ⓐ Ⓑ Ⓒ Ⓓ Ⓔ	65 Ⓐ Ⓑ Ⓒ Ⓓ Ⓔ	87 Ⓐ Ⓑ ● Ⓓ Ⓔ
22 ● Ⓑ Ⓒ Ⓓ Ⓔ	44 Ⓐ Ⓑ Ⓒ Ⓓ Ⓔ	66 Ⓐ Ⓑ Ⓒ Ⓓ Ⓔ	88 Ⓐ Ⓑ Ⓒ Ⓓ Ⓔ

Model Examination 4
Answer Sheet

Exam 91

Garageman-Driver
Tractor-Trailer Operator
Motor Vehicle Operator

The exam that follows is very much like the actual examination. Tear out the answer sheets and use them to record your answers to the examination questions. There are two parts to this exam. Each part has its own directions and time limits. Correct answers for all questions are on pages 214–17.

PART ONE

1. _____

2. _____
   _____

3. _____
   _____

4. _____
   _____

5. _____
   _____

6. _____
   _____

7. _____
   _____

8. _____
   _____

9. _____

10.

11. _____
    _____
12. _____
    _____
13. _____
14. _____
15. _____
    _____
16. _____
    _____
17. _____
18. _____
19. _____
20. _____
21. _____
22. _____

Chart A

	Truck License Number	Kind of Service	Odometer Reading When Serviced
	835 XYZ	tune up	22,305
23.			
24.			

TEAR HERE

Chart B

Driver ID Number	Truck License Number	Odometer Reading
8723	997 IUP	88,141

25.

26.

Chart C

Driver ID Number	Odometer Reading When Taken Out	Odometer Reading When Returned
3406	12,562	12,591

27.

28.

Chart D

Vehicle License Number	Kind of Service	Serviceperson ID Number
592 TJD	grease job	8452

29.

30.

Chart E

Truck License Number	Driver ID Number	Serviceperson ID Number
042 RVB	5842	4307

31.

32.

33. _____

_____

34. _____

_____

35. _____

_____

36. _____

37. _____

38. _____

_____

39. _____

_____

40. _____

PART TWO

41. (A) (B) (C) (D) (E)   49. (A) (B) (C) (D) (E)   57. (A) (B) (C) (D) (E)   65. (A) (B) (C) (D) (E)   73. (A) (B) (C) (D) (E)
42. (A) (B) (C) (D) (E)   50. (A) (B) (C) (D) (E)   58. (A) (B) (C) (D) (E)   66. (A) (B) (C) (D) (E)   74. (A) (B) (C) (D) (E)
43. (A) (B) (C) (D) (E)   51. (A) (B) (C) (D) (E)   59. (A) (B) (C) (D) (E)   67. (A) (B) (C) (D) (E)   75. (A) (B) (C) (D) (E)
44. (A) (B) (C) (D) (E)   52. (A) (B) (C) (D) (E)   60. (A) (B) (C) (D) (E)   68. (A) (B) (C) (D) (E)   76. (A) (B) (C) (D) (E)
45. (A) (B) (C) (D) (E)   53. (A) (B) (C) (D) (E)   61. (A) (B) (C) (D) (E)   69. (A) (B) (C) (D) (E)   77. (A) (B) (C) (D) (E)
46. (A) (B) (C) (D) (E)   54. (A) (B) (C) (D) (E)   62. (A) (B) (C) (D) (E)   70. (A) (B) (C) (D) (E)   78. (A) (B) (C) (D) (E)
47. (A) (B) (C) (D) (E)   55. (A) (B) (C) (D) (E)   63. (A) (B) (C) (D) (E)   71. (A) (B) (C) (D) (E)   79. (A) (B) (C) (D) (E)
48. (A) (B) (C) (D) (E)   56. (A) (B) (C) (D) (E)   64. (A) (B) (C) (D) (E)   72. (A) (B) (C) (D) (E)   80. (A) (B) (C) (D) (E)

Score Yourself

How did you do? This exam is machine scored. Your official score will therefore be based on the number of questions you answered correctly in *Part Two only*. Because answering Part One questions correctly is so important to getting the correct answers in Part Two, however, it will be helpful to you to find your raw score for each section so you can identify and correct your problems.

Part One	40 Questions	Number Right _____
Part Two	40 Questions	Number Right _____

On a scale of Poor to Excellent, where does your score fall?

Self Evaluation Chart

	Excellent	Good	Average	Fair	Poor
Part One	36–40	32–35	28–31	24–27	0–23
Part Two	36–40	32–35	28–31	24–27	0–23

TEAR HERE

PART ONE

Time: 60 Minutes. 40 Questions.

Directions: *Read the questions carefully. Be sure you know what the questions are about and then answer each question in the way you are told. Write or diagram your answers on the separate answer sheet for Part One. Correct answers are on pages 214–16.*

Questions 1 and 2 are about Picture 1 below. Look at the picture.

Picture 1

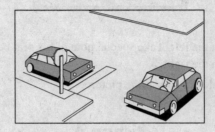

1. How many vehicles are shown in the picture?
2. What is happening in this picture?

Question 3 is about Picture 2 below. Look at the picture.

Picture 2

3. What does the driver see in his rearview mirror? Be as complete as possible in your description. When you answer the questions in Part Two, you may not look back at the pictures.

Questions 4 and 5 are about Picture 3 below. Look at the picture.

Picture 3

4. Describe the man on the left. Take special note of his seat belt.
5. Describe the man on the right.

Question 6 is about Picture 4 below. Look at the picture.

Picture 4

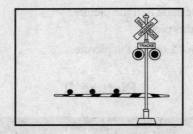

6. If you come upon the scene shown in Picture 4 as you are driving along the road, what must you do?

Question 7 is about Picture 5 below. Look at the picture.

Picture 5

7. What are the vehicles in the picture doing?

Question 8 is about Picture 6 below. Look at the picture.

Picture 6

8. How is the sign on the left related to the vehicle on the right? What does it mean?

Questions 9 and 10 are about Picture 7 below. Look at the picture.

Picture 7

9. The roadway in Picture 7 is
   (A) a four-lane superhighway
   (B) a no-passing zone
   (C) a two-way street
   (D) a single-lane street
(Write the letter of your answer on the answer sheet.)

10. On your answer sheet, draw arrows in the roadway indicating the direction of traffic flow.

Question 11 is about Picture 8 below. Look at the picture.

Picture 8

11. Write as complete a description as you can of the objects and activities in Picture 8.

Question 12 is about Picture 9 below. Look at the picture.

Picture 9

12. Describe the pattern of wear on this tire.

Question 13 is about Picture 10 below. Look at the picture.

Picture 10

13. The meaning of this sign is
   (A) no parking
   (B) no truck parking
   (C) no trucks
   (D) trucks only

(Write the letter of your answer on the answer sheet.)

Question 14 is about Picture 11 below. Look at the picture.

Picture 11

14. What should you look for when you see this sign?

Questions 15 and 16 are about Picture 12 below. Look at the picture.

Picture 12

15. What is the boy doing?
16. What else is happening in this picture?

Question 17 is about Picture 13 below. Look at the picture.

Picture 13

17. The purpose of this sign is to caution you against
    (A) a winding road
    (B) drunk drivers
    (C) a road that may be slippery when wet
    (D) a steep hill
(Write the letter of your answer on the answer sheet.)

Question 18 is about the words on Picture 14 below. Look at the picture.

Picture 14

18. The words on this sign mean the same as
    (A) Dead End, No Exit
    (B) One Way Traffic
    (C) No U Turn, Keep Out
    (D) Special Parking Rules Today, Do Not Park Here
(Write the letter of your answer on the answer sheet.)

Questions 19 and 20 are about Picture 15 below. Look at the picture.

Picture 15

19. What is the vehicle in the picture?
20. Who are the passengers?

Question 21 is about words that might appear on a traffic sign. Decide which line—A, B, C, or D—means most nearly the same as the first line, and write the letter of that line on the answer sheet.

21. Bridge Freezes Before Roadway
    (A) Bridge May Be Icy
    (B) Detour—Bridge Under Repair
    (C) Yield to Road Maintenance Crews
    (D) Cold Weather Forecast for Tonight

Question 22 is about Picture 16 below. Look at the picture.

Picture 16

ROAD
WORK
1000 FT

22. The words on this sign mean that
    (A) 500 people are working in the road
    (B) for the next 1000 feet, people will be working in the road
    (C) in 1000 feet, expect to find people working in the road
    (D) please help the people working in the road for the next 1000 feet
(Write the letter of your answer on the answer sheet.)

Questions 23 and 24 have to do with filling in a chart. You are given the following information to put in Chart A.

Truck, license number 835 XZY, had a tune up at odometer reading 22,305.
Truck, license number 673 PUR, received a new fuel pump at odometer reading 67,422.
Truck, license number 441 RTG, had an oil change at odometer reading 46,098.

The information for the first truck has already been filled in. For question 23, write the information for the second truck in the proper columns in Chart A on the answer sheet. For question 24, write the information for the third truck in the proper columns in Chart A on the answer sheet.

Questions 25 and 26 have to do with filling in another chart. You are given the following information to put in Chart B.

Driver, ID number 8723, took truck license number 997 IUP at odometer reading 88,141.
Driver, ID number 6309, took truck license number 534 TRE at odometer reading 35,790.
Driver, ID number 7342, took truck license number 256 TAE at odometer reading 56,798.

The information for the first driver has already been filled in. For question 25, write the information for the second driver in the proper columns in Chart B on the answer sheet. For question 26, write the information for the third driver in the proper columns in Chart B on the answer sheet.

Questions 27 and 28 have to do with filling in another chart. You are given the following information to put in Chart C.

Driver, ID number 3406, took his jeep at odometer reading 12,562 and returned it at odometer reading 12,591.
Driver, ID number 9845, took his jeep at odometer reading 54,970 and returned it at odometer reading 54,997.
Driver, ID number 4785, took her jeep at odometer reading 43,054 and returned it at odometer reading 43,086.

The information for the first driver has already been filled in. For question 27, write the information for the second driver in the proper columns in Chart C on the answer sheet. For question 28, write the information for the third driver in the proper columns in Chart C on the answer sheet.

Questions 29 and 30 have to do with filling in another chart. You are given the following information to put in Chart D.

Vehicle license number 592 TJD had a grease job by mechanic ID number 8452.
Vehicle license number 447 IKT had its carburetor adjusted by serviceperson ID number 7092.
Vehicle license number 837 PRE had a tire changed by serviceperson ID number 6052.

The information for the first vehicle has already been filled in. For question 29, write the information for the second vehicle in the proper columns in Chart D on the answer sheet. For question 30, write the information for the third vehicle in the proper columns in Chart D on the answer sheet.

Questions 31 and 32 have to do with filling in one more chart. You are given the following information to put in Chart E.

Truck license number 042 RVB is to be driven into the yard by driver ID number 5842 and turned over to serviceperson ID number 4307 for service.
Truck license number 759 YUX is to be driven into the yard by driver ID number 8372 and turned over to serviceperson ID number 3987 for service.
Truck license number 943 WCG is to be driven into the yard by driver ID number 6241 and turned over to serviceperson ID number 4273 for service.

The information for the first truck has already been filled in. For question **31,** write the information for the second truck in the proper columns in Chart E on the answer sheet. For question **32,** write the information for the third truck in the proper columns in Chart E on the answer sheet.

Questions 33 and 34 are about pictures of lane-control lights. Each picture has a letter. You are to tell what each picture shows by writing a short description of the picture on the answer sheet.

X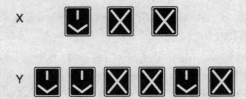

Y

33. What does Picture X show?
34. What does Picture Y show?

Question 35 is about Picture 17 below. Look at the picture.

Picture 17

35. Describe this picture in the space on the answer sheet.

Question 36 is about the word on Picture 18 below. Look at the picture.

Picture 18

36. The word on this sign means that the driver should
(A) stop
(B) turn around
(C) let merging traffic enter the roadway
(D) look carefully before proceeding
(Write the letter of your answer on the answer sheet.)

Question 37 is about Picture 19 below. Look at the picture.

Picture 19

37. The meaning of this sign is
(A) Right Turn Only
(B) No Right Turn
(C) No Left Turn
(D) Left Turn Only
(Write the letter of your answer on the answer sheet.)

Question 38 is about Picture 20 below. Look at the picture.

Picture 20

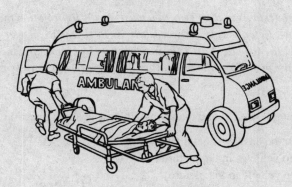

38. Describe what is happening in this picture.

Question 39 is about Picture 21 below. Look at the picture.

Picture 21

39. What is happening in this picture? Write your description in the space on the answer sheet.

Question 40 is about the sign in Picture 22 below. Look at the picture.

Picture 22

40. The driver who approaches this sign must
(A) stop
(B) slow down and look both ways
(C) turn around
(D) back up
(Write the letter of your answer on the answer sheet.)

PART TWO

Time: 60 Minutes. 40 Questions.

Directions: To answer the questions in Part Two, you must use the information that you wrote in answer to the questions in Part One. Refer to your answer sheet for Part One to answer these questions. Mark the answers to questions 41 to 80 on the Part Two answer sheet by blackening the letter of your answer. You may not look back at the pictures while answering the questions in Part Two. The correct answers are on page 217.

Question 41 below is about question 1, and question 42 below is about question 2.

41. For number 41 on the answer sheet, mark space
(A) if there are no vehicles in the picture
(B) if there is one vehicle in the picture
(C) if there are two vehicles in the picture
(D) if there are three vehicles in the picture
(E) if there are four vehicles in the picture

42. For number 42 on the answer sheet, mark space

(A) if there is about to be a crash
(B) if a vehicle just went through a stop sign
(C) if a car is driving on the wrong side of the street
(D) if there are no vehicles in the intersection
(E) if one car has stopped at a stop sign

Question 43 is about question 3.

43. For number 43 on the answer sheet, mark space
(A) if a motorcycle is passing a car
(B) if a motorcycle is directly behind a car
(C) if a truck is behind a car
(D) if two motorcycles are in the left lane
(E) if there is nothing in the rearview mirror

Question 44 below is about question 4, and question 45 below is about question 5.

44. For number 44 on the answer sheet, mark space

(A) if the man is likely to suffer internal injuries in case of a crash
(B) if the man is wearing his seat belt properly
(C) if the man is well protected in case of auto crash
(D) if the man is wearing his seat belt across his right shoulder
(E) if the man is likely to be thrown from the car in an accident

45. For number 45 on the answer sheet, mark space

(A) if the man's shoulder strap goes under his tie
(B) if the man's lap strap is unfastened
(C) if the man is likely to be thrown through the windshield in a crash
(D) if the man is wearing his seat belt and shoulder harness properly
(E) if the man is wearing a jacket

Question 46 below is about question 6.

46. For number 46 on the answer sheet, mark space

(A) if you should blow your horn
(B) if you should get out of your car and move the barrier
(C) if you should come to a full stop and wait
(D) if you should accelerate and continue
(E) if you should stop, look, and proceed

Question 47 below is about question 7.

47. For number 47 on the answer sheet, mark space

(A) if a car is about to hit a pedestrian
(B) if a person is jaywalking
(C) if a police officer is directing traffic
(D) if a cyclist is going the wrong way on a one-way street
(E) if a woman and child are crossing in the crosswalk

Question 48 below is about question 8.

48. For number 48 on the answer sheet, mark space

(A) if the sign should be blue and orange
(B) if the sign signifies that this is a slow-moving vehicle
(C) if the sign means "pass when safe"
(D) if the sign should be worn on the driver's back
(E) if the sign means that you should yield the right of way to the vehicle to which it is attached

For number 49 on the answer sheet, mark the space that has the same letter as the letter you wrote on the answer line for question 9.

Question 50 below is about question 10.

50. For number 50 on the answer sheet, mark space

   (A) if the arrow in one lane points in one direction and the arrow in the other lane points in the opposite direction
   (B) if the arrows in both lanes point to the right
   (C) if the arrows in both lanes point to the left
   (D) if there are arrows pointing in both directions in both lanes
   (E) if there is an arrow in only one lane

Question 51 below is about question 11.

51. For number 51 on the answer sheet, mark space

   (A) if it is raining
   (B) if there is one balloon on the ground
   (C) if there are four balloons
   (D) if there is heavy road traffic
   (E) if it would be wise for the motorist to pull over to the side of the road to watch the show

Question 52 below is about question 12.

52. For number 52 on the answer sheet, mark space

   (A) if the wear on the tire indicates the effect of overinflation
   (B) if the wear on the tire indicates the effect of excessive caster
   (C) if the wear on the tire indicates the effect of improper balance
   (D) if the wear on the tire indicates the effect of underinflation
   (E) if the wear on the tire indicates the effect of toe-out

   For number 53 on the answer sheet, mark the space that has the same letter as the letter you wrote on the answer line for question 13.

Question 54 below is about question 14.

54. For number 54 on the answer sheet, mark space

   (A) if you should look for hitchhikers
   (B) if you should look for schoolchildren
   (C) if you should look for a garage sale
   (D) if you should watch out for a flagman
   (E) if you should watch for deaf pedestrians

Question 55 below is about question 15, and question 56 below is about question 16.

55. For number 55 on the answer sheet, mark space

   (A) if a little boy is running across the street
   (B) if a little boy is sleeping
   (C) if a little boy is helping an old lady cross the street
   (D) if a little boy is lying in the street
   (E) if a little boy is getting out of the car

56. For number 56 on the answer sheet, mark space

   (A) if an ambulance has just pulled up
   (B) if a man is getting out of the car
   (C) if there has been a hit-and-run accident
   (D) if a crowd is gathering around the little boy
   (E) if a woman is crying

For number 57 on the answer sheet, mark the space that has the same letter as the letter you wrote on the answer line for question 17.

For Number 58 on the answer sheet, mark the space that has the same letter as the letter you wrote on the answer line for question 18.

Question 59 below is about question 19, and question 60 below is about question 20.

59.   For number 59 on the answer sheet, mark space

(A) if the vehicle is a taxicab
(B) if the vehicle is a bus
(C) if the vehicle is a tractor-trailer
(D) if the vehicle is a farm tractor
(E) if the vehicle is a jeep

60.   For number 60 on the answer sheet, mark space

(A) if the passengers are schoolchildren
(B) if the passengers are campers
(C) if the passengers are farmers
(D) if the passengers are military personnel
(E) if the passengers are senior citizens

For number 61 on the answer sheet, mark the space that has the same letter as the letter you wrote on the answer line for question 21.

For number 62 on the answer sheet, mark the space that has the same letter as the letter you wrote on the answer line for question 22.

Questions 63 and 64 below are about Chart A, which you filled in. Mark on the answer sheet the letter of the answer.

63.   What is the license number of the truck that received a new fuel pump? Look at what you wrote on the chart. Do not try to answer from memory.

(A) 673 PUR
(B) 835 XZY
(C) 441 RTG
(D) 637 RUP

64.   At what odometer reading did truck 441 RTG have its oil changed?

(A) 46,908
(B) 64,809
(C) 46,098
(D) 46,089

Questions 65 and 66 below are about Chart B, which you filled in. Look at what you wrote on the chart and mark the answer sheet with the letter of the correct answer.

65.   What was the ID number of the driver who took truck license number 534 TRE?

(A) 6390
(B) 6309
(C) 7342
(D) 7243

66. At what odometer reading did driver number 7342 take out his truck?

(A) 56,798
(B) 88,141
(C) 35,790
(D) 65,798

Questions 67 and 68 below are about Chart C, which you filled in. Look at what you wrote on the chart and mark the answer sheet with the letter of the correct answer.

67. What was the odometer reading when driver number 9845 returned her jeep?
(A) 54,997
(B) 54,970
(C) 15,591
(D) 43,086

68. What was the odometer reading when driver number 4785 took out his jeep?
(A) 12,562
(B) 43,086
(C) 54,970
(D) 43,054

Questions 69 and 70 below are about Chart D, which you filled in. Look at what you wrote on the chart and mark the answer sheet with the letter of the correct answer.

69. What service was performed on vehicle license number 447 IKT?
(A) lubrication
(B) replacement of air hose
(C) carburetor adjustment
(D) tire change

70. What was the ID number of the serviceperson who changed a tire?

(A) 837 PRE
(B) 6052
(C) 6025
(D) 7092

Questions 71 and 72 below are about Chart E, which you filled in. Look at what you wrote on the chart and mark the answer sheet with the letter of the correct answer.

71. What was the ID number of the serviceperson to whom driver ID number 8372 turned over her truck?

(A) 3978
(B) 3987
(C) 3897
(D) 3879

72. What was the ID number of the driver who turned over her truck to serviceperson ID 4273?

(A) 943 WCG
(B) 5842
(C) 959 YUX
(D) 6241

Question 73 below is about question 33 under Picture X, and question 74 below is about question 34 under Picture Y.

73.   For number 73 on the answer sheet, mark space

(A) if there are no lanes open in Picture X
(B) if there is only one lane open in Picture X
(C) if there are only two lanes open in Picture X
(D) if there are only three lanes open in Picture X
(E) if there is only one lane closed in Picture X

74.   For number 74 on the answer sheet, mark space

(A) if there is only one lane closed in Picture Y
(B) if there are only two lanes closed in Picture Y
(C) if there are only three lanes closed in Picture Y
(D) if there are only four lanes closed in Picture Y
(E) if there are only five lanes closed in Picture Y

Question 75 below is about question 35.

75.   For number 75 on the answer sheet, mark space

(A) if drivers approaching from the right cannot see any traffic signals
(B) if drivers approaching this light straight ahead have a green arrow pointing to the right
(C) if drivers approaching from the left are guided by five different traffic signals
(D) if drivers approaching this light straight ahead have a red arrow pointing to the left
(E) if drivers approaching this light straight ahead have a green arrow pointing to the left

For number 76 on the answer sheet, mark the space that has the same letter as the letter you wrote on the answer line for question 36.

For number 77 on the answer sheet, mark the space that has the same letter as the letter you wrote on the answer line for question 37.

Question 78 below is about question 38.

78.   For number 78 on the answer sheet, mark space

(A) if a person is being pushed in a wheelchair
(B) if there has been a traffic accident
(C) if two men are putting a person into an ambulance
(D) if a police officer is directing traffic
(E) if a woman is wringing her hands in despair

Question 79 below is about question 39.

79.   For number 79 on the answer sheet, mark space

(A) if there is a mail truck in the picture
(B) if a car is about to enter an intersection
(C) if three people are walking abreast
(D) if children are playing in the street
(E) if a young man is walking with an elderly woman

For number 80 on the answer sheet, mark the space that has the same letter as the letter you wrote on the answer line for question 40.

END OF EXAM

CORRECT ANSWERS
FOR MODEL EXAMINATION 4

PART ONE

1. Two
2. The car on the left has stopped at the stop sign; the car on the right is passing through the intersection.
3. In the rearview mirror, the driver sees that there is a motorcycle directly behind the car.
4. The man on the left is wearing his seat belt incorrectly. The shoulder strap is under his arm instead of across his shoulder.
5. The man on the right is wearing his seat belt correctly.
6. Stop and wait for the train to pass and the barrier to be lifted.
7. The vehicles have stopped for pedestrians in the crosswalk.
8. The sign on the left should be mounted on the tractor. The sign is a warning to other vehicles on the road that the vehicle upon which it is mounted is a slow-moving vehicle.
9. **(C)**
10.

11. There is one car on the road. There are three hot air balloons in the sky. The sun is peeking from behind some clouds.
12. The tire is worn right down the middle.
13. **(C)**
14. Look for a flagman.
15. The young boy is lying in the roadway.
16. A man is getting out of a car.
17. **(C)**
18. **(B)**
19. The vehicle is a bus.
20. The passengers are a group of well-dressed elderly men and women, some with suitcases.
21. **(A)**
22. **(C)**

Chart A

Truck License Number	Kind of Service	Odometer Reading When Serviced
835 XYZ	tune up	22,305
673 PUR	new fuel pump	67,422
441 RTG	oil change	46,098

23. (row 673 PUR)
24. (row 441 RTG)

Chart B

Driver ID Number	Truck License Number	Odometer Reading
8723	997 IUP	88,141
6309	534 TRE	35,790
7342	256 TAE	56,798

25. (row 6309)
26. (row 7342)

Chart C

Driver ID Number	Odometer Reading When Taken Out	Odometer Reading When Returned
3406	12,562	12,591
9845	54,970	54,997
4785	43,054	43,086

27. (row 9845)
28. (row 4785)

Chart D

Vehicle License Number	Kind of Service	Serviceperson ID Number
592 TJD	grease job	8452
447 IKT	carburetor adjustment	7092
837 PRE	tire change	6052

29. (row 447 IKT)
30. (row 837 PRE)

Chart E

Truck License Number	Driver ID Number	Serviceperson ID Number
042 RVB	5842	4307
759 YUX	8372	3987
943 WCG	6241	4273

31. 759 YUX
32. 943 WCG

33. Picture X shows the left lane is open to traffic (shown by arrow) and the two lanes to the right are closed to traffic (shown by Xs).

34. Picture Y shows six traffic lanes. Starting from the left, lanes 1 and 2 are open to traffic, lanes 3 and 4 are closed to traffic, lane 5 is open, and lane 6 is closed.

35. There is a signal light at a three- or four-way intersection. Cars coming straight at the signal light can have a red, yellow, or green light, or a green arrow pointing left. Cars coming from left and right probably have only a red, yellow, or green light.

36. **(C)**

37. **(B)**

38. Two men are putting a person on a stretcher into an ambulance.

39. A young man and an older woman are walking together.

40. **(A)**

PART TWO

41. **C**	55. **D**	68. **D**
42. **E**	56. **B**	69. **C**
43. **B**	57. **C**	70. **B**
44. **A**	58. **B**	71. **B**
45. **D**	59. **B**	72. **D**
46. **C**	60. **E**	73. **B**
47. **E**	61. **A**	74. **C**
48. **B**	62. **C**	75. **E**
49. **C**	63. **A**	76. **C**
50. **A**	64. **C**	77. **B**
51. **E**	65. **B**	78. **C**
52. **A**	66. **A**	79. **E**
53. **C**	67. **A**	80. **A**
54. **D**		

Model Examination 5
Answer Sheet

Exam 630

Postal Police Officer

The exam that follows is very much like the actual postal police officer examination. Tear out the answer sheet and use it to record your answers to the examination questions. Listen carefully and follow the additional instructions as given by the examiner. Correct answers for Book A questions are on page 242.

BOOK A
PART A—NAME AND NUMBER COMPARISONS

1. Ⓐ Ⓑ Ⓒ Ⓓ Ⓔ   11. Ⓐ Ⓑ Ⓒ Ⓓ Ⓔ   21. Ⓐ Ⓑ Ⓒ Ⓓ Ⓔ   31. Ⓐ Ⓑ Ⓒ Ⓓ Ⓔ   41. Ⓐ Ⓑ Ⓒ Ⓓ Ⓔ
2. Ⓐ Ⓑ Ⓒ Ⓓ Ⓔ   12. Ⓐ Ⓑ Ⓒ Ⓓ Ⓔ   22. Ⓐ Ⓑ Ⓒ Ⓓ Ⓔ   32. Ⓐ Ⓑ Ⓒ Ⓓ Ⓔ   42. Ⓐ Ⓑ Ⓒ Ⓓ Ⓔ
3. Ⓐ Ⓑ Ⓒ Ⓓ Ⓔ   13. Ⓐ Ⓑ Ⓒ Ⓓ Ⓔ   23. Ⓐ Ⓑ Ⓒ Ⓓ Ⓔ   33. Ⓐ Ⓑ Ⓒ Ⓓ Ⓔ   43. Ⓐ Ⓑ Ⓒ Ⓓ Ⓔ
4. Ⓐ Ⓑ Ⓒ Ⓓ Ⓔ   14. Ⓐ Ⓑ Ⓒ Ⓓ Ⓔ   24. Ⓐ Ⓑ Ⓒ Ⓓ Ⓔ   34. Ⓐ Ⓑ Ⓒ Ⓓ Ⓔ   44. Ⓐ Ⓑ Ⓒ Ⓓ Ⓔ
5. Ⓐ Ⓑ Ⓒ Ⓓ Ⓔ   15. Ⓐ Ⓑ Ⓒ Ⓓ Ⓔ   25. Ⓐ Ⓑ Ⓒ Ⓓ Ⓔ   35. Ⓐ Ⓑ Ⓒ Ⓓ Ⓔ   45. Ⓐ Ⓑ Ⓒ Ⓓ Ⓔ
6. Ⓐ Ⓑ Ⓒ Ⓓ Ⓔ   16. Ⓐ Ⓑ Ⓒ Ⓓ Ⓔ   26. Ⓐ Ⓑ Ⓒ Ⓓ Ⓔ   36. Ⓐ Ⓑ Ⓒ Ⓓ Ⓔ   46. Ⓐ Ⓑ Ⓒ Ⓓ Ⓔ
7. Ⓐ Ⓑ Ⓒ Ⓓ Ⓔ   17. Ⓐ Ⓑ Ⓒ Ⓓ Ⓔ   27. Ⓐ Ⓑ Ⓒ Ⓓ Ⓔ   37. Ⓐ Ⓑ Ⓒ Ⓓ Ⓔ   47. Ⓐ Ⓑ Ⓒ Ⓓ Ⓔ
8. Ⓐ Ⓑ Ⓒ Ⓓ Ⓔ   18. Ⓐ Ⓑ Ⓒ Ⓓ Ⓔ   28. Ⓐ Ⓑ Ⓒ Ⓓ Ⓔ   38. Ⓐ Ⓑ Ⓒ Ⓓ Ⓔ   48. Ⓐ Ⓑ Ⓒ Ⓓ Ⓔ
9. Ⓐ Ⓑ Ⓒ Ⓓ Ⓔ   19. Ⓐ Ⓑ Ⓒ Ⓓ Ⓔ   29. Ⓐ Ⓑ Ⓒ Ⓓ Ⓔ   39. Ⓐ Ⓑ Ⓒ Ⓓ Ⓔ   49. Ⓐ Ⓑ Ⓒ Ⓓ Ⓔ
10. Ⓐ Ⓑ Ⓒ Ⓓ Ⓔ   20. Ⓐ Ⓑ Ⓒ Ⓓ Ⓔ   30. Ⓐ Ⓑ Ⓒ Ⓓ Ⓔ   40. Ⓐ Ⓑ Ⓒ Ⓓ Ⓔ   50. Ⓐ Ⓑ Ⓒ Ⓓ Ⓔ

PART B—READING COMPREHENSION

1. Ⓐ Ⓑ Ⓒ Ⓓ Ⓔ   7. Ⓐ Ⓑ Ⓒ Ⓓ Ⓔ   13. Ⓐ Ⓑ Ⓒ Ⓓ Ⓔ   19. Ⓐ Ⓑ Ⓒ Ⓓ Ⓔ   25. Ⓐ Ⓑ Ⓒ Ⓓ Ⓔ
2. Ⓐ Ⓑ Ⓒ Ⓓ Ⓔ   8. Ⓐ Ⓑ Ⓒ Ⓓ Ⓔ   14. Ⓐ Ⓑ Ⓒ Ⓓ Ⓔ   20. Ⓐ Ⓑ Ⓒ Ⓓ Ⓔ   26. Ⓐ Ⓑ Ⓒ Ⓓ Ⓔ
3. Ⓐ Ⓑ Ⓒ Ⓓ Ⓔ   9. Ⓐ Ⓑ Ⓒ Ⓓ Ⓔ   15. Ⓐ Ⓑ Ⓒ Ⓓ Ⓔ   21. Ⓐ Ⓑ Ⓒ Ⓓ Ⓔ   27. Ⓐ Ⓑ Ⓒ Ⓓ Ⓔ
4. Ⓐ Ⓑ Ⓒ Ⓓ Ⓔ   10. Ⓐ Ⓑ Ⓒ Ⓓ Ⓔ   16. Ⓐ Ⓑ Ⓒ Ⓓ Ⓔ   22. Ⓐ Ⓑ Ⓒ Ⓓ Ⓔ   28. Ⓐ Ⓑ Ⓒ Ⓓ Ⓔ
5. Ⓐ Ⓑ Ⓒ Ⓓ Ⓔ   11. Ⓐ Ⓑ Ⓒ Ⓓ Ⓔ   17. Ⓐ Ⓑ Ⓒ Ⓓ Ⓔ   23. Ⓐ Ⓑ Ⓒ Ⓓ Ⓔ   29. Ⓐ Ⓑ Ⓒ Ⓓ Ⓔ
6. Ⓐ Ⓑ Ⓒ Ⓓ Ⓔ   12. Ⓐ Ⓑ Ⓒ Ⓓ Ⓔ   18. Ⓐ Ⓑ Ⓒ Ⓓ Ⓔ   24. Ⓐ Ⓑ Ⓒ Ⓓ Ⓔ   30. Ⓐ Ⓑ Ⓒ Ⓓ Ⓔ

TEAR HERE

PART C—ARITHMETIC REASONING

1. Ⓐ Ⓑ Ⓒ Ⓓ Ⓔ   5. Ⓐ Ⓑ Ⓒ Ⓓ Ⓔ   9. Ⓐ Ⓑ Ⓒ Ⓓ Ⓔ   13. Ⓐ Ⓑ Ⓒ Ⓓ Ⓔ   17. Ⓐ Ⓑ Ⓒ Ⓓ Ⓔ
2. Ⓐ Ⓑ Ⓒ Ⓓ Ⓔ   6. Ⓐ Ⓑ Ⓒ Ⓓ Ⓔ   10. Ⓐ Ⓑ Ⓒ Ⓓ Ⓔ   14. Ⓐ Ⓑ Ⓒ Ⓓ Ⓔ   18. Ⓐ Ⓑ Ⓒ Ⓓ Ⓔ
3. Ⓐ Ⓑ Ⓒ Ⓓ Ⓔ   7. Ⓐ Ⓑ Ⓒ Ⓓ Ⓔ   11. Ⓐ Ⓑ Ⓒ Ⓓ Ⓔ   15. Ⓐ Ⓑ Ⓒ Ⓓ Ⓔ   19. Ⓐ Ⓑ Ⓒ Ⓓ Ⓔ
4. Ⓐ Ⓑ Ⓒ Ⓓ Ⓔ   8. Ⓐ Ⓑ Ⓒ Ⓓ Ⓔ   12. Ⓐ Ⓑ Ⓒ Ⓓ Ⓔ   16. Ⓐ Ⓑ Ⓒ Ⓓ Ⓔ   20. Ⓐ Ⓑ Ⓒ Ⓓ Ⓔ

BOOK B

There are 122 questions in Book B of the Postal Police Officer Exam. The questions in Book B are questions about you—about your school and work records, about your likes and dislikes, and about your personality. There are no right and wrong answers to these Book B questions, so there is no answer key and no scoring method. In this model exam we include forty questions that are typical of the questions you'll be asked. You may want to look at old report cards or yearbooks so that you are prepared to answer these questions.

1. Ⓐ Ⓑ Ⓒ Ⓓ Ⓔ   26. Ⓐ Ⓑ Ⓒ Ⓓ Ⓔ   51. Ⓐ Ⓑ Ⓒ Ⓓ Ⓔ   76. Ⓐ Ⓑ Ⓒ Ⓓ Ⓔ   101. Ⓐ Ⓑ Ⓒ Ⓓ Ⓔ
2. Ⓐ Ⓑ Ⓒ Ⓓ Ⓔ   27. Ⓐ Ⓑ Ⓒ Ⓓ Ⓔ   52. Ⓐ Ⓑ Ⓒ Ⓓ Ⓔ   77. Ⓐ Ⓑ Ⓒ Ⓓ Ⓔ   102. Ⓐ Ⓑ Ⓒ Ⓓ Ⓔ
3. Ⓐ Ⓑ Ⓒ Ⓓ Ⓔ   28. Ⓐ Ⓑ Ⓒ Ⓓ Ⓔ   53. Ⓐ Ⓑ Ⓒ Ⓓ Ⓔ   78. Ⓐ Ⓑ Ⓒ Ⓓ Ⓔ   103. Ⓐ Ⓑ Ⓒ Ⓓ Ⓔ
4. Ⓐ Ⓑ Ⓒ Ⓓ Ⓔ   29. Ⓐ Ⓑ Ⓒ Ⓓ Ⓔ   54. Ⓐ Ⓑ Ⓒ Ⓓ Ⓔ   79. Ⓐ Ⓑ Ⓒ Ⓓ Ⓔ   104. Ⓐ Ⓑ Ⓒ Ⓓ Ⓔ
5. Ⓐ Ⓑ Ⓒ Ⓓ Ⓔ   30. Ⓐ Ⓑ Ⓒ Ⓓ Ⓔ   55. Ⓐ Ⓑ Ⓒ Ⓓ Ⓔ   80. Ⓐ Ⓑ Ⓒ Ⓓ Ⓔ   105. Ⓐ Ⓑ Ⓒ Ⓓ Ⓔ
6. Ⓐ Ⓑ Ⓒ Ⓓ Ⓔ   31. Ⓐ Ⓑ Ⓒ Ⓓ Ⓔ   56. Ⓐ Ⓑ Ⓒ Ⓓ Ⓔ   81. Ⓐ Ⓑ Ⓒ Ⓓ Ⓔ   106. Ⓐ Ⓑ Ⓒ Ⓓ Ⓔ
7. Ⓐ Ⓑ Ⓒ Ⓓ Ⓔ   32. Ⓐ Ⓑ Ⓒ Ⓓ Ⓔ   57. Ⓐ Ⓑ Ⓒ Ⓓ Ⓔ   82. Ⓐ Ⓑ Ⓒ Ⓓ Ⓔ   107. Ⓐ Ⓑ Ⓒ Ⓓ Ⓔ
8. Ⓐ Ⓑ Ⓒ Ⓓ Ⓔ   33. Ⓐ Ⓑ Ⓒ Ⓓ Ⓔ   58. Ⓐ Ⓑ Ⓒ Ⓓ Ⓔ   83. Ⓐ Ⓑ Ⓒ Ⓓ Ⓔ   108. Ⓐ Ⓑ Ⓒ Ⓓ Ⓔ
9. Ⓐ Ⓑ Ⓒ Ⓓ Ⓔ   34. Ⓐ Ⓑ Ⓒ Ⓓ Ⓔ   59. Ⓐ Ⓑ Ⓒ Ⓓ Ⓔ   84. Ⓐ Ⓑ Ⓒ Ⓓ Ⓔ   109. Ⓐ Ⓑ Ⓒ Ⓓ Ⓔ
10. Ⓐ Ⓑ Ⓒ Ⓓ Ⓔ   35. Ⓐ Ⓑ Ⓒ Ⓓ Ⓔ   60. Ⓐ Ⓑ Ⓒ Ⓓ Ⓔ   85. Ⓐ Ⓑ Ⓒ Ⓓ Ⓔ   110. Ⓐ Ⓑ Ⓒ Ⓓ Ⓔ
11. Ⓐ Ⓑ Ⓒ Ⓓ Ⓔ   36. Ⓐ Ⓑ Ⓒ Ⓓ Ⓔ   61. Ⓐ Ⓑ Ⓒ Ⓓ Ⓔ   86. Ⓐ Ⓑ Ⓒ Ⓓ Ⓔ   111. Ⓐ Ⓑ Ⓒ Ⓓ Ⓔ
12. Ⓐ Ⓑ Ⓒ Ⓓ Ⓔ   37. Ⓐ Ⓑ Ⓒ Ⓓ Ⓔ   62. Ⓐ Ⓑ Ⓒ Ⓓ Ⓔ   87. Ⓐ Ⓑ Ⓒ Ⓓ Ⓔ   112. Ⓐ Ⓑ Ⓒ Ⓓ Ⓔ
13. Ⓐ Ⓑ Ⓒ Ⓓ Ⓔ   38. Ⓐ Ⓑ Ⓒ Ⓓ Ⓔ   63. Ⓐ Ⓑ Ⓒ Ⓓ Ⓔ   88. Ⓐ Ⓑ Ⓒ Ⓓ Ⓔ   113. Ⓐ Ⓑ Ⓒ Ⓓ Ⓔ
14. Ⓐ Ⓑ Ⓒ Ⓓ Ⓔ   39. Ⓐ Ⓑ Ⓒ Ⓓ Ⓔ   64. Ⓐ Ⓑ Ⓒ Ⓓ Ⓔ   89. Ⓐ Ⓑ Ⓒ Ⓓ Ⓔ   114. Ⓐ Ⓑ Ⓒ Ⓓ Ⓔ
15. Ⓐ Ⓑ Ⓒ Ⓓ Ⓔ   40. Ⓐ Ⓑ Ⓒ Ⓓ Ⓔ   65. Ⓐ Ⓑ Ⓒ Ⓓ Ⓔ   90. Ⓐ Ⓑ Ⓒ Ⓓ Ⓔ   115. Ⓐ Ⓑ Ⓒ Ⓓ Ⓔ
16. Ⓐ Ⓑ Ⓒ Ⓓ Ⓔ   41. Ⓐ Ⓑ Ⓒ Ⓓ Ⓔ   66. Ⓐ Ⓑ Ⓒ Ⓓ Ⓔ   91. Ⓐ Ⓑ Ⓒ Ⓓ Ⓔ   116. Ⓐ Ⓑ Ⓒ Ⓓ Ⓔ
17. Ⓐ Ⓑ Ⓒ Ⓓ Ⓔ   42. Ⓐ Ⓑ Ⓒ Ⓓ Ⓔ   67. Ⓐ Ⓑ Ⓒ Ⓓ Ⓔ   92. Ⓐ Ⓑ Ⓒ Ⓓ Ⓔ   117. Ⓐ Ⓑ Ⓒ Ⓓ Ⓔ
18. Ⓐ Ⓑ Ⓒ Ⓓ Ⓔ   43. Ⓐ Ⓑ Ⓒ Ⓓ Ⓔ   68. Ⓐ Ⓑ Ⓒ Ⓓ Ⓔ   93. Ⓐ Ⓑ Ⓒ Ⓓ Ⓔ   118. Ⓐ Ⓑ Ⓒ Ⓓ Ⓔ
19. Ⓐ Ⓑ Ⓒ Ⓓ Ⓔ   44. Ⓐ Ⓑ Ⓒ Ⓓ Ⓔ   69. Ⓐ Ⓑ Ⓒ Ⓓ Ⓔ   94. Ⓐ Ⓑ Ⓒ Ⓓ Ⓔ   119. Ⓐ Ⓑ Ⓒ Ⓓ Ⓔ
20. Ⓐ Ⓑ Ⓒ Ⓓ Ⓔ   45. Ⓐ Ⓑ Ⓒ Ⓓ Ⓔ   70. Ⓐ Ⓑ Ⓒ Ⓓ Ⓔ   95. Ⓐ Ⓑ Ⓒ Ⓓ Ⓔ   120. Ⓐ Ⓑ Ⓒ Ⓓ Ⓔ
21. Ⓐ Ⓑ Ⓒ Ⓓ Ⓔ   46. Ⓐ Ⓑ Ⓒ Ⓓ Ⓔ   71. Ⓐ Ⓑ Ⓒ Ⓓ Ⓔ   96. Ⓐ Ⓑ Ⓒ Ⓓ Ⓔ   121. Ⓐ Ⓑ Ⓒ Ⓓ Ⓔ
22. Ⓐ Ⓑ Ⓒ Ⓓ Ⓔ   47. Ⓐ Ⓑ Ⓒ Ⓓ Ⓔ   72. Ⓐ Ⓑ Ⓒ Ⓓ Ⓔ   97. Ⓐ Ⓑ Ⓒ Ⓓ Ⓔ   122. Ⓐ Ⓑ Ⓒ Ⓓ Ⓔ
23. Ⓐ Ⓑ Ⓒ Ⓓ Ⓔ   48. Ⓐ Ⓑ Ⓒ Ⓓ Ⓔ   73. Ⓐ Ⓑ Ⓒ Ⓓ Ⓔ   98. Ⓐ Ⓑ Ⓒ Ⓓ Ⓔ
24. Ⓐ Ⓑ Ⓒ Ⓓ Ⓔ   49. Ⓐ Ⓑ Ⓒ Ⓓ Ⓔ   74. Ⓐ Ⓑ Ⓒ Ⓓ Ⓔ   99. Ⓐ Ⓑ Ⓒ Ⓓ Ⓔ
25. Ⓐ Ⓑ Ⓒ Ⓓ Ⓔ   50. Ⓐ Ⓑ Ⓒ Ⓓ Ⓔ   75. Ⓐ Ⓑ Ⓒ Ⓓ Ⓔ   100. Ⓐ Ⓑ Ⓒ Ⓓ Ⓔ

BOOK A

PART A—NAME AND NUMBER COMPARISONS

Time: 8 Minutes. 50 Questions.

Directions: For each question, compare the three names or numbers and mark your answer:

    A   if **ALL THREE** names or numbers are exactly **ALIKE**
    B   if only the **FIRST** and **SECOND** names or numbers are exactly **ALIKE**
    C   if only the **FIRST** and **THIRD** names or numbers are exactly **ALIKE**
    D   if only the **SECOND** and **THIRD** names or numbers are exactly **ALIKE**
    E   if **ALL THREE** names or numbers are **DIFFERENT**

1.	Thomas L. Kershaw	Thomas L. Kershaw	Thomas J. Kershaw
2.	Takahide E. Moro	Takahide E. Moru	Takahide E. Moru
3.	Carlota Cosentino	Carlotta Cosentino	Carlotta Constentino
4.	Albertina Andriuolo	Albertina Andriuolo	Albertina Andriuolo
5.	Francis J. Czukor	Francis Z. Czukor	Frances J. Czukor
6.	7692138	7692138	7692138
7.	2633342	2633342	2633342
8.	2454803	2548403	2454803
9.	9670243	9670423	9670423
10.	2789350	2789350	2798350
11.	Darlene P. Tenenbaum	Darlene P. Tenenbaum	Darlene P. Tanenbaum
12.	Maxwell Macmillan	Maxwell MacMillan	Maxwell Macmillian
13.	Frank D. Stanick	Frank D. Satanic	Frank D. Satanich
14.	J. Robert Schunk	J. Robert Schunh	Robert J. Schunk
15.	Fernando Silva, Jr.	Fernando Silva, Jr.	Fernand Silva, Jr.
16.	2797630	2797360	2797360
17.	6312192	6312192	6312192
18.	7412032	7412032	7412032
19.	2789327	2879327	2789327
20.	5927681	5927861	5927681
21.	Wendy A. Courtney	Wendy A. Courtney	Wendy A. Courtnay
22.	Lambert Forman, MD	Lambert Forman, MD	Lambert Forman, MD
23.	Joseph A. Gurreri	Joseph A. Gurreri	Joseph A. Gurreri
24.	Sylnette Lynch	Sylnette Lynch	Sylnette Lynch
25.	Zion McKenzie, Jr.	Zion McKenzie, Sr.	Zion MacKenzie, Jr.
26.	6932976	6939276	6932796
27.	9631695	9636195	9631695
28.	7370527	7375027	7370537
29.	2799379	2739779	2799379
30.	5261383	5261383	5261338
31.	J. Randolph Rea	J. Randolph Rea	J. Randolphe Rea
32.	W. E. Johnston	W. E. Johnson	W. E. Johnson
33.	Vergil L. Muller	Vergil L. Muller	Vergil L. Muller
34.	Atherton R. Warde	Asheton R. Warde	Atherton P. Warde

35.	E. Owens McVey	E. Owen McVey	E. Owen McVay
36.	8125690	8126690	8125609
37.	2395890	2395890	2395890
38.	1926341	1926347	1926314
39.	6219354	6219354	6219354
40.	2312793	2312793	2312793
41.	Alexander Majthenyi	Alexander Majthenyi	Alexander Majthenyi
42.	James T. Harbison	James T. Harbinson	James T. Harbison
43.	Margareta Goldenkoff	Margaretta Goldenkoff	Margaretha Goldenkoff
44.	Cornelius Detwiler	Cornelius Detwiler	Cornelius Detwiler
45.	Benjamin A. D'Ortona	Benjamin A. D'Ortoni	Benjamin D'Ortonia
46.	1065407	1065407	1065047
47.	6452054	6452654	6452054
48.	8501268	8501268	8501286
49.	3457988	3457986	3457986
50.	4695682	4695862	4695682

END OF PART A

PART B—READING COMPREHENSION

Time: 60 Minutes. 30 Questions.

Directions: For each reading question you will be given a paragraph that contains all the information necessary to infer the correct answer. Use only the information provided in the paragraph. Do not speculate or make assumptions that go beyond this information. Also, assume that all information given in the paragraph is true, even if it conflicts with some fact known to you. Only one correct answer can be validly inferred from the information contained in the paragraph. Mark its letter on your answer sheet.

1.   A member of the department shall not indulge in liquor while in uniform. A member of the department not required to wear a uniform and a uniformed member while out of uniform shall not indulge in intoxicants to an extent unfitting the member for duty.

The paragraph best supports the statement that

(A) an off-duty member, not in uniform, may drink liquor to the extent that it does not unfit the member for duty
(B) a member not on duty, but in uniform and not unfit for duty, may drink liquor
(C) an on-duty member, unfit for duty in uniform, may drink intoxicants
(D) a uniformed member in civilian clothes may not drink intoxicants unless unfit for duty
(E) a civilian member of the department, in uniform, may drink liquor if fit for duty

2.   Tax law specialists may authorize their assistants to sign their names to reports, letters, and papers that are not specially required to be signed personally by the tax law specialist. The signature should be: "Jane Doe, tax law specialist, by Richard Roe, tax technician." The name of the tax law specialist may be written or stamped, but the signature of the tax technician shall be in ink.

The paragraph best supports the statement that

(A) if a tax law specialist's assistant signs official papers both by rubber stamp and in ink, the assistant has authority to sign
(B) if a tax technician does not neglect to include his or her title in ink along with his or her signature following the word "by," the technician may sign papers that are not specially required to be signed personally by the tax law specialist
(C) no signatory authority delegated to the tax technician by the tax law specialist may be redelegated by the tax technician to an assistant unless so authorized in ink by the tax law specialist
(D) if a tax law specialist personally signs written requisitions in ink, the technician is not required to identify the source of the order with a rubber stamp
(E) when a tax technician signs authorized papers for a tax law specialist, the tax technician must write out the tax law specialist's signature in full with pen and ink

3. Upon retirement from service, a member shall receive a retirement allowance consisting of an annuity that shall be the actuarial equivalent of his accumulated deductions at the time of retirement; a pension in addition to his annuity that shall be one service-fraction of his final compensation multiplied by the number of years of government service since he last became a member; and a pension that is the actuarial equivalent of the reserve-for-increased-take-home-pay to which he may then be entitled, if any.

The paragraph best supports the statement that

(A) a retirement allowance shall consist of an annuity plus a pension plus an actuarial equivalent of a service-fraction

(B) upon retirement from service, a member shall receive an annuity plus a pension plus an actuarial equivalent of reserve-for-increased-take-home-pay if he is entitled

(C) a retiring member shall receive an annuity plus reserve-for-increased-take-home-pay, if any, plus final compensation

(D) a retirement allowance shall consist of a pension plus reserve-for-increased-take-home-pay, if any, plus accumulated deductions

(E) a retirement allowance shall consist of an annuity that is equal to one service-fraction of final compensation, a pension multiplied by the number of years of government service, and the actuarial equivalent of accumulated deductions from increased take-home-pay

4. If you are in doubt as to whether any matter is legally mailable, you should ask the postmaster. Even though the Postal Service has not expressly declared any matter to be nonmailable, the sender of such matter may be held fully liable for violation of law if he or she does actually send nonmailable matter through the mail.

The paragraph best supports the statement that

(A) if the postmaster is in doubt as to whether any matter is legally mailable, the postmaster may be held liable for any sender's sending nonmailable matter through the mail

(B) if the sender is ignorant of what it is that constitutes nonmailable matter, the sender is relieved of all responsibility for mailing nonmailable matter

(C) if a sender sends nonmailable matter, the sender is fully liable for law violation even though doubt may have existed about the mailability of the matter

(D) if the Postal Service has not expressly declared material mailable, it is nonmailable

(E) if the Postal Service has not expressly declared material nonmailable, it is mailable

5. In evaluating education for a particular position, education in and of itself is of no value except to the degree in which it contributes to knowledges, skills and abilities needed in the particular job. On its face, such a statement would seem to contend that general educational development need not be considered in evaluating education and training. Much to the contrary, such a proposition favors the consideration of any and all training, but only as it pertains to the position for which the applicant applies.

    The paragraph best supports the statement that

    (A) if general education is supplemented by specialized education, it is of no value
    (B) if a high school education is desirable in any occupation, special training need not be evaluated
    (C) in evaluating education, a contradiction arises in assigning equal weight to general and specialized education
    (D) unless it is supplemented by general education, specialized education is of no value
    (E) education is of value to the degree to which it is needed in the particular position

6. Statistics tell us that heart disease kills more people than any other illness, and the death rate continues to rise. People over 30 have a fifty-fifty chance of escaping, for heart disease is chiefly an illness of people in late middle age and advanced years. Because there are more people in this age group living today than there were some years ago, heart disease is able to find more victims.

    The paragraph best supports the statement that

    (A) if a person has heart disease, there is a 50 percent chance that he or she is over 30 years of age
    (B) according to statistics, more middle-aged and elderly people die of heart disease than of all other causes
    (C) because heart disease is chiefly an illness of people in late middle age, young people are less likely to be the victims of heart disease
    (D) the rising birth rate has increased the possibility that the average person will die of heart disease
    (E) if the stress of modern living were not increasing, there would be a slower increase in the risk of heart disease.

7. Racketeers are primarily concerned with business affairs, legitimate or otherwise, and prefer those that are close to the margin of legitimacy. They get their best opportunities from business organizations that meet the need of large sections of the public for goods or services that are defined as illegitimate by the same public, such as prostitution, gambling, illicit drugs or liquor. In contrast to the thief, the racketeer and the establishments he or she controls deliver goods and services for money received.

    The paragraph best supports the statement that

    (A) since racketeers deliver goods and services for money received, their business affairs are not illegitimate
    (B) since racketeering involves objects of value, it is unlike theft
    (C) victims of racketeers are not guilty of violating the law, therefore racketeering is a victimless crime
    (D) since many people want services which are not obtainable through legitimate sources, they contribute to the difficulty of suppressing racketeers
    (E) if large sections of the public are engaged in legitimate business with racketeers, the businesses are not illegitimate

8. The housing authority not only faces every problem of the private developer, it must also assume responsibilities of which private building is free. The authority must account to the community; it must conform to federal regulations; it must provide durable buildings of good standard at low cost; and it must overcome the prejudices of contractors, bankers and prospective tenants against public operations. These authorities are being watched by antihousing enthusiasts for the first error of judgment or the first evidence of high costs that can be torn to bits before a Congressional committee.

    The paragraph best supports the statement that

    (A) since private developers are not accountable to the community, they do not have the opposition of contractors, bankers and prospective tenants
    (B) if Congressional committees are watched by antihousing enthusiasts, they may discover errors of judgment and high costs on the part of a housing authority
    (C) while a housing authority must deal with all the difficulties encountered by a private builder, it must also deal with antihousing enthusiasts
    (D) if housing authorities are not immune to errors in judgment, they must provide durable buildings of good standard and low cost just like private developers
    (E) if a housing authority is to conform to federal regulations, it must overcome the prejudices of contractors, builders and prospective tenants

9. Security of tenure in the public service must be viewed in the context of the universal quest for security. If we narrow our application of the term to employment, the problem of security in the public service is seen to differ from that in private industry only in the need to meet the peculiar threats to security in governmental organizations—principally the danger of making employment contingent upon factors other than the performance of the workers.

The paragraph best supports the statement that

(A) if workers seek security, they should enter public service

(B) if employment is contingent upon factors other than work performance, workers will feel more secure

(C) if employees believe that their security is threatened, they are employed in private industry

(D) the term of employment in public service differs from that in private industry

(E) the employment status of the public servant with respect to security of tenure differs from that of the private employee by encompassing factors beyond those affecting the private employee

10. The wide use of antibiotics has presented a number of problems. Some patients become allergic to the drugs, so that they cannot be used when they are needed. In other cases, after prolonged treatment with antibiotics, certain organisms no longer respond to them. This is one of the reasons for the constant search for more potent drugs.

The paragraph best supports the statement that

(A) since a number of problems have been presented by long term treatment with antibiotics, antibiotics should never be used on a long term basis

(B) because some people have developed an allergy to specific drugs, potent antibiotics cannot always be used

(C) since antibiotics have been used successfully for certain allergies, there must be a constant search for more potent drugs

(D) if antibiotics are used for a prolonged period of time, certain organisms become allergic to them

(E) since so many diseases have been successfully treated with antibiotics, there must be a constant search for new drugs

11. The noncompetitive class consists of positions for which there are minimum qualifications but for which no reliable exam has been developed. In the noncompetitive class, every applicant must meet minimum qualifications in terms of education, experience, and medical or physical qualifications. There may even be an examination on a pass/fail basis.

The paragraph best supports the statement that

(A) if an exam is unreliable, the position is in the noncompetitive class

(B) if an applicant has met minimum qualifications in terms of education, experience, medical, or physical requirements, the applicant must pass a test

(C) if an applicant has met minimum qualifications in terms of education, experience, medical, or physical requirements, the applicant may fail a test

(D) if an applicant passes an exam for a noncompetitive position, the applicant must also meet minimum qualifications

(E) if there are minimum qualifications for a position, the position is in the noncompetitive class

12. Two independent clauses cannot share one sentence without some form of connective. If they do, they form a run-on sentence. Two principal clauses may be joined by a coordinating conjunction, by a comma followed by a coordinating conjunction, or by a semicolon. They may also form two distinct sentences. Two main clauses may never be joined by a comma without a coordinating conjunction. This error is called a comma splice.

The paragraph best supports the statement that

(A) if the violation is called a comma splice, two main clauses are joined by a comma without a coordinating conjunction
(B) if two distinct sentences share one sentence and are joined by a coordinating conjunction, the result is a run-on sentence
(C) when a coordinating conjunction is not followed by a semicolon, the writer has committed an error of punctuation
(D) while a comma and a semicolon may not be used in the same principal clause, they may be used in the same sentence
(E) a bad remedy for a run-on sentence is not a comma splice

13. The pay in some job titles is hourly; in others it is annual. Official work weeks vary from 35 hours to 37-$\frac{1}{2}$ hours to 40 hours. In some positions, overtime is earned for all time worked beyond the set number of hours, and differentials are paid for night, weekend, and holiday work. Other positions offer compensatory time off for overtime or for work during unpopular times. Still other positions require the jobholder to devote as must extra time as needed to do the work without any extra compensation. And in some positions, employees who work overtime are given a meal allowance.

The paragraph best supports the statement that

(A) if a meal allowance is given, there is compensation for overtime
(B) if the work week is 35 hours long, the job is unpopular
(C) if overtime is earned, pay in the job title is hourly
(D) if a jobholder has earned a weekend differential, the employee has worked beyond the set number of hours
(E) if compensatory time is offered, it is offered as a substitute for overtime pay

14. All applicants must be of satisfactory character and reputation and must meet all requirements set forth in the Notice of Examination for the position for which they are applying. Applicants may be summoned for the written test prior to investigation of their qualifications and background. Admission to the test does not mean that the applicant has met the qualifications for the position.

    The paragraph best supports the statement that

    (A) if an applicant has been admitted to the test, the applicant has not met requirements for the position
    (B) if an applicant has not been investigated, the applicant will not be admitted to the written test
    (C) if an applicant has met all requirements for the position, the applicant will be admitted to the test
    (D) if an applicant has satisfactory character and reputation, the applicant will not have his or her background investigated
    (E) if an applicant has met all the requirements set forth in the Notice of Examination, the applicant will pass the test

15. Although it has in the past been illegal for undocumented aliens to work in the United States, it has not, until now, been unlawful for employers to hire these aliens. With the passage of the new immigration law, employers will now be subject to civil penalties and ultimately imprisonment if they "knowingly" hire, recruit, or refer for a fee any unauthorized alien. Similarly, it is also unlawful for employers to continue to employ an undocumented alien who was hired after November 6, 1986, knowing that he or she was or is unauthorized to work.

    The paragraph best supports the statement that

    (A) under the new immigration law, it is no longer illegal for undocumented aliens to be denied employment in the United States
    (B) if an undocumented alien is not remaining on the job illegally, the worker was not hired after November 6, 1986
    (C) if a person wishes to avoid the penalties of the new immigration law, the person must not knowingly employ aliens
    (D) if an employer inadvertently hires undocumented aliens, the employer may be subject to fine or imprisonment but not both
    (E) if an unauthorized alien is able to find an employer who will hire him or her after November 6, 1986, the alien is welcome to go to work

16. The law requires that the government offer employees, retirees, and their families the opportunity to continue group health and/or welfare fund coverage at 102 percent of the group rate in certain instances where the coverage would otherwise terminate. All group benefits, including optional benefits riders, are available. Welfare fund benefits that can be continued under COBRA are dental, vision, prescription drugs, and other related medical benefits. The period of coverage varies from 18 to 36 months, depending on the reason for continuation.

The paragraph best supports the statement that

(A) the period of coverage continuation varies depending on the reason for termination
(B) upon retirement, welfare fund benefits continue at a 102 percent rate
(C) the law requires employees, retirees, and their families to continue health coverage
(D) COBRA is a program for acquiring welfare fund benefits
(E) if retirees or their families do not desire to terminate them, they can continue group benefits at 102 percent of the group rate

17. Historical records as such rarely constitute an adequate or, more importantly, a reliable basis for estimating earthquake potential. In most regions of the world, recorded history is short relative to the time between the largest earthquakes. Thus, the fact that there have been no historic earthquakes larger than a given size does not make us confident that they will also be absent in the future. It may, alternatively, be due to the short length of available historical records relative to the long repeat time for large earthquakes.

The paragraph best supports the statement that

(A) if historic earthquakes are no larger than a given size, they are unlikely to recur
(B) potential earthquakes do not inspire confidence in historical records as predictors of time between earthquakes
(C) if the time span between major earthquakes were not longer than the length of available records, history would have greater predictive value
(D) since there have been no historic earthquakes larger than a given size, we are confident that there will be a long time span between major earthquakes
(E) in those regions of the world where recorded history is long, the time between the largest earthquakes is short

18. A language can be thought of as a number of strings or sequences of symbols. The definition of a language defines which strings belong to the language, but since most languages of interest consist of an infinite number of strings, this definition is impossible to accomplish by listing the strings (or sentences). While the number of *sentences* in a language can be infinite, the rules by which they are constructed are not. This may explain why we are able to speak sentences in a language that we have never spoken before, and to understand sentences that we have never heard before.

The paragraph best supports the statement that

(A) if there is an infinite number of sequences of symbols in a language, there is an infinite number of rules for their construction

(B) if we have never spoken a language, we can understand its sentences provided that we know the rules by which they were constructed

(C) a language is defined by its strings

(D) if the number of sentences in an unnatural language were not infinite, we would be able to define it

(E) if sequences of symbols are governed by rules of construction, then the number of sentences can be determined

19. An assumption commonly made in regard to the reliability of testimony is that when a number of persons report the same matter, those details upon which there is an agreement may generally be considered substantiated. Experiments have shown, however, that there is a tendency for the same errors to appear in the testimony of different individuals, and that, apart from any collusion, agreement of testimony is no proof of dependability.

The paragraph best supports the statement that

(A) if details of the testimony are true, all witnesses will agree to it

(B) unless there is collusion, it is impossible for a number of persons to give the same report

(C) if most witnesses do not independently attest to the same facts, the facts cannot be true

(D) if the testimony of a group of people is in substantial agreement, it cannot be ruled out that those witnesses have not all made the same mistake

(E) under experimental conditions, witnesses tend to give reliable testimony

20. In some instances, changes are made in a contract after it has been signed and accepted by both parties. This is done either by inserting a new clause in a contract or by annexing a *rider* to the contract. If a contract is changed by a rider, both parties must sign the rider in order for it to be legal. The basic contract should also note that a rider is attached by inserting new words to the contract, and both parties should also initial and date the new insertion. The same requirement applies if they later change any wording in the contract. What two people agree to do, they can mutually agree not to do—as long as they both agree.

The paragraph best supports the statement that

(A) if two people mutually agree not to do something, they must sign a rider

(B) if both parties to a contract do not agree to attach a rider, they must initial the contract to render it legal

(C) if a rider to a contract is to be legal, that rider must be agreed to and signed by both parties, who must not neglect to initial and date that portion of the contract to which the rider refers

(D) if a party to a contract does not agree to a change, that party should initial the change and annex a rider detailing the disagreement

(E) if the wording of a contract is not to be changed, both parties must initial and date a rider

21. Personnel administration begins with the process of defining the quantities of people needed to do the job. Thereafter, people must be recruited, selected, trained, directed, rewarded, transferred, promoted, and perhaps released or retired. However, it is not true that all organizations are structured so that workers can be dealt with as individuals. In some organizations, employees are represented by unions, and managers bargain directly only with these associations.

The paragraph best supports the statement that

(A) no organizations are structured so that workers cannot be dealt with as individuals

(B) some working environments other than organizations are structured so that workers can be dealt with as individuals

(C) all organizations are structured so that employees are represented by unions

(D) no organizations are structured so that managers bargain with unions

(E) some organizations are not structured so that workers can be dealt with as individuals

22. Explosives are substances or devices capable of producing a volume of rapidly expanding gases that exert a sudden pressure on their surroundings. Chemical explosives are the most commonly used, although there are mechanical and nuclear explosives. All mechanical explosives are devices in which a physical reaction is produced, such as that caused by overloading a container with compressed air. While nuclear explosives are by far the most powerful, all nuclear explosives have been restricted to military weapons.

The paragraph best supports the statement that

(A) all explosives that have been restricted to military weapons are nuclear explosives
(B) no mechanical explosives are devices in which a physical reaction is produced, such as that caused by overloading a container with compressed air
(C) some nuclear explosives have not been restricted to military weapons
(D) all mechanical explosives have been restricted to military weapons
(E) some devices in which a physical reaction is produced, such as that caused by overloading a container with compressed air, are mechanical explosives

23. The modern conception of the economic role of the public sector (government), as distinct from the private sector, is that every level of government is a link in the economic process. Government's contribution to political and economic welfare must, however, be evaluated not merely in terms of its technical efficiency, but also in the light of its acceptability to a particular society at a particular state of political and economic development. Even in a dictatorship, this principle is formally observed, although the authorities usually destroy the substance by presuming to interpret to the public its collective desires.

The paragraph best supports the statement that

(A) it is not true that some levels of government are not links in the economic process
(B) all dictatorships observe the same economic principles as other governments
(C) all links in the economic process are levels of government
(D) the contributions of some levels of government do not need to be evaluated for technical efficiency and acceptability to society
(E) no links in the economic process are institutions other than levels of government

24. All property is classified as either personal property or real property, but not both. In general, if something is classified as personal property, it is transient and transportable in nature, while real property is not. Things such as leaseholds, animals, money, and intangible and other moveable goods are examples of personal property. Permanent buildings and land, on the other hand, are fixed in nature and are not transportable.

The paragraph best supports the statement that

(A) if something is classified as personal property, it is not transient and transportable in nature
(B) some forms of property are considered to be both personal property and real property
(C) permanent buildings and land are real property
(D) permanent buildings and land are personal property
(E) tangible goods are considered to be real property

25. The Supreme Court's power to invalidate legislation that violates the Constitution is a strong restriction on the powers of Congress. If an Act of Congress is deemed unconstitutional by the Supreme Court, then the Act is voided. Unlike a presidential veto, which can be overridden by a two-thirds vote of the House and the Senate, a constitutional ruling by the Supreme Court must be accepted by the Congress.

The paragraph best supports the statement that

(A) if an Act of Congress is voided, then it has been deemed unconstitutional by the Supreme Court
(B) if an Act of Congress has not been voided, then it has not been deemed unconstitutional by the Supreme Court
(C) if an Act of Congress has not been deemed unconstitutional by the Supreme Court, then it is voided
(D) if an Act of Congress is deemed unconstitutional by the Supreme Court, then it is not voided
(E) if an Act of Congress has not been voided, then it has been deemed unconstitutional by the Supreme Court

26. All child-welfare agencies are organizations that seek to promote the healthy growth and development of children. Supplying or supplementing family income so that parents can maintain a home for their children is usually the first such service to be provided. In addition to programs of general family relief, some special programs for broken families are offered when parental care is temporarily or permanently unavailable.

The paragraph best supports the statement that

(A) it is not true that some organizations that seek to promote the healthy growth and development of children are child-welfare agencies
(B) some programs offered when parental care is temporarily or permanently unavailable are not special programs for broken families
(C) it is not true that no special programs for broken families are offered when temporary or permanent parental care is unavailable
(D) all programs offered when parental care is temporarily or permanently unavailable are special programs for broken families
(E) some organizations that seek to promote the healthy growth and development of children are not child-welfare agencies.

27. Information centers can be categorized according to the primary activity or service they provide. For example, some information centers are document depots. These depots, generally government-sponsored, serve as archives for the acquisition, storage, retrieval, and dissemination of a variety of documents. All document depots have the capacity to provide a great range of user services, which may include preparing specialized bibliographies, publishing announcements, indexes, and abstracts, as well as providing copies.

The paragraph best supports the statement that

(A) some information centers are categorized by features other than the primary activity or service they provide
(B) some document depots lack the capacity to provide a great range of user services
(C) no document depot lacks the capacity to provide a great range of user services
(D) all information centers are document depots
(E) some places that provide a great range of user services are not document depots

28. Authorities generally agree that the use of hyphens tends to defy most rules. The best advice that can be given is to consult the dictionary to determine whether a given prefix is joined solidly to a root word or is hyphenated. One reliable rule, however, is that if an expression is a familiar one, such as overtime and hatchback, then it is a nonhyphenated compound.

The paragraph best supports the statement that

(A) if an expression is a familiar one, then it is a hyphenated compound
(B) if an expression is a nonhyphenated compound, then it is a familiar expression
(C) if an expression is not a familiar one, then it is a hyphenated compound
(D) if an expression is a hyphenated compound, containing a suffix rather than a prefix, then it is not a familiar one
(E) if an expression is a hyphenated compound, then it is not a familiar one

29. One use for wild land is the protection of certain species of wild animals or plants in wildlife refuges or in botanical reservations. Some general types of land use are activities that conflict with this stated purpose. All activities that exhibit such conflict are, of course, excluded from refuges and reservations.

The paragraph best supports the statement that

(A) all activities that conflict with the purpose of wildlife refuges or botanical reservations are general types of land use
(B) all activities excluded from wildlife refuges and botanical reservations are those that conflict with the purpose of the refuge or reservation
(C) some activities excluded from wildlife refuges and botanical reservations are general types of land use
(D) no activities that conflict with the purpose of wildlife refuges and botanical reservations are general types of land use
(E) some general types of land use are not excluded from wildlife refuges and botanical reservations

30. Many kinds of computer programming languages have been developed over the years. Initially, programmers had to write instructions in machine language. If a computer programming language is a machine language, then it is a code that can be read directly by a computer. Most high-level computer programming languages, such as Fortran and Cobol, use strings of common English phrases that communicate with the computer only after being converted or translated into a machine code.

The paragraph best supports the statement that

(A) all high-level computer programming languages use strings of common English phrases that are converted to a machine code
(B) if a computer programming language is a machine language, then it is not a code that can be read directly by a computer
(C) if a computer programming language is a code that can be read directly by a computer, then it is not a machine language
(D) if a computer programming language is not a code that can be read directly by a computer, then it is not a machine language
(E) if a computer programming language is not a machine language, then it is a code that can be read directly by a computer

END OF PART B

PART C—ARITHMETIC REASONING

Time: 50 Minutes. 20 Questions.

Directions: *Analyze each paragraph to set up each problem; then solve it. Mark your answer sheet with the letter of the correct answer. If the correct answer is not given as one of the response choices, you should select response E, "none of these."*

1. Twelve clerks are assigned to enter certain data on index cards. This number of clerks could perform the task in 18 days. After these clerks have worked on this assignment for 6 days, 4 more clerks are added to the staff to do this work. Assuming that all the clerks work at the same rate of speed, the entire task, instead of taking 18 days, will be performed in

    (A) 9 days
    (B) 12 days
    (C) 15 days
    (D) 16 days
    (E) none of these

2. In a low-cost public-health dental clinic, an adult cleaning costs twice as much as the same treatment for a child. If a family of three children and two adults can visit the clinic for cleanings for a cost of $49, what is the cost for each adult?

    (A) $7
    (B) $10
    (C) $12
    (D) $14
    (E) none of these

3. A government employee is relocated to a new region of the country and purchases a new home. The purchase price of the house is $87,250. Taxes to be paid on this house include: county tax of $424 per year; town tax of $783 per year; and school tax of $466 every six months. The aggregate tax rate is $.132 per $1000 of assessed value. The assessed value of this house is what percent of the purchase price?

    (A) 14.52%
    (B) 18.57%
    (C) 22.81%
    (D) 29.05%
    (E) none of these

4. The Social Security Administration has ordered an intensive check of 756 SSI payment recipients who are suspected of having above-standard incomes. Four clerical assistants have been assigned to this task. At the end of six days at 7 hours each, they have checked on 336 recipients. In order to speed up the investigation, two more assistants are assigned at this point. If they work at the same rate, the number of additional 7-hour days it will take to complete the job is, most nearly

(A) 1
(B) 2
(C) 3
(D) 4
(E) none of these

5. A family spends 30 percent of its take-home income for food, 8 percent for clothing, 25 percent for shelter, 4 percent for recreation, 13 percent for education, and 5 percent for miscellaneous items. The remainder goes into the family savings account. If the weekly net earnings of this household are $500, how many weeks will it take this family to accumulate $15,000 in savings, before interest?

(A) 200
(B) 175
(C) 150
(D) 100
(E) none of these

6. An Internal Revenue Service (IRS) officer is making spot-checks of income reported on income tax returns. A cab driver being audited works on a commission basis, receiving $42^1/_2$ percent of fares collected. The IRS allocates that earnings from tips should be valued at 29 percent of commissions. If the cab driver's weekly fare collections average $520, then the IRS projects his reportable monthly earnings to be

(A) between $900 and $1000
(B) between $1000 and $1100
(C) between $1100 and $1200
(D) between $1200 and $1250
(E) none of these

7. A department head hired a total of 60 temporary employees to handle a seasonal increase in the department's workload. The following lists the number of temporary employees hired, their rates of pay, and the duration of their employment:

> One-third of the total were hired as clerks, each at the rate of $12,700 a year, for two months

> 30 percent of the total were hired as office machine operators, each at the rate of $13,150 a year, for four months

> 22 stenographers were hired, each at the rate of $13,000 a year, for three months.

The total amount paid to these temporary employees to the nearest dollar was

(A) $194,499
(B) $192,900
(C) $130,000
(D) $127,500
(E) none of these

8. A government worker whose personal car gets 24 miles to the gallon was required to use this car for government business. He filled the tank before he began, requiring 18 gallons, for which he paid $1.349 per gallon. He drove 336 miles, then filled the tank again at a cost of $1.419 per gallon. The government reimburses him at the rate of $.20 per mile. What was the actual cost of gasoline for this trip?

(A) $19.87
(B) $23.05
(C) $24.28
(D) $44.15
(E) none of these

9. The visitors' section of a courtroom seats 105 people. The court is in session 6 hours a day. On one particular day, 486 people visited the court and were given seats. What is the average length of time spent by each visitor in the court? Assume that as soon as a person leaves a seat it is immediately filled and that at no time during the day is one of the 105 seats vacant. Express your answer in hours and minutes.

(A) 1 hour 18 minutes
(B) 1 hour 20 minutes
(C) 1 hour 30 minutes
(D) 2 hours
(E) none of these

10. A worker is paid at the rate of $8.60 per hour for the first 40 hours worked in a week and time-and-a-half for overtime. The FICA (social security) deduction is 7.13 percent; federal tax withholding is 15 percent; state tax withholding, 5 percent; and local tax withholding, $2\frac{1}{2}$ percent. If a worker works 48 hours a week for two consecutive weeks, she will take home

(A) $314.69
(B) $580.97
(C) $629.39
(D) $693.16
(E) none of these

11. A court clerk estimates that the untried cases on the docket will occupy the court for 150 trial days. If new cases are accumulating at the rate of 1.6 trial days per day and the court sits five days a week, how many days' business will remain to be heard at the end of 60 trial days?

    (A) 168
    (B) 184
    (C) 185
    (D) 186
    (E) none of these

12. A criminal investigator has an appointment to meet with an important informant at 4 P.M. in a city that is 480 kilometers from his base location. If the investigator estimates that his average speed will be 40 mph, what time must he leave home to make his appointment?

    (A) 8:15 A.M.
    (B) 8:30 A.M.
    (C) 8:45 A.M.
    (D) 9:30 A.M.
    (E) none of these

13. A program analysis office is taking bids for a new office machine. One machine is offered at a list price of $1360 with successive discounts of 20 percent and 10 percent, a delivery charge of $35 and an installation charge of $52. The other machine is offered at a list price of $1385 with a single discount of 30 percent, a delivery charge of $40 and an installation charge of $50. If the office chooses the less expensive machine, the savings will amount to just about

    (A) .6 percent
    (B) 1.9 percent
    (C) 2.0 percent
    (D) 2.6 percent
    (E) none of these

14. An assignment is completed by 32 clerks in 22 days. Assuming that all the clerks work at the same rate of speed, the number of clerks that would be needed to complete this assignment in 16 days is

    (A) 27
    (B) 38
    (C) 44
    (D) 52
    (E) none of these

15. The paralegals in a large legal department have decided to establish a "sunshine fund" for charitable purposes. Paralegal A has proposed that each worker chip in one-half of 1 percent of weekly salary; paralegal B thinks 1 percent would be just right; paralegal C suggests that one-third of 1 percent would be adequate; and paralegal D, who is strapped for funds, argues for one-fifth of 1 percent. The payroll department will cooperate and make an automatic deduction, but the paralegals must agree on a uniform percentage. The average of their suggested contributions is approximately

   (A) ¹/₄ percent
   (B) ¹/₃ percent
   (C) ¹/₂ percent
   (D) ⁵/₈ percent
   (E) none of these

16. A federal agency had a personal computer repaired at a cost of $49.20. This amount included a charge of $22 per hour for labor and a charge for a new switch that cost $18 before a 10 percent government discount was applied. How long did the repair job take?

   (A) 1 hour, 6 minutes
   (B) 1 hour, 11 minutes
   (C) 1 hour, 22 minutes
   (D) 1 hour, 30 minutes
   (E) none of these

17. In a large agency where mail is delivered in motorized carts, two tires were replaced on a cart at a cost of $34.00 per tire. If the agency had expected to pay $80 for a pair of tires, what percent of its expected cost did it save?

   (A) 7.5 percent
   (B) 17.6 percent
   (C) 57.5 percent
   (D) 75.0 percent
   (E) none of these

18. An experimental anti-pollution vehicle powered by electricity traveled 33 kilometers (km) at a constant speed of 110 kilometers per hour (km/h). How many minutes did it take this vehicle to complete its experimental run?

   (A) 3
   (B) 10
   (C) 18
   (D) 20
   (E) none of these

19. In one Federal office, $^1/_6$ of the employees favored abandoning a flexible work schedule system. In a second office that had the same number of employees, $^1/_4$ of the workers favored abandoning it. What is the average of the fractions of the workers in the two offices who favored abandoning the system?

(A) $^1/_{10}$
(B) $^1/_5$
(C) $^5/_{24}$
(D) $^5/_{12}$
(E) none of the these

20. A clerk is able to process 40 unemployment compensation claims in one hour. After deductions of 18 percent for benefits and taxes, the clerk's net pay is $6.97 per hour. If the clerk processed 1,200 claims, how much would the government have to pay for the work, based on the clerk's hourly wage *before* deductions?

(A) $278.80
(B) $255.00
(C) $246.74
(D) $209.10
(E) none of these

END OF PART C

CORRECT ANSWERS FOR MODEL EXAMINATION 5

BOOK A

PART A—NAME AND NUMBER COMPARISONS

1. B	11. B	21. B	31. B	41. A
2. D	12. E	22. A	32. D	42. C
3. E	13. E	23. A	33. A	43. E
4. A	14. E	24. A	34. E	44. A
5. E	15. B	25. E	35. E	45. E
6. A	16. D	26. E	36. E	46. B
7. A	17. A	27. C	37. A	47. C
8. C	18. A	28. E	38. E	48. B
9. D	19. C	29. C	39. A	49. D
10. B	20. C	30. B	40. A	50. C

Explanations

1. **(B)** The first two names are exactly alike, but the third name has a different initial.

2. **(D)** In the second and third names, the surname is Moru. In the first name, it is Moro.

3. **(E)** The given name is alike in the second and third names only; the surname is alike in only the first and second names.

4. **(A)** All three names are exactly alike.

5. **(E)** The middle initial in the second name is different from that of the other two. In the third name, Francis becomes Frances.

6. **(A)** All three numbers are exactly alike.

7. **(A)** All three numbers are exactly alike.

8. **(C)** The "254" of the beginning of the second number is different from the "245" opening of the first and third numbers.

9. **(D)** The "243" ending of the first number is different from the "423" ending of the second and third numbers.

10. **(B)** The "2798" opening of the third number is different from the "2789" opening of the first and second numbers.

11. **(B)** In the third name, the surname changes from Tenenbaum to Tanenbaum.

12. **(E)** The surname is different in each of the three names.

13. **(E)** Again, all three surnames are different.

14. **(E)** "Robert J." of the third name is the reverse of "J. Robert" of the first two names; the spelling of the surname in the second name differs from that of the first and third.

15. **(B)** "Fernand" of the third name is different from "Fernando" of the first two.

16. **(D)** The "630" ending of the first number is different from the "360" ending of the second and third.

17. **(A)** All three numbers are exactly alike.

18. **(A)** All three numbers are exactly alike.

19. **(C)** The "287" beginning of the second number is different from the "278" beginning of the first and third numbers.

20. **(C)** The "861" ending of the second number is different from the "681" ending of the first and third.

21. **(B)** "Courtnay" of the third name is different from "Courtney" of the first and second.

22. **(A)** All three names are exactly alike.

23. **(A)** All three names are exactly alike.

24. **(A)** All three names are exactly alike.

25. **(E)** The second name is "Sr.," while the first and third names are "Jr."; the third surname begins with "Mac," while the first and second surnames begin with "Mc."

26. **(E)** The three numbers end: 2976, 9276, 2796.

27. **(C)** The first and third numbers end, 1695; the second ends, 6195.

28. **(E)** The three numbers end: 0527, 5027, 0537.

29. **(C)** The first and third numbers are identical; the second number differs in a number of digits.

30. **(B)** The last two digits of the third number are reversed.

31. **(B)** "Randolphe" of the third name is different from "Randolph" of the first two.

32. **(D)** The surname of the second and third names, "Johnson," is different from the surname of the first name, "Johnston."

33. **(A)** All three names are exactly alike.

34. **(E)** The middle initial of the third name differs from the other two. "Asheton" of the second name differs from "Atherton" of the other two.

35. **(E)** The given name in the second and third names is "Owen" while in the first it is "Owens." The surname of the first two names is "McVey" while in the third it is "McVay."

36. **(E)** The three numbers end: 5690, 6690, 5609.

37. **(A)** All three numbers are exactly alike.

38. **(E)** The last two digits are, respectively: 41, 47, 14.

39. **(A)** All three numbers are exactly alike.

40. **(A)** All three numbers are exactly alike.

41. **(A)** All three names are exactly alike.

42. **(C)** The first and third names are exactly alike, but the second name inserts an "n" in the surname.

43. **(E)** The given name is different in all three names.

44. **(A)** All three names are exactly alike.

45. **(E)** The surname is different in each of the three names.

46. **(B)** In the third number, the fifth and sixth digits are reversed.

47. **(C)** In the second number, the fifth digit is "6" while in the other numbers the fifth digit is "0."

48. **(B)** In the third number, the last two digits are reversed.

49. **(D)** The last digit of the second and third numbers is "6"; the first number ends with "8."

50. **(C)** In the second number, the order of the fifth and sixth digits is reversed.

PART B—READING COMPREHENSION

1. A	7. D	13. E	19. D	25. B
2. B	8. C	14. C	20. C	26. C
3. B	9. E	15. B	21. E	27. C
4. C	10. B	16. E	22. E	28. E
5. E	11. D	17. C	23. A	29. C
6. C	12. A	18. B	24. C	30. D

Explanations

1. **(A)** The essential information from which the answer can be inferred is found in the second sentence. Since *a uniformed member while out of uniform* (in other words, an off-duty member) *may **not** indulge in intoxicants to an extent unfitting the member for duty,* it follows that the same member may drink liquor in moderation. Response B is incorrect because it directly contradicts the first sentence. Response C is incorrect because it introduces a concept not addressed in the paragraph—that of the uniformed member who reports unfit for duty. Response D is wrong because it reverses the meaning of the second sentence— the uniformed member in civilian clothes may drink only to the extent that the member remains fit for duty. Response E is incorrect because it raises a topic never mentioned in the paragraph—that of the civilian member of the department in a uniform (what uniform?).

2. **(B)** The paragraph makes the statement that the technician may sign that which it is not required that the specialist personally sign and states the rules that apply to the technician: name and title of tax law specialist followed by "by" and the name and title of the tax technician in ink. Response B is incorrect in that the assistant does not have authority to sign all papers. Responses C and D are incorrect because they address topics not mentioned in the paragraph—redelegation and requisitions. Response E is incorrect; the tax law specialist's name may be affixed by rubber stamp.

3. **(B)** The first clause states that the retiree is entitled to an annuity; the second clause tells of the pension that is the equal of one service-fraction of final compensation multiplied by number of years of government service; and the last clause describes an additional pension that is the actuarial equivalent of any reserve-for-increased-take-home-pay to which the retiree might at that time be entitled. Response A is incorrect because it does not complete the explanation of the basis for the second pension. Responses C, D, and E are all hopelessly garbled misstatements.

4. **(C)** In effect, the paragraph is saying, "When in doubt, check it out." Ignorance of the nature of the material to be mailed or of how the law pertains to it does not excuse the mailer if the material was indeed subject to a prohibition. Response A misinterprets the role of the postmaster. The postmaster is the final authority as to mailability. Response B is incorrect in its direct contradiction of the paragraph, which states, "Ignorance is no excuse." Responses D and E both interpret beyond the paragraph. The paragraph places all burden on the mailer.

5. **(E)** The last sentence makes the point that *any and all training* is valuable, *but only as it pertains to the position for which the applicant applies.* Responses A and D miss the point. Any training or education is valuable *if it contributes to knowledges, skills, and abilities needed in the particular job.* Responses B and C make statements unsupported by the paragraph.

6. **(C)** The second sentence tells us that heart disease is an illness of late middle age and old age. Response A is totally wrong. Since heart disease is an illness of older people, the odds of a person with heart disease being over 30 are much more than 50%. The fifty-fifty statement refers to the likelihood of persons over 30 sometime developing heart disease. Response B confuses death from *all causes* with death from *all other illnesses.* Response D makes an unsupported assumption that only the rising birth rate contributes to the number of people above a certain age. Actually, the longevity rate is much more crucial to this figure. Response E makes a statement that, whether true or false, is in no way supported by the paragraph.

7. **(D)** If people want what they can't get through legitimate, entirely legal channels, they will turn to those who supply those products or services. The consumers of less than legitimate products or services are unlikely to betray their suppliers. Response A is incorrect. Since racketeers deliver goods and services for money received, they are not engaged in theft, but not all "non-thieves" are engaged in legitimate business. Response B is incorrect because both racketeering and theft involve objects of value; the differences are along other dimensions. Response C makes no sense at all. Response E is unsupported by the paragraph.

8. **(C)** The first sentence tells us that the problems of the housing authority are legion, that it faces all the problems of private developers and problems peculiar to a public authority. Being *watched by antihousing enthusiasts* is one of these problems. Response A makes an unsupported statement. The paragraph does not enumerate the problems of private developers. Response B is incorrect. It is the antihousing authorities who watch for errors and cost overruns and then bring them to the attention of Congressional committees. Responses D and E make unsupported statements that do not make much sense as statements.

9. **(E)** *The peculiar threats to security in governmental organizations* to which the paragraph alludes are factors related to partisan, electoral politics. Other factors—job performance, needs of the marketplace, interpersonal relationships, and internal power plays—affect private and public employees in about equal proportions. Response A is unsupported by the paragraph. Response B directly contradicts the paragraph. Responses C and D are entirely unsupported by the paragraph.

10. **(B)** Some people develop allergies to antibiotics so that although those specific antibiotics might be the drug of choice to counter illness, the antibiotics cannot be used for those people. Response A makes a categorical statement that is unsupported by the paragraph. Response C is incorrect because antibiotics do not cure allergies; they may cause allergies. Response D is incorrect because the organisms do not become allergic to antibiotics (people become allergic). Response E is incorrect because there would be no need to search for new drugs if the existing ones were unfailingly effective. We need new drugs precisely because some organisms have become resistant to current ones.

11. **(D)** The paragraph clearly states that *in the competitive class every applicant must meet minimum qualifications.* . . . There may or may not be a pass/fail examination, but there most definitely are minimum qualifications that must be fulfilled. Response A is a distortion of the first sentence. The sentence means that there are no reliable exams for noncompetitive positions, not that noncompetitive positions are filled by unreliable exams. Response B is incorrect because the paragraph states that there *may* be an exam, not that there will be an exam. Response C is incorrect because if there is a test, the applicant must pass it. Response E goes beyond the scope of the paragraph. The paragraph does not state that *all* positions for which there are minimum qualifications are in the noncompetitive class.

12. **(A)** The paragraph defines a comma splice as the joining of two main clauses by a comma without a coordinating conjunction. Response B is incorrect because a run-on sentence is defined as two independent clauses sharing one sentence with no connective. Response C is incorrect because the paragraph suggests that a semicolon used as a connective can stand alone. Response D touches on a subject not addressed in the paragraph. Response E reverses the intent of the paragraph. A comma splice *is* a bad remedy for a run-on sentence.

13. **(E)** In *some* positions overtime is earned for time worked beyond the set number of hours; *other* positions offer compensatory time for overtime. Compensatory time is an alternative to overtime pay. Responses A, B, and C make unsupported statements. Response D combines the additional payments for two different classes of services. Overtime pay is for hours in excess of the standard number; weekend differentials are for work on weekends, even if within the standard number of workweek hours.

14. **(C)** The paragraph makes clear that applicants may take the test before their backgrounds and qualifications have been investigated. If qualification is not even prerequisite to testing, certainly a qualified applicant will not be barred from the exam. Response A is incorrect in assuming that all persons admitted to the test are unqualified. The paragraph indicates only that their qualifications need not have yet been verified. Response B contradicts the paragraph. Response D is incorrect. The investigation is made to verify satisfactory character and reputation. Response E is unsupported by the paragraph.

15. **(B)** Since it is illegal to continue employing an undocumented alien hired after November 6, 1986, it must not be illegal to retain an employee who was hired before that date. Response A is incorrect. It never was illegal to *deny* employment to undocumented aliens; it is now illegal to employ them. Response C misinterprets the paragraph. The paragraph applies only to undocumented or unauthorized aliens. Aliens who have authorizing documents or "green cards" may be employed legally. Response D is incorrect. Penalties are for "knowingly" hiring illegal aliens, not for inadvertent hiring. (You must limit your answers to the material presented in the paragraph, even though you may know of the burden on employers to verify documentation or face penalties.) Response E is in contradiction to the paragraph.

16. **(E)** COBRA provides for the continuation of health and welfare benefits upon payment of 102% of the group premium. Response A misinterprets the variation in the length of continuing coverage to depend upon the reason for termination of coverage rather than upon the reason for continuation of coverage. Response B is incorrect because it is the cost to the subscriber that jumps to 102% of the group rate, not the extent of the coverage. Response C is incorrect because the law requires the employer to offer the opportunity to continue health coverage; it does not require employees, retirees, or their families to continue that coverage. Response D is wrong because under COBRA terminated employees and retirees can continue coverage, but they cannot acquire new benefits.

17. **(C)** Recorded history is short relative to the time span between major earthquakes; therefore, history is inadequate as a predictive tool. Either a much longer period of recorded history or a much shorter span between major earthquakes would enhance the predictive value of historical data. Response A is not supported by the paragraph. Responses B and D are not only unsupported, but also make no sense. Response E makes an assumption that goes beyond the paragraph.

18. **(B)** Basically, the last sentence of the paragraph is saying that if we know the rules of construction of a language, we can understand it. Response A contradicts the paragraph. The paragraph states that the number of rules is finite. Response C twists the second sentence, which states that definition of a language by listing its strings is impossible because the number of strings is infinite. Response D introduces unnatural languages, which is not a subject of the paragraph. Response E makes an unsupported statement.

19. **(D)** Just as *agreement of testimony is no proof of dependability,* so agreement of testimony is no proof of undependability. Response A is incorrect because the thrust of the paragraph is that people's perceptions are sometimes in error. Response B contradicts the paragraph. It is reported that a number of witnesses may report the same erroneous observation even apart from collusion. Response C misses the point. Since witnesses can make mistakes, they are just as likely to have not noticed the truth as to have "observed" that which did not happen. Response E is a misstatement.

20. **(C)** If a contract is changed by a rider, both parties must sign the rider. The basic contract should note that a rider is being attached, and both parties should initial and date the notice in the basic contract. Response A is incorrect in that it creates a rider without necessarily having created a contract. A mutual agreement to refrain from an act may be a first point of agreement and not a change. Responses B and D are both incorrect because there can be no change unless both parties agree. Response E is incorrect because if there is to be no change there is no call for a rider.

21. **(E)** The third sentence of the paragraph states that *it is not true that all organizations are structured so that workers can be dealt with as individuals.* From this statement we can infer that *some organizations are not structured so that workers can be dealt with as individuals.* Response A contradicts both the third and fourth sentences by ignoring the information that *in some organizations, employees are represented by unions, and managers bargain with these associations.* Responses C and D are incorrect because they generalize *some* to mean *all.* Response B is unsupported because the paragraph gives no information about working environments other than organizations.

22. **(E)** The third sentence states that *all mechanical explosives are devices in which a physical reaction is produced, such as that caused by overloading a container with compressed air.* From this we can safely conclude that *some* devices in which a physical reaction is produced, such as that caused by overloading a container with compressed air, are mechanical explosives. We cannot infer response A because the paragraph does not provide sufficient information to enable the conclusion that all explosives that have been restricted to military weapons are nuclear weapons. It may be that other explosives that are not nuclear weapons also have been restricted to military weapons. Responses B and C contradict the paragraph. Response D is wrong because the paragraph provides no information at all about whether or not mechanical explosives are restricted to military weapons.

23. **(A)** *Every level of government is a link in the economic process.* It can be deduced that its contradictory statement, *some levels of government are not links in the economic process,* cannot be true. Response B is not supported by the paragraph because it goes beyond the information given. It cannot be concluded that dictatorships observe more than one principle in common with other governments. Responses C and E represent incorrect interpretations of the information that *every level of government is a link in the economic process.* It cannot be inferred from this statement that *all links in the economic process are levels of government,* only that some are. We know that the category "all levels of government" is contained in the category "links in the economic process," but we do not

know if other links in the economic process exist that are not levels of government. Response D is not supported by the passage; there is nothing to suggest that the contributions of some levels of society do *not* need to be evaluated.

24.   **(C)**   The first sentence presents two mutually exclusive alternatives—*all property is classified as either personal property or real property, but not both.* The second sentence states that *if something is classified as personal property, it is transient and transportable in nature.* The fourth sentence states that *permanent buildings and land . . . are fixed in nature and are not transportable.* From that we can conclude that since permanent buildings and land are not transient and transportable in nature, they are not personal property; they must, therefore, be real property. All other responses contradict the paragraph in some way.

25.   **(B)**   The essential information from which the answer is to be inferred is contained in the second sentence, which states that if an Act of Congress has been deemed unconstitutional, then it is voided. In response B we are told that an Act of Congress is not voided; therefore, we can conclude that *it has not been deemed unconstitutional by the Supreme Court.* Responses A and C are not supported because the paragraph does not indicate whether an Act of Congress is voided *only* when it has been deemed unconstitutional or if it could be voided for other reasons. Responses D and E contradict the paragraph.

26.   **(C)**   The last sentence states that *some special programs for broken families are offered when parental care is temporarily or permanently unavailable.* If this statement is true, then its negation cannot be true. Response A contradicts the paragraph. Responses B and D cannot be validly inferred because the paragraph does not provide sufficient information to support the inferences made. Response E is wrong because the paragraph states that *all child-welfare agencies are organizations that seek to promote the healthy growth and development of children.* There is no way of knowing from this statement whether or not there are organizations other than child-welfare agencies that seek to promote the healthy growth and welfare of children.

27.   **(C)**   This answer can be inferred from the information presented in the last sentence of the paragraph, which says in part that *all document depots have the capacity to provide a great range of user services.* In view of this statement, it is clearly the case that *no* document depot lacks such a capacity. Response A goes beyond the information given in the paragraph. Response B contradicts the information presented. Response D draws an overly general conclusion from the information presented. One can infer that *some* document depots are information centers, but one cannot infer that *all* information centers are document depots. Response E goes beyond the information that is implicit in the last sentence.

28.   **(E)**   The last sentence says that *if an expression is a familiar one . . . then it is a nonhyphenated compound.* Therefore, if an expression is a hyphenated compound, it cannot be a familiar one. Response A contradicts the information. Response B is incorrect because the paragraph does not give us information about *all* nonhyphenated compounds, only those that are familiar expressions. Response C is incorrect because the paragraph does not give us enough information about all unfamiliar expressions. Response D cannot be correct because the paragraph provides no information about compounds that have suffixes.

29.   **(C)**   The second sentence tells us that *some general types of land use are activities that conflict with* the purpose of wildlife refuges and botanical reservations. The third sentence explains that *all activities that exhibit such conflict are . . . excluded from refuges and reservations.* Therefore, we can conclude that *some activities excluded from refuges and reservations* (the ones that conflict with the purpose of refuges and reservations) *are general types of land use.* Response A is wrong because the paragraph does not give any information as to

whether all activities that conflict with the purpose of refuges and reservations are general types of land use. Response B cannot be inferred because the paragraph does not give enough information about *all* activities that are excluded. Response D is incorrect because it is too inclusive. Response E is based upon insufficient information.

30. **(D)** The third sentence states that *if a computer programming language is a machine language, then it is a code that can be read directly by a computer.* From this statement it can be seen that all machine languages are codes that can be read directly by a computer and that if a computer programming language is not such a code, then it is not a machine language. Response A goes beyond the information presented in the paragraph. Responses B and C contradict the paragraph. Response E is incorrect because the paragraph does not say whether or not computer languages that are *not* machine languages are codes that can be read directly by a computer.

PART C—ARITHMETIC REASONING

1. C	5. A	9. A	13. A	17. E
2. D	6. C	10. C	14. C	18. C
3. B	7. B	11. D	15. C	19. C
4. E	8. A	12. B	16. D	20. B

Explanations

1. **(C)** The first 12 clerks complete $^6/_{18}$, or $^1/_3$ of the job in 6 days, leaving $^2/_3$ of the job to be completed.

    One clerk would require $12 \times 18 = 216$ days to complete the job, working alone. Sixteen clerks require $216 \div 16$, or $13^1/_2$ days for the entire job. But only $^2/_3$ of the job remains. To do $^2/_3$ of the job, sixteen clerks require

    $$^2/_3 \times 13^1/_2 = ^2/_3 \times ^{27}/_2 = 9 \text{ days}$$

    The entire job takes 6 days + 9 days = 15 days.

2. **(D)** Let x = cost of a child's cleaning

    Then $2x$ = cost of an adult's cleaning

    $$2(2x) + 3(x) = \$49$$
    $$4x + 3x = \$49$$
    $$7x = \$49$$
    $$x = \$\ 7$$

    $7 is the cost of a child's cleaning; $2 \times \$7$ or $14 is the cost of an adult's cleaning.

3. **(B)** First determine the total annual tax:

    $$\$424 + \$783 + (2)\$466 = \$424 + \$783 + \$932 = \$2139$$

    Divide the total taxes by the tax rate to find the assessed valuation.

    $$\$2139 \div .132 = \$16,204$$

    To find what percent one number is of another, create a fraction by putting the part over the whole and convert to a decimal by dividing.

    $$\frac{\$16,205}{\$87,250} = \$16,205 \div \$87,250 = 18.57\%$$

4. **(E)** The correct answer, not given, is five additional days.

    Four assistants completed 336 cases in 42 hours (6 days at 7 hours per day). Therefore, each assistant completed $336 \div 4$, or 84 cases in 42 hours, for a rate of 2 cases per hour per assistant.

    After the first 6 days, the number of cases remaining is

    $$756 - 336 = 420$$

    It will take 6 assistants, working at the rate of 2 cases per hour per assistant, $420 \div 12$ or 35 hours to complete the work. If each workday has 7 hours, then $35 \div 7$ or 5 days are needed.

5. **(A)** Add what the family spends
   $$30\% + 8\% + 25\% + 4\% + 13\% + 5\% = 85\%$$

   Since it spends 85 percent, it has 100 percent − 85 percent = 15 percent remaining for savings.

   15% of $500 = .15 × $500 = $75 per week
   $15,000 ÷ $75 = 200 weeks

6. **(C)** Commission   = 42½% of fares
   42½% of $520 = .425 × $520
   $\qquad\qquad\qquad$ = $221 commission

   Tips   = 29% of commission
   29% of $221 = .29 × $221
   $\qquad\qquad\qquad$ = $64.09 tips

   Weekly earnings:
   $221.00
   + 64.09
   _____
   $285.09

   Monthly earnings, based on four-week month
   $285.09
   ×   4
   _____
   $1140.36

   Earnings in a month a few days longer than four weeks clearly fall between $1100 and $1200.

7. **(B)** Take this problem one step at a time. Of the 60 employees, one-third, or 20, were clerks. 30 percent, or 18, were machine operators. 22 were stenographers.
   The clerks earned $12,750 ÷ 12 = $1,062.50 per month
   Machine operators earned $13,150 ÷ 12 = $1,095.83 per month
   Stenographers earned $13,000 ÷ 12 = $1,083.33 per month

   20 clerks × $1,062.50 × 2 months = $42,500.00
   18 machine operators × $1,095.83 × 4 months = $78,899.76
   22 stenographers × $1,083.33 × 3 months = $71,499.78
   $42,500.00 + $78,889.76 + $71,499.78 = $192,899.54 total cost

8. **(A)** The government worker drove 336 miles, and his car got 24 miles per gallon; therefore, he used 336 ÷ 24 = 14 gallons for which he paid $1.419 per gallon or $1.419 × 14 = $19.87. All other information is irrelevant; disregard it.

9. **(A)** There are 360 minutes in a six-hour day. If each seat is occupied all day there are 105 × 360 = 37,800 minutes of seating time to be divided among 486 people. 37,800 ÷ 486 = 77.77 minutes of seating time per person = 1 hour 17.7 minutes per person.

10. **(C)** The worker earns $8.60 per hour for two 40-hour weeks or $8.60 × 80 hours = $688 and $12.90 per hour for an additional 16 hours ($12.90 × 16 hours = $206.40), so her gross pay is $688 + $206.40 = $894.40. From this are deducted: FICA at 7.13 percent = $63.77 and the three withholding taxes at the combined rate of 22.5% = $201.24. Add the deductions: $63.77 + $201.24 = $265.01, and subtract the sum from the gross pay: $894.40 − $265.01= $629.39.

11.   **(D)** Since the court does one day's work per day, at the end of 60 days there will be 150 – 60 = 90 trial days of old cases remaining. New cases are accumulating at the rate of 1.6 trial days per day; therefore, there will be $60 \times 1.6 = 96$ trial days of new cases at the end of 60 days. 96 new trial days added to the backlog of 90 trial days would make the total backlog 186 trial days.

12.   **(B)** A kilometer is $^5/_8$ of a mile.
$480 \text{ km} \times {}^5/_8 = 300 \text{ miles}$; $300 \text{ miles} \div 40 \text{ mph} = 7.5 \text{ hours}$
Subtract 7.5 hours from the required arrival time of 4 P.M. to find that he must leave at 8:30 A.M. (noon to 4 P.M. is 4 hours + 8:30 to noon is $3^1/_2$ hours).

13.   **(A)** Calculate the cost of the first machine:
$\$1360 - 20\% = \$1360 \times 80\% = \$1088$
then
$\$1088 - 10\% = \$1088 \times 90\% = \$979.20 + \$35 + \$52 = \$1066.20$

Calculate the cost of the second machine:
$\$1385 - 30\% = \$1385 \times 70\% = \$969.50 + \$40 + \$50 = \$1059.50$
The second machine is $\$1066.20 - \$1059.50 = \$6.70$ less expensive; $\$6.70 \div \$1066.20 = .6\%$ savings by buying the second machine.

14.   **(C)** The proportion is $32 \times 22 = x \times 16$
$16x = 704$
$x = 704 \div 16 = 44$

15.   **(C)** Add the suggested contributions and divide by the number of paralegals to get the average.
$1/2\% = 15/30\%$
$1/1\% = 30/30\%$
$1/3\% = 10/30\%$
$+\ 1/5\% = \underline{16/30\%}$
$61/30\% = 2\% \div 4 \text{ paralegals} = 1/2\%$

16.   **(D)** Compute the following:
$[49.20 - (18 - (18 \times .10))]/22 = x$
$x = 33/22 = 1.5 \text{ hours or 1 hour, 30 minutes}$

The cost of the switch after the government discount of 10% is applied is $18 - (18 \times .10)$ or \$16.20. This amount, when subtracted from the total charge of \$49.20, leaves \$33, which represents the charge for labor. A charge of \$33 at the rate of \$22 per hour represents 1.5 hours, or 1 hour and 30 minutes, of work.

17.   **(E)** The correct answer is not given as one of the response choices. The answer can be obtained by computing the following:
$(80/2 - 34)/40 = x$
$x = 6/40 = .15$
$.15 \times 100 = 15\%$

The expected \$80 cost for a pair of tires would make the cost of a single tire \$40. The difference between the actual cost of \$34 per tire and the expected cost of \$40 per tire is \$6, which is 15 percent of the \$40 expected cost.

18. **(C)** Obtain the answer by setting up a simple proportion:

110 km/60 min = 33 km/x min

Solving this proportion, we obtain $110x = 1980$; $x = {}^{1980}/_{110} = 18$.

19. **(C)** Compute the following:

$(1/6 + 1/4)/2 = x$

This simple arithmetic averaging of two fractions can be accomplished by first finding their lowest common denominator:

$1/6 = 2/12$ and $1/4 = 3/12$

The sum of 2/12 and 3/12 is 5/12. This fraction, when multiplied by 1/2 (which is the same as dividing by 2) gives the correct answer:

$5/12 \times 1/2 = 5/24$

20. **(B)** Compute the following:

(1) $.82S = 6.97$

and

(2) $1200/40 \times S = Y$

The clerk's net pay of $6.97 per hour represents .82 of his or her gross pay (100% − 18% = 82% or .82). Solving equation 1 we find that the clerk's hourly salary *(S)* before deductions is $8.50. Substituting this figure in equation (2), we compute the total number of hours of work involved (1200 forms divided by 40 forms per hour equals 30 hours of work), and then multiply 30 hours by an hourly wage of $8.50 to get $255.00, the amount the government would have to pay for the work.

SCORE SHEET

NAME AND NUMBER COMPARISONS: Your score on the Name and Number Comparisons part is based upon the number of questions you answered correctly minus one-fourth of the questions you answered incorrectly (number wrong divided by 4). Calculate this now: Number Wrong ÷ 4 =   .

Number Right– Number Wrong ÷ 4 = Raw Score

_____   –_____ =_____

READING COMPREHENSION: Your score on the Reading Comprehension part is based only on the number of questions you answered correctly. Wrong answers do not count against you.

Number Right = Raw Score

_____= _____

ARITHMETIC REASONING: Your score on the Arithmetic Reasoning part is based only upon the number of questions you answered correctly. Wrong answers do not count against you.

Number Right = Raw Score

_____= _____

TOTAL SCORE: To find your total raw score, add together the raw scores for each section of the exam.

Name and Number Comparisons Score   _____

+

Reading Comprehension Score   _____

+

Arithmetic Reasoning Score   _____

=   _____

Total Raw Score   _____

Self Evaluation Chart

Calculate your raw score for each test as shown above. Then check to see where your score falls on the scale from Poor to Excellent. Lightly shade in the boxes in which your scores fall.

Part	Excellent	Good	Average	Fair	Poor
Name and Number Comparisons	43–50	35–42	26–34	19–25	0–18
Reading Comprehension	25–30	20–24	15–19	11–14	0–10
Arithmetic Reasoning	18–20	15–17	12–14	9–11	0–8
Total Score	85–100	70–84	51–69	31–50	0–30

BOOK B

Book B is set up to look like a multiple-choice test and it is timed like a test, but it is not a test at all. There are no right or wrong answers, and there is no score. You cannot study for Book B, and your only preparation can consist of gathering statistical records from your school years and thinking about what you achieved and when.

Book B consists of 122 questions to be answered in 40 minutes. Questions ask about your best and worst grades in school and about your favorite subjects. They ask about your extracurricular activities and about your participation in sports. There are questions about attendance, part-time jobs, and leadership positions. Some questions ask you how you think your teachers or employers might rate you. Similar questions ask you to suggest what your friends might say about you. Still other questions ask how you rate yourself against others. Answer honestly and to the best of your ability.

Mini-Model Book B

1. My favorite subject in high school was

   (A) math
   (B) English
   (C) physical education
   (D) social studies
   (E) science

2. My GPA upon graduation from high school (on a 4.0 scale) was

   (A) lower than 2.51
   (B) 2.51 to 2.80
   (C) 2.81 to 3.25
   (D) 3.26 to 3.60
   (E) higher than 3.60

3. In my second year of high school I was absent

   (A) never
   (B) not more than 3 days
   (C) 4 to 10 days
   (D) more often than 10 days
   (E) do not recall

4. My best grades in high school were in

   (A) art
   (B) math
   (C) English
   (D) social studies
   (E) music

5. While in high school I participated in

   (A) one sport
   (B) two sports and one other extracurricular activity
   (C) three nonathletic extracurricular activities
   (D) no extracurricular activities
   (E) other than the above

6. During my senior year in high school I held a paying job

(A) 0 hours a week
(B) 1 to 5 hours a week
(C) 6 to 10 hours a week
(D) 11 to 16 hours a week
(E) more than 16 hours a week

7. The number of semesters in which I failed a course in high school was

(A) none
(B) one
(C) two or three
(D) four or five
(E) more than five

8. In high school I did volunteer work

(A) more than 10 hours a week
(B) 5 to 10 hours a week on a regular basis
(C) sporadically
(D) seldom
(E) not at all

If you did not go to college, skip questions 9–24. Go to Question 25.

9. My general area of concentration in college was

(A) performing arts
(B) humanities
(C) social sciences
(D) business
(E) none of the above

10. At graduation from college, my age was

(A) under 20
(B) 20
(C) 21 to 24
(D) 25 to 29
(E) 30 or over

11. My standing in my graduating class was in the

(A) bottom third
(B) middle third
(C) top third
(D) top quarter
(E) top 10 percent

12. In college, I was elected to a major office in a class or in a club or organization

(A) more than six times
(B) four or five times
(C) two or three times
(D) once
(E) never

13. In comparison to my peers, I cut classes

 (A) much less often than most
 (B) somewhat less often than most
 (C) just about the same as most
 (D) somewhat more often than most
 (E) much more often than most

14. The campus activities in which I participated most were

 (A) social service
 (B) political
 (C) literary
 (D) did not participate in campus activities
 (E) did not participate in any of these activities

15. My name appeared on the dean's list

 (A) never
 (B) once or twice
 (C) in three or more terms
 (D) in more terms than it did not appear
 (E) do not remember

16. The volunteer work I did while in college was predominantly

 (A) health-care related
 (B) religious
 (C) political
 (D) educational
 (E) did not volunteer

17. While a college student, I spent most of my summers

 (A) in summer school
 (B) earning money
 (C) traveling
 (D) in service activities
 (E) resting

18. My college education was financed

 (A) entirely by my parents
 (B) by my parents and my own earnings
 (C) by scholarships, loans, and my own earnings
 (D) by my parents and loans
 (E) by a combination of sources not listed above

19. In the college classroom I was considered

 (A) a listener
 (B) an occasional contributor
 (C) an average participant
 (D) a frequent contributor
 (E) a leader

20.   The person on campus whom I most admired was

    (A) another student
    (B) an athletic coach
    (C) a teacher
    (D) an administrator
    (E) a journalist

21.   Of the skills I developed at college, the one I value most is

    (A) foreign language ability
    (B) oral expression
    (C) writing skills
    (D) facility with computers
    (E) analytical skills

22.   I made my greatest mark in college through my

    (A) athletic prowess
    (B) success in performing arts
    (C) academic success
    (D) partying reputation
    (E) conciliatory skill with my peers

23.   My cumulative GPA (on a 4.0 scale) in courses in my major was

    (A) lower than 3.00
    (B) 3.00 to 3.25
    (C) 3.26 to 3.50
    (D) 3.51 to 3.75
    (E) higher than 3.75

24.   While in college I

    (A) worked full-time and was a part-time student
    (B) worked 20 hours a week and was a full-time student
    (C) worked 20 hours a week and was a part-time student
    (D) was a full-time student working more than 10 but less than 20 hours a week
    (E) was a full-time student

25.   In the past six months, I have been late to work (or school)

    (A) never
    (B) only one time
    (C) very seldom
    (D) more than five times
    (E) I don't recall

26.   My supervisors (or teachers) would be most likely to describe me as

    (A) competent
    (B) gifted
    (C) intelligent
    (D) fast working
    (E) detail oriented

27. My peers would probably describe me as

(A) analytical
(B) glib
(C) organized
(D) funny
(E) helpful

28. According to my supervisors (or teachers), my greatest asset is my

(A) ability to communicate orally
(B) written expression
(C) ability to motivate others
(D) organization of time
(E) friendly personality

29. In the past two years, I have applied for

(A) no jobs other than this one
(B) one other job
(C) two to four other jobs
(D) five to eight other jobs
(E) more than eight jobs

30. In the past year, I read strictly for pleasure

(A) no books
(B) one book
(C) two books
(D) three to six books
(E) more than six books

31. When I read for pleasure, I read mostly

(A) history
(B) fiction
(C) poetry
(D) biography
(E) current events

32. My peers would say of me that, when they ask me a question, I am

(A) helpful
(B) brusque
(C) condescending
(D) generous
(E) patient

33. My supervisors (or teachers) would say that my area of least competence is

(A) analytical ability
(B) written communication
(C) attention to detail
(D) public speaking
(E) self-control

34. In the past two years, the number of full-time (35 hours or more) jobs I have held is

   (A) none
   (B) one
   (C) two or three
   (D) four
   (E) five or more

35. Compared to my peers, my supervisors (or teachers) would rank my dependability

   (A) much better than average
   (B) somewhat better than average
   (C) about average
   (D) somewhat less than average
   (E) much less than average

36. In my opinion, the most important of the following attributes in an employee is

   (A) discretion
   (B) loyalty
   (C) open-mindedness
   (D) courtesy
   (E) competence

37. My peers would say that the word that describes me least is

   (A) sociable
   (B) reserved
   (C) impatient
   (D) judgmental
   (E) independent

38. My supervisors (or teachers) would say that I react to criticism with

   (A) a defensive attitude
   (B) quick capitulation
   (C) anger
   (D) interest
   (E) shame

39. My attendance record over the past year has been

   (A) not as good as I would like it to be
   (B) not as good as my supervisors (or teachers) would like it to be
   (C) a source of embarrassment
   (D) satisfactory
   (E) a source of pride

40. My peers would say that when I feel challenged my reaction is one of

   (A) determination
   (B) energy
   (C) defiance
   (D) caution
   (E) compromise

There are no "right" answers to these questions, so there is no answer key.

BOOKS FOR JOB HUNTERS

CAREERS / STUDY GUIDES

Airline Pilot
Allied Health Professions
Automobile Technician Certification Tests
Federal Jobs for College Graduates
Federal Jobs in Law Enforcement
Getting Started in Film
How You Really Get Hired
Internships
Law Enforcement Exams Handbook
Make Your Job Interview a Success
Mechanical Aptitude and Spatial Relations Tests
Mid-Career Job Hunting
Office Guide to Business English
Office Guide to Buiness Letters, Memos & Reports
Office Guide to Business Math
Office Guide to Spelling & Word Division
100 Best Careers for the Year 2000
100 Best Careers in Entertainment
Passport to Overseas Employment
Postal Exams Handbook
Real Estate License Examinations
Refrigeration License Examinations
The Telephone Company Test
Travel Agent

RESUME GUIDES

The Complete Resume Guide
Resumes for Better Jobs
Resumes That Get Jobs
Your Resume: Key to a Better Job

AVAILABLE AT BOOKSTORES EVERYWHERE

MACMILLAN • USA